War and Drugs

War and Drugs

The Role of Military Conflict in the Development of Substance Abuse

Dessa K. Bergen-Cico

Routledge
Taylor & Francis Group

LONDON AND NEW YORK

First published 2012 by Paradigm Publishers

Published 2016 by Routledge
2 Park Square, Milton Park, Abingdon, Oxon OX14 4RN
711 Third Avenue, New York, NY 10017, USA

Routledge is an imprint of the Taylor & Francis Group, an informa business

Library of Congress Cataloging-in-Publication Data
Bergen-Cico, Dessa K.
  War and drugs : the role of military conflict in the development of substance abuse /
Dessa K. Bergen-Cico.
    p. cm.
  Includes bibliographical references and index.
  ISBN 978-1-59451-894-2 (hbk. : alk. paper) — ISBN 978-1-59451-895-9 (pbk. : alk. paper)
  1. Drug traffic—Political aspects—History. 2. Soldiers—Drug use—History.
3. Soldiers—Drug use—United States—History. 4. War and society. I. Title.
  HV5801.B445 2012
  362.29088'355—dc23

                                                                2011024729

ISBN 13: 978-1-59451-894-2 (hbk)
ISBN 13: 978-1-59451-895-9 (pbk)

The artwork on the cover, titled "Duality of Humanity," is used with special permission from the artist, Shepard Fairey. ©2008

Designed and Typeset by Straight Creek Bookmakers.

*This book is dedicated to my family—
my husband, John; daughter, Rachael; and son, Johnny—
for their love, support, and inspiration.*

Contents

Preface

In its current iteration, the War on Drugs appears to be a spectacular failure of domestic and foreign policy. As the drug war has grown increasingly militaristic, legalistic, and moralistic, the levels of drug use and addiction have remained relatively constant for decades, rising in recent years. The original declaration of a War on Drugs was instituted by President Richard Nixon on June 17, 1971—a response to the nation's concerns regarding drug use and related criminal activity among returning Vietnam veterans and the role of drugs within the anti-war movement. There are misgivings about its current status, but when the War on Drugs was first declared in 1971, it was primarily a public-health policy centered on access to treatment on demand. In the 1980s, the emphasis on treatment was displaced by bureaucratic militaristic infrastructures and paramilitary tactics to create a "Drug-Free America." With the move away from primary prevention and treatment came the infantilized "Just Say No" and red-ribbon campaigns, epic failures that created delusions of public action.

As we will examine in Chapter 7, "The Cold War Was Hot for the Drug Trade," it was under cover of these Drug-Free America campaigns that a number of top U.S. officials turned a blind eye toward drug trafficking in Afghanistan, Pakistan, Nicaragua, Mexico, and even the United States. In several cases, top officials were complicit in transnational drug trafficking because the revenue supported anti-communist and anti-Soviet objectives of the Cold War, which superseded the importance of drug-war objectives. The synergistic relationship between drugs and war and the history of the drug war are much more nuanced than the monolith it now appears to be.

Although I have worked in the field of substance-abuse prevention and addictions treatment for decades, I was not aware of many of these historical connections prior to initiating research for this book. Certainly, I had heard about conspiracy theories that were vaguely reminiscent of this history; however, couched as conspiratorial, these facts were largely veiled as "counterculture paranoia," dismissed by practitioners and academics alike. These factors contribute to the complicit and complex history of drugs and war, which underscores the fundamental problems in our ability to make any real progress in the erstwhile drug war.

The political history that has driven the ebb and flow of drugs is studied and documented by historians, political scientists, and journalists, but it is cleaved from the consciousness of those of us working in the prevention and treatment field. Once I began to incorporate this type of geopolitical history into the courses I teach on the dynamics of addiction, I found that students dramatically reframed their legalistic and moralistic views toward those affected by drugs. This widening perspective has been accompanied by a more adult dialogue about effective demand reduction and treatment strategies.

The emphasis on drug interdiction (supply reduction) and the moralistic views held by institutions and society have done nothing more than alienate those affected by addiction. As a country, we have struggled with the drug-war issue since the Vietnam War, an era that represented a turning point in the confluence of drugs and war, when use of drugs became synonymous with opposition to the war; the nation sought to numb itself from the images of bloodshed and the anxiety of being conscripted.

Born in the 1960s, I grew up exposed to the wrenching, violent imagery of the Vietnam War—flashing pictures of war on the nightly news and in the pages of *Time* and *Life* magazines daily. Terrified mothers running with their bleeding infants, terrified children running naked from burning villages, and children sobbing over their parents' decapitated bodies touched on the deepest fears of every child. One picture that particularly haunts me was that of a South Vietnamese man executing a Vietcong operative. The force of the shot blew the man's head back, his hair flying, although the bullet had not yet struck. I grapple with the idea that the photographer did not intervene—or could not or should not have intervened—to halt this murder. I was equally confused by the fact that both men were Vietnamese. My exposure to these images has undoubtedly played an important role in my staunch opposition to violence and my lifelong interest in the impact of war on survivors. I grieve alongside all forced to see these images and more so for those whose lives are directly affected by warfare.

During these formative years, I was also exposed to the intergenerational arguments between those who supported and those who opposed U.S. involvement in the Vietnam War. Viewpoints for and against the war tended to coincide with viewpoints on the use of drugs. Therefore, I came of age when smoking marijuana and hash was inextricably linked to the anti-war movement, and drug use was in and of itself a political anti-authoritarian statement. As a very young child, I remember watching with disbelief and some amusement as a "rebellious" teenage neighbor strolled down the middle of our suburban street, wearing an Army jacket and smoking a joint, as he waved hello to a group of adults idly chatting in a neighbor's yard. After the young man walked by, the adults made no mention of the fact that he was smoking weed. They did, however, grumble about the disrespectful juxtaposition of the young man sprouting long hair and wearing an Army jacket he had not earned through military service. I'm pretty sure the reason they did not comment on the fact that he was smoking a joint was because they honestly did not know what a joint was.

These are the types of memories that, for me, created a logic model in which I understood that I was unnerved by the violence of Vietnam and I conceptually opposed the war. Marijuana and other drug use was a symbolic gesture of opposition to the war, and that created what I felt was a social connection to the anti-war movement. Because of these early observations, I have long understood that people initially choose to use drugs (including alcohol) for intensely personal reasons, in addition to making social or political statements. The reasons they may continue to use—and for some, become addicted—are more complex and have much to do with the depth of their emotional reservoirs and coping strategies. The humanity behind these issues drew me into the professional study of alcohol and other drugs, which has circuitously brought me back to complex issues of violence and wars and the War on Drugs, *ad infinitum*.

Despite unabashed opposition to violence, I do support and have the utmost respect for the men and women who serve in the military. As a graduate of West Point, my brother served in the military. My husband was a Marine in the Reserve Officers Training Corp, and my father-in-law was a World War II Marine vet. In recent years, I have worked closely with veterans suffering from post-traumatic stress disorder (PTSD), including 70-year-old Vietnam War veterans and 22-year-old men and women from Operation Iraqi Freedom (OIF) and Operation Enduring Freedom (OEF) in Afghanistan. In addition to work with military veterans, I have worked with former gang members, who often refer to themselves as "street soldiers" of a different type of drug war—many exhibiting similar PTSD symptomology. PTSD, a consequence of war for soldiers and civilians, results in hyper-arousal, hyper-vigilance, emotional and physical reactivity, re-experiencing of traumatic events, avoidance, isolation, and emotional numbing. The emotional numbing that alcohol and other drugs can provide has made them a perennial means of PTSD symptom management.

With each name, age, photograph, and hometown flashed across the television to momentarily honor fallen soldiers in Iraq and Afghanistan, I can only imagine the utter fear they faced in their final moments and the unending agony of their families. As my own son approached 18, the poignancy of each life lost took on a deeper meaning for me. Regardless of my son's stoic nature, he would be irretrievably damaged if he witnessed the carnage of war. I also know that the young soldiers affected by war are not altogether different from my son in this regard. These observations of humanity led me to expand my research of alcohol and other drug use to encompass its connection with the human impact of war.

During my research for this book, I interviewed veterans and their families, reviewed historical footage, and read innumerable accounts of the human experiences of war and the escalating use of alcohol and other drugs in connection to war-related trauma. Among the film footage and photographs were haunting images of survivors' shattered nerves and their soulful eyes—a glimpse into the vulnerable child within each of them. They are eyes that witnessed the slaughter of combat and experienced terror.

The latter part of this book examines the fact that the rate of suicides among U.S. veterans of the Iraq (OIF) and Afghan (OEF) wars is double that of the general U.S. population, and the level of alcohol and other drug abuse among OEF and OIF service members and veterans has soared. In fact, I began development of this book focused on the escalation of war and drugs in response to one another, as evidenced by the current wars in Iraq and Afghanistan with the content that makes up Chapters 11 through 13. My research continuously brought me back to lessons learned from the neglectful and negative experiences of Vietnam veterans. Researching drug use among troops in Vietnam and understanding the links between the anti-war movement and drugs in the U.S. brought to the surface the connections with the original declaration of the War on Drugs in 1971. This book has limited its scope of focus on the War on Drugs to a cursory overview of U.S. political rhetoric since 1971 and the drug-war smokescreen invoked by President Ronald Reagan, while simultaneously providing coverage for Nicaraguans trafficking cocaine into the U.S., the militarization of the drug war under George H.W. Bush, and finally, the current drug-war crises in Mexico.

As I researched this book, each military incursion was socially, politically, or ideologically linked to previous incursions that were quite apparently funded increasingly by regional and transnational drug trafficking. It was like pulling on a rope in search of an anchor buried in the murky abyss of war, the economics of the drug trade, and the human propensity for numbing oneself to the pain by using alcohol and other drugs. I anchored this book with the most obvious drug-related war, the Opium Wars of 1839–1842 and 1856–1860.

The Opium Wars illustrate how modern-day mass-consumption markets were developed in conjunction with mass addiction of the Chinese through forced trade of opium as a commodity to acquire silver bullion, which became the European financial model for funding colonial empires for the next century. The French funded their colonization of French Indochina through an opium monopoly in the region until 1950, after which point the opium trade became a source of clandestine funding for forces on each side of the split that would divide North and South Vietnam and spur the war.

Although there were numerous military incursions between the Opium Wars and the Vietnam War, this book focuses on the wars that most notably potentiate alcohol and other drug use as relief from the suffering of war (the U.S. Civil War), government involvement in the provision of these substances for troops (World War II), and the trafficking or use of drugs as tools of the Cold War.

This book covers diverse topics and timelines related to war and the roles that drugs have played in military incursions. However, I also examine the drug war and the role that government actions have played in the War on Drugs. The timeline on the following pages provides the reader with a fundamental background of the events that have shaped the history of the synergy between drugs and war.

Timeline

1620s–1670s: The use of opium rises among soldiers in Asia. Rajput troops, fighting for the Mughal Empire, introduce the use of opium to Assam (a region south of the Himalayas); opium is given daily to Rajput soldiers.

1839–1842: First Opium War fought between the United Kingdom and Qing Dynasty of China.

1850: The British arrive in lower Burma, importing large quantities of opium from India and selling it through a government-controlled opium monopoly.

1856–1860: Second Opium War between the United Kingdom and French Empire and the Qing Dynasty of China to open all Chinese ports for trade and to legalize the opium trade in China.

1899: France establishes the opium monopoly to control all opium trade in Indochina.

1909: The first federal drug-prohibition law passes; the U.S. outlaws the importation of opium. U.S. presses International Opium Commission (IOC) for legislation aimed at suppressing the sale of opium to China.

1912–1917: Chinese warlords encourage Chinese hill tribes to cultivate opium poppy. It is used to generate tax revenue and finance their war efforts.

1914: Harrison Narcotics Act implemented and U.S. federal control of narcotics established; nonmedical use of heroin and cocaine made illegal.

1917: Exportation of opium from India to China is banned.

1919: The establishment of the League of Nations following World War I provides the international community with a centralized body for the administration of drug-control policies.

1919: Congress passes Eighteenth Amendment to U.S. Constitution, establishing national alcohol prohibition.

1920: The League of Nations creates the Advisory Committee on the Traffic in Opium and Other Dangerous Drugs, commonly known as the Opium Advisory Committee (OAC), the precursor to the United Nations Commission on Narcotic Drugs and the United Nations Office of Drugs and Crime (UNODC).

1933: Congress repeals national alcohol prohibition and reverses the Eighteenth Amendment to U.S. Constitution.

1935–1939: Among the first signs of trouble in the international community prior to World War II is the withdrawal of Germany and Japan from the League of Nations OAC.

1937: Marijuana Tax Act enacted, making possession of marijuana illegal and placing it under federal control.

1940: Production of amphetamines escalates in anticipation of wartime needs for Germany and Japan.

1946: France abolishes their opium monopoly in Indochina. The French Corsican underworld moves in to fill the gap.

1947: French intelligence service seizes control of Vietnamese opium trade, which becomes funding source for clandestine operations against Viet Minh.

1946–1950: Post World War II stockpiles of amphetamines from Europe are dumped into the Japanese market, resulting in epidemic rates of amphetamine addiction in Japan.

1947: United States establishes the Central Intelligence Agency (CIA) for the primary purpose of preventing the spread of communism. CIA begins establishing clandestine alliances along the Iron Curtain in regions where the threat of communism is greatest in Southeast Asia.

1940s–1970s: In its anti-communist efforts in postwar France, the U.S. intelligence agencies (OSS, CIA) ally with French Corsicans to disrupt pro-communist organizations in Marseille and provide support for Corsicans involved in the narcotics trade. Corsican gangsters and Italian mafia dominate U.S. heroin market. Marseille laboratories refine opium into heroin that is trafficked through New York City; a heroin epidemic ensues.

1950s: The Kuomintang (KMT) Army living in northeast Burma and northern Thailand is aided by the U.S. (through the CIA) in its fight against the communist Chinese government. Opium is used to pay soldiers in northern Burma, and the KMT finance its anti-communist resistance through the sale of opium and heroin. The region becomes known as the Golden Triangle.

1950: The CIA establishes the regional charter airline Air America.

1954: The Eisenhower Administration establishes the U.S. Interdepartmental Committee on Narcotics.

1955–1965: Corsican gangsters establish and run "Air Opium," a collection of commuter airplanes that transport opium and revive the Laotian drug trade.

1955–1972: As part of their Cold War efforts, the CIA and the Department of Defense conduct ongoing human experiments with LSD, marijuana, and other psychedelics in their quest for the development of mind-control methods; e.g., MK-ULTRA, Project Bluebird.

1961: The United Nations Single Convention on Narcotic Drugs is adopted, replacing existing multilateral treaties concerned with control of narcotic drugs. The referent object in the UN Single convention is mankind, and the existential threat is the evil of drug addiction. To protect mankind from addiction, global prohibition is the method of protection.

1965–1975: U.S. involvement in Vietnam correlates with a surge in illegal heroin being smuggled into America. Air America is used by Southeast Asian allies to transport raw opium from the Golden Triangle to Marseille by Corsican gangsters, where their refined heroin is shipped to the U.S.

1966: LSD is declared illegal in the United States.

1966–1974: The Brotherhood of Eternal Love is established as an outgrowth of the Vietnam anti-war movement in California. The

Brotherhood initiates a hash-smuggling trade between Afghanistan and the U.S. and becomes one of the top producers of LSD with its trademark Orange Sunshine.

1971: President Richard M. Nixon declares a War on Drugs and creates a Special Action Office for Drug Abuse Prevention. Nixon declares drug abuse "public enemy number one."

1970s: The number of heroin addicts in the U.S. reaches an estimated 750,000. Once Saigon falls and the Vietnam War ends, the heroin epidemic subsides, along with heroin supplies in U.S. The end of the Vietnam War and the War on Drugs disrupt the flow of heroin from the Golden Triangle. The search for a new source of raw opium is fulfilled in Mexico's Sierra Madre mountains, and "Mexican Mud" replaces "China White" heroin until 1978.

1972: Convention on Psychotropic Substances ratified, amending the 1961 United Nations Single Convention.

1973: Nixon creates the Drug Enforcement Administration (DEA) to coordinate the efforts of all other agencies.

1979–1990: Opium and heroin production in Afghanistan, Pakistan, and Iran escalate, and the region becomes known as the "Golden Crescent," a formidable epicenter for opium and heroin. Opium and heroin production escalate amid the confluence of regional wars: the Soviet invasion of Afghanistan (1979), the Islamic revolution in Iran (1979), and the Iran-Iraq War (1980–90). U.S. supports the mujahideen in Afghanistan in their fight against the Soviets.

1981: U.S. authorizes CIA to support and conduct political and paramilitary operations in Nicaragua and elsewhere in Central America. Approves $19 million to fund Contra military to fight the Sandinistas for control of Nicaragua.

1988: United Nations Convention Against Illicit Traffic in Narcotic Drugs and Psychotropic Substances is ratified. The referent object in the third UN convention is "nation states"; the existential threats are organized crime and drug trafficking. To protect "nation states" from transnational organized crime, the drug war escalates to militarized operations.

1982–1983: Boland Amendment enacted; prohibits CIA and Department of Defense (DoD) from spending money to support the Contras and activities designed to overthrow the Sandinista, yet it still allows arms interdiction. Nicaraguan exiles in the U.S. use drug trafficking to fund the Contras.

1984: Nancy Reagan launches the "Just Say No" anti-drug campaign. The Washington Times reports that the Nicaraguan Sandinistas are involved in the drug trade.

1986: Senate Subcommittee on Terrorism, Narcotics, and International Operations (Kerry Committee) opens investigation into alleged illegal gun-running and narcotics trafficking associated with the Contra War. Independent counsel initiates investigation of Iran-Contra Affair.

1988: The Kerry Committee's report, "Drugs, Law Enforcement and

Foreign Policy," concludes that drug traffickers used the Contra war and their ties to the Contras as a cover for drug trafficking, and funding from drug traffickers provided financial support for the Contras. Nicaraguan exiles living in the U.S. engages in mass trafficking of cocaine into the U.S., primarily through Florida and California. Influx of cocaine results in the national expansion of the Bloods and the Crips gangs.

1988: The U.S. and Mexican governments attempt to eliminate opium cultivation in Mexico ("Mexican Mud") by spraying poppy fields with Agent Orange, a toxic defoliant used during the Vietnam War. As a result, the amount of "Mexican Mud" in the U.S. drug market declines; the Golden Crescent becomes the top source.

1989: President George H.W. Bush creates the Office of National Drug Control Policy (ONDCP). William Bennett appointed first "drug czar," with the mission of making drug abuse socially unacceptable.

1990: General Manuel Noriega surrenders to the DEA on January 3, during U.S. invasion of Panama. Noriega convicted of drug trafficking in 1992.

1992: Columbia's drug lords introduce high-grade heroin into the United States.

1996: Afghanistan replaces Myanmar (formerly Burma) as the leading producer of illicit opium; Afghanistan continues to increase opium cultivation until the Taliban's brief prohibition of drug production in 2001.

2001: Taliban prohibits the cultivation and production of poppies and opium; consequently, opium and heroin prices skyrocket.

2001: In response to the September 11th attacks, the U.S. invades Afghanistan in an effort to break the foothold the Taliban, Al Qaeda, and Osama Bin Laden have in the region.

2002–2007: Cannabis and opium poppy cultivation and narcotics production escalate in Afghanistan. Regional drug trafficking provides significant funding for the Taliban and Al Qaeda.

2004: DEA announces its involvement alongside the State Department and the Department of Defense in the U.S. Embassy Kabul Counternarcotics Implementation Plan in efforts to reduce heroin production in Afghanistan, now the world's leading opium producer.

2006: Felipe Calderón elected President of Mexico; he reinvigorates the War on Drugs, targeting the drug cartels in Mexico.

2006–2011: Mexico's drug war claims more than 34,612 lives.

June 1, 2011: Report of the Global Commission on Drug Policy published, calling for an end to the War on Drugs. Among the 19 commissioners are the former presidents of several nations, the former U.S. secretary of state, the former chairman of the U.S. Federal Reserve, and former secretary general of the United Nations.

June 23, 2011: U.S. Congressional Representatives Ron Paul (R: TX) and Barney Frank (D: MA) introduce the "Ending Federal Marijuana Prohibition Act of 2011," a bipartisan bill to end U.S. federal marijuana prohibition.

Acknowledgments

Many people have directly and indirectly contributed to the development of this book. The threads that have pulled together the conceptual framework include Shepard Fairey's inspirational artwork, thousands of scholarly books and historical documents, my direct work with veterans, the National Security Archives, the Cold War History Project, and the Veterans History Project through the Library of Congress. One particular Veterans History Project photograph by Aldo Stephen Panzieri, Air Force veteran of the Vietnam War, captured the subtlety of the personal experiences of Vietnam troops and their use of drugs overseas. The image was Aldo's photograph of a young soldier with a rifle at his side while he snorted dope out of a paper bag. Aldo's pictures are included in Chapter 9, "The Vietnam War and Blowback at Home." I also want to acknowledge the scholarly support and guidance of my mentor, Dr. Sandra Lane, who encouraged me throughout the writing process, provided feedback, and served as a sounding board in my efforts to articulate the connections between war and drugs and their escalation in response to one another. A special thank you to my editor, Jennifer Knerr, for believing in this project and shepherding me through the process of completing my first full-length book. In closing, I want to thank my family—my husband, John, our daughter, Rachael, and our son, Johnny—for their inspiration and support throughout the writing and research process of this book.

CHAPTER I

Introduction

The Escalation of War and Drugs in Relation to One Another

Call off the Global Drug War.

Jimmy Carter, June 16, 2011,[1]
U.S. president, recipient of the 2002 Nobel Peace Prize

ON JULY 14, 1969, President Richard Nixon identified drug abuse as "a serious national threat." Two years later, on June 17, 1971, President Nixon sternly faced television cameras, calling drug abuse "public enemy number one in the United States," and declared a national War on Drugs. The War on Drugs was declared in response to the turmoil of the 1960s, rising crime, and the blowback of the Vietnam War. Recreational use of psychoactive drugs had become popular among the hippie subculture, the white middle class, and black urban populations. Marijuana was part of the larger counterculture tapestry opposing Nixon's actions in Vietnam.[2] There was also widespread marijuana, heroin, and amphetamine use among U.S. soldiers in Vietnam. With no end in sight to an unpopular—and unwinnable—Vietnam War, Nixon waged a war that might be won more easily: an all-out offensive on drugs at home.

At the height of the Vietnam War, opiates, such as heroin, marijuana, and amphetamines, were widely available in Vietnam and on the streets of America. As the U.S. negotiated a war settlement, thousands of servicemen would be returning home, addicted to heroin. Fearful of the social ramifications of the influx of potential addicts, the Nixon Administration dedicated the majority of drug-war funding to treatment rather than to interdiction and law enforcement, which currently receive the majority of funding.

I

In the early days of the War on Drugs, there was also substantial emphasis on addiction prevention, treatment, and rehabilitation, which presented a balanced approach to the country's drug problems, but this balance was fleeting. Drug use and addiction were intentionally shifted away from what they are—a health issue—and framed administratively and socially as criminal and a threat to national security. President Nixon strategically pulled the authority for drugs out of the National Institute on Mental Health (NIMH), where it belonged, and in January 1972, with Executive Order 11641, he created the Office of Drug Abuse Law Enforcement (ODALE) to coalesce federal and local forces to fight the illegal drug trade at the street level.[3] ODALE enabled the U.S. to launch strategic efforts to prevent the import of illegal drugs and combat the use, manufacturing, and trade of all illicit drugs within its borders.

In a speech on January 3, 1973, New York Governor Nelson Rockefeller proclaimed the crime associated with addiction as a "reign of terror" and neighborhoods were being "as effectively destroyed by addicts as by an invading army."[4] In July 1973, Nixon established the Drug Enforcement Administration (DEA), and from that point forward, the drug war became increasingly focused on securitization and militarization.[5] The phrase "War on Drugs" implies a militaristic response to the cultivation, distribution, and use of a commodity (psychoactive drugs). What the phrase fails to capture is that drugs are both a byproduct and a tool of war, and that drugs and war are mutually reinforcing and intensifying phenomena. Narcotic trafficking escalates in regions where there are military incursions, often becoming the primary source of funding for many rebel groups and paramilitary operations. At the same time, illicit drugs numb the fear, pain, and grief of military personnel and their victims. Drug use also trends upward among civilians from the countries who deploy troops to combat. An endemic drug trade had taken root with burgeoning groups of narco-traffickers, gunrunners, and paramilitary factions in Central America, South America, and Southeast Asia.

The declaration of the War on Drugs near the end of the Vietnam War was not the beginning of drug warfare. History reveals a lethal synergy between military confrontation and the consumption of mind-altering substances. Nowhere is this more evident than in the two Opium Wars of 1839–1842 and 1856–1860 between Britain and China, during which Britain actively sought to force the sale of the addictive drug opium to the Chinese in order to achieve colonial hegemony. Britain saturated China's population, government, royalty, and much of its army with highly addictive opium. When China attempted to ban the trafficking of opium, England launched a war to retain access to the Chinese market. England's victory had devastating consequences for the Chinese people that would last for nearly 100 years.

The Opium Wars further accelerated global trade, not just in opium, but in other addictive consumables such as sugar, tea, and tobacco. Profits from the commercial farming and sale of opium funded Britain's colonial wars and the resulting expansion of the British Empire, creating a precedent that would be followed by France, the Netherlands, Burma (Myanmar), the CIA, Afghan insurgents, Nicaraguan Contras, and numerous paramilitary groups.[6,7,8]

In all of these associated conflicts and countless others before and since, soldiers, refugees, and civilians have reacted to war-induced suffering by heavy use and abuse of alcohol and other drugs. Escalating drug cultivation, trafficking, and use is a demonstrable and predictable consequence of war. Addiction and drug-related violence in turn produce waves of turbulence that sustain and intensify military conflict.

Two threads connect war and drugs: human suffering and the intent to serve as a defense mechanism. Armed conflict is frequently a mechanism for the defense of territory, resources, and values, as well as a vehicle for greed and aggression. Drugs, including alcohol, are mechanisms of defense from one's thoughts, emotions, and physical pain. Both war and addiction feed on human frailty, as illustrated by the Vietnam War (1965–1975) and Operation Enduring Freedom (OEF) in Afghanistan (2001–present). The Cold War conflict in Vietnam triggered a tsunami-like global escalation of addiction and drug trafficking in the Golden Triangle, Vietnam, Laos, Thailand, and Burma (now Myanmar), as well as among U.S. Vietnam veterans and civilians. Meanwhile, the war in Afghanistan (OEF) has coincided with the exponential growth of opium cultivation in that region. Within two years of OEF, Afghanistan had regained its position as the world's largest producer of opium, accounting for nearly 90 percent of the world's illicit market.

With lethal force begetting more violence in classic tit-for-tat fashion, an approach more in line with peace promotion would seem to hold out greater promise of progress.[9] The amplification of armed conflict occasioned by the War on Drugs can be seen in the escalating violence in Mexico. The Mexican drug cartels' response to President Felipe Calderón's crackdown on narcotics trafficking has been like attempting to douse a fire with gasoline. Police and government officials who have dared to take action against the cartels have, in tragic retribution, been decapitated and savagely tortured.[10] This nexus suggests that waging a War on Drugs may promote drug use and trade, rather than reducing drug trafficking (through economic development) and addiction (through treatment). With the martial approach to combating addiction having largely failed, a chorus of scholars and policy experts has called for a different tactic.[11,12,13,14,15,16,17]

I certainly do not advocate inaction. For the Mexican and Afghan governments to sit idly by would be to enable lower-level narco-terrorism to escalate into narco-statehood. Thwarting efforts to control this phenomenon, however, is the durable and enormous market for illicit drugs in America, Europe, and the Russian Federation. To effectively reduce the demand for drugs, we must first conduct a global examination of the entwined histories of war and drugs. To date, most efforts to address the intersection of war and drugs have failed to consider the profound influence of each upon the other. Peace studies, for example, focus on the history of conflict, conflict resolution, and avoidance of war. Addiction studies focus on the dynamics of addiction in the hope of treating, preventing, and reversing its progression. Looking at the relationship between addiction and warfare and examining their mutual escalation in response to one another provides fresh insight into the prevention of these problems.

Some wars are nebulous, such as the Cold War (1945–1991), yet its relationship to the proliferation of psychedelic drug use in the United States is clear. In the chapters covering the Cold War, we will examine the triangulation between the peace movement, psychedelic drugs, and the U.S. government. During the Cold War, the U.S. government developed and tested the use of psychedelic drugs as a means of mind-control social manipulation. However, when the CIA lost control over the dissemination of the drugs, and they became synonymous with the anti-war movement, people involved in the peace movement were investigated by the U.S. House Committee on Un-American Activities.[18]

For purposes of this book, drugs are defined as psychoactive substances that are capable of being used recreationally and have addictive potential. War is broadly delineated and refers to three frameworks: conflict or armed hostility between nations or between factions within a state or region (e.g., the Vietnam War, the Colombian conflict pitting the government against FARC rebels); antagonistic campaigns against something perceived as destructive (e.g., the War on Drugs); and more generally and often personally, a struggle to overcome (e.g., battling addiction). In the context of armed hostility between nations or factions within nation-states, drugs have long been intertwined with issues of defense, national security, economics, and politics.

This book challenges the reader to consider a broader perspective of alcohol and other drugs in relation to war by dissecting the duality of their relationship to one another. At each level I advance a thesis, and collectively these frame the argument of the book.

1. For those affected by war (soldiers, veterans, refugees, their families, and the countries involved), alcohol and other drugs are pursued as a refuge from suffering.
2. For centuries, drugs have been used as a commodity to fund wars, para-political groups, and governments.
3. The militaristic approach embodied in the War on Drugs has intensified conflict in regions associated with drug production and consumption, due in large part to the triad of unaddressed addiction, poverty, and the trafficking of drugs and munitions.

If we are to make any progress in controlling the expansion of drug markets and the escalation of drug use, we need to focus on the roots of addiction, drug cultivation, and trafficking and revisit the long-term multigenerational effect of engaging in war—whether war is understood as the drug war, an international conflict, a civil war, a terrorist organization, or another paramilitary conflict. War shapes lives for generations, taking an inevitable and immeasurable human toll.

This book does not endorse a particular policy or solution. Addiction is a multifaceted problem that needs to be examined at the individual (micro) level, the community (mezzo) level, and the national and international (macro) levels; thus, the solutions must be more nuanced and complex than simple prohibition or legalization.

Campaigns against psychoactive substances, such as the temperance movement and the War on Drugs, have been analyzed in relation to issues of power, cultural privilege, and class distinction.[19] Further, war has been appropriated as a metaphor to describe the interpersonal struggle involved in battling addiction. Yet not enough attention has been devoted to the historical examination of the ripple effects of war-related drug trafficking and addiction.

The covert nature of drug use impedes a full assessment of the economic and human impact of war-related addiction. Consumer spending on illicit drugs is virtually impossible to tabulate. Further complicating the historical analysis of rates of addiction and the financial cost of the War on Drugs is the unreliability of statistical evidence.[20,21,22] Precise rates of addiction prior to the late 1970s, when valid survey and data-collection methodologies were established, are difficult to track. Furthermore, tallying the financial costs of drug wars can be misleading because spending is dispersed among numerous government agencies and is rarely transparent. For example, funds spent by the U.S. military on drug control in the early 2000s were removed from the total figure of what the United States spends annually in the War on Drugs.[23] The data in this book are drawn from both governmental and non-governmental organizations, as well as government accountability and oversight agencies.

This book begins its examination of the duality of war and drugs with the Opium Wars of 1839–1842 and 1856–1860, from which we are currently some seven generations removed, and continues chronologically covering the major U.S. wars that most contributed to global trends in drug use, including the period known as the Cold War (1947–1991); I conclude with the wars in Afghanistan (OEF, 2001 to present) and Iraq (Operation Iraqi Freedom [OIF], 2003–2010).

The Opium Wars established a precedent for the use of drug trafficking to fund governments, military incursions, and colonialism. Colonial-era opium trade played an important role in funding the European, French, and Asian empires and their world trade. Opium provided the capital that built the British and French colonial infrastructure and administration.[24,25] The drug abuse and addiction that plague countries around the world today have roots in these conflicts.

The after-effects of war reverberate for years with anyone exposed to armed conflict—soldiers, civilians, and refugees. This book examines the suffering that has long plagued survivors of war: posttraumatic stress disorder (PTSD) and the use of alcohol and other drugs to block psychological and physical pain. Veterans and civilians who have witnessed atrocities or who have faced or caused death and injury are psychologically unsettled for years, and many suffer from depression, mood swings, emotional numbness, outbursts of rage, aggressive impulses, alcoholism, drug addiction, isolation, and the deterioration of relationships as a result of their unsettled behavior. For each individual affected by war-related PTSD, there are family and community members affected by their aggressive behaviors, moods, and addictions. Veterans with PTSD suffer from impaired memory and attention, insomnia, and anxiety, and are more likely to use drugs and alcohol in excess later in life.[26,27]

CHAPTER 2

Drugs and War

T HERE IS A SYNERGISTIC relationship between warfare and substance abuse. Drugs
have been used to weaken enemies, relieve pain, and stimulate troops to fight.
The connection between mind-altering substances and armed fighting has
a long and complicated history. Since Alexander the Great launched his assault on
the Persian Empire in 334 BCE, the "fruits of the poppy" (sap of the flower *Papaver
somniferum*) have been used to relieve the pain of war.[1] Alexander and his Greek
army introduced opium to Turkey, Afghanistan, Persia, and Central and Southeast
Asia.[2] Drugs have also served as a source of funding for clandestine military and
paramilitary activity for centuries.

An example from 13th-century Persia (Iran) demonstrates the use of drugs as
a tool of war and a method to train young soldiers to overcome their reluctance to
harm others. The Persian ruler al-Hassan bin Sabbah, the Sheikh of Alamut, used
hashish as an incentive to coax young disciples to carry out lethal "hits" against their
enemies. They came to be known as *hashisheen*, or assassins.[3] The hash disinhibited
the would-be assassins psychologically, enabling them to carry out the murders.
The promise of a continued supply of hash maintained the allegiance of the young
soldiers to the rulers.

Alcohol and other drugs often create physical and psychological states that result
in violence. There is a long history of soldiers turning to alcohol and other drugs for
"liquid courage" and disinhibition, to settle their nerves, or to increase their aggression, all depending on the type of drug ingested.

During battle, 25 percent of soldiers lose control of their bladder and bowels from
the intense fear and anxiety; some resort to mind-altering drugs, including alcohol,
to counter and dull the emotional horror.[4,5] To counter loss of bowel control, Rajputs,
members of a royal warrior caste of India, took opium, long recognized as effective
in decreasing bowel peristalsis and even today occasionally used as a treatment for
diarrhea.

Vikings and ancient Russian warriors drank an infusion of the hallucinogenic mushroom *Amanita muscaria* before battle.[6] Scythian soldiers of Central Asia smoked hashish and marijuana. Anthropologists have documented that the Massai of East Africa prepare for war by drinking potent narcotic herbs made from the bark of the thorny olkiloriti tree, an ancient practice that continues to this day.[7] During both world wars, Russian soldiers took valerian, an herbal sedative.[8]

Of all the substances used to mitigate the fear of battle, alcohol has been the most widely used to dull emotions and reduce inhibitions. Historians note that the Chinese and the Greeks drank before battles. In 1415, French knights got drunk on the eve of the Battle of Agincourt (a victory for the English). The term "Dutch courage" refers to drinking alcohol to disguise fear and gain courage for a fight. The term is said to have originated from English soldiers drinking Genever gin before their battles against the formidable Dutch navy in the 1600s. Genocidal killers in Bosnia and Kosovo also drank heavily to prepare for the ethnic-cleansing atrocities they would subsequently commit. The Nazi Einsatzgruppen was given schnapps before and after mass killings. In 1945, Soviet troops in Berlin fueled their rape atrocities by drinking an enormous variety of substances, including toxic chemicals.[9,10]

Historian Niall Ferguson says World War I could not have been fought without alcohol.[11] Ferguson's observation echoes the sentiments of a medical officer for the Royal Sussex Regiment, who declared the British would not have won the war without the rum rations issued to British soldiers before battle.[12] Italian troops were likewise issued two bottles of cognac each day; officers and soldiers alike reportedly got drunk at every opportunity.[13] During World War II, U.S. soldiers who ran out of liquor reportedly improvised and made cocktails with juice and Aqua Velva aftershave (which contained pure alcohol).[14]

The following poem, written by a World War I soldier in 1918, describes the prevalence of alcohol and the need to drink heavily during this brutal war.

> *You say we're mad when we strike the beer,*
> *But if you'd stood in shivering fear*
> *With the boys who bring the wounded back*
> *Cross no-man's land where there ain't no track*
> *You'd read no psalms to the men that fight*
> *You'd take the drink to forget the sight*
> *Of torn out limbs and sightless eyes*
> *Or the passing of a pal that dies.*[15]

During World War II, amphetamines were used extensively by forces on each side of the conflict. Japanese Kamikaze pilots, primed with stimulants, were high on methamphetamines during their suicide missions.[16] During World War II, the Luftwaffe surged across Europe at lightning speed, fueled by methamphetamines. During the blitzkrieg, more than 35 million tablets of the methamphetamine Pervitin were shipped to the German army between April and June of 1940.[17]

The use of stimulant drugs distorts thinking and enhances physical tolerance; amphetamines are highly addictive, and dependency develops quickly, potentially triggering psychosis. The use of amphetamines and other drugs by Nazi military leaders, including Hitler, is believed to have greatly fueled their aggression, grandiose ideations, and paranoia. This paranoia and psychotic behavior of commanders, fueled by stimulant drugs, may have been a factor in enabling the Nazi administration to carry out heinous acts of violence against humanity.[18] The Nazis' genocide of the Jewish people clearly stems from their aberrant ideology, and those who participated in atrocities are responsible for their behavior. However, the use of alcohol and other drugs did play a part in the behavior of many Nazis, including the physicians who oversaw the mass murders at the concentration camps. They primed themselves to commit atrocities, and alcohol was served as a means of coping afterward.[19]

As a means of survival during the Gulf War, Operation Enduring Freedom (OEF), and Operation Iraqi Freedom (OIF), U.S. soldiers used amphetamines in prescribed doses to stay alert during patrols, nighttime duty, and long missions conducted in extreme heat. During these wars, combinations of stimulants and narcotics—known as "go-pills" and "no-pills"—were issued to pilots and other military personnel.[20,21] Amphetamines (the "go-pills") helped the pilots and soldiers stay awake on long missions, and sedatives (the "no-pills") helped to induce sleep. Whereas many Vietnam veterans developed heroin addiction in Southeast Asia, veterans of the wars in Afghanistan and Iraq are more likely to develop addictions to such prescription medications as opiates for pain relief, sedatives for sleep, or amphetamines.[22]

During the civil war in Sierra Leone (1991–2002), members of the Revolutionary United Front (RUF) abducted children and got them addicted to cocaine, amphetamines, and a heinous concoction of gunpowder and cocaine known as *brown brown*. Physical dependence on these stimulant drugs fostered aggression in the youngsters, allowing the RUF to build its opposition army through the use of "boy soldiers" for their cause.[23] The practice of recruiting child soldiers, drugging them as a means of control, and keeping them dependent on their "captors" is pervasive among paramilitary groups in Afghanistan, the Congo, Liberia, Myanmar, Sierra Leone, and Sri Lanka (Liberation Tigers of Tamil Eelam [LTTE]).[24]

The war-torn regions of Africa are particularly vulnerable to drug trafficking and addiction. Presently, the majority of the wars in Africa are civil wars, which result in very high rates of trauma and devastation of the country's economic system. As such, the survivors are susceptible to addiction as a means of escaping the trauma of war, while drugs such as heroin and cocaine flood the region because of security vulnerabilities. Cocaine traffickers from Colombia use West Africa as a transshipment point to Europe because it provides the path of least resistance, with thousands of miles of unsecured coastline. The Camorra syndicate, which dominates the drug trade in Naples and Castel Volturno, Italy, prey on the vulnerable citizens of war-torn countries and enslave them in their narcotics trafficking.[25,26]

The United Nations has recognized illicit drug production as one of the highest-risk activities for inducing conflict in regions of economic instability. Underlying patterns of drug cultivation, production, international trafficking, and domestic consumption have made dramatic gains following each war in which the U.S. has engaged.[27,28] Regions where drugs are cultivated and traded tend to have the highest rates of addiction.

One contemporary example is Afghanistan. The current war in Afghanistan, known as Operation Enduring Freedom (OEF), continues to escalate in violence, while opium production has skyrocketed from its nadir of 185 tons in 2001 to 8,200 tons in 2007, capturing most of the world's heroin market.[29] The growth in production provides funds for insurgent paramilitary groups, contributing to widespread corruption and destabilization of the new government. Afghanistan is at risk of becoming a narco-state. During the Soviet-Afghan war, the CIA protected Afghan drug lords who served U.S. anti-communist political interests. The U.S. befriended Afghan and Pakistani rebel tribesmen in their fight against the Soviets, while the CIA provided cover for Afghan drug lords whose money funded their rebellion.[30] When the Soviet-Afghan war was over, a million people were dead, and Afghan heroin had captured 60% of the U.S. market.[31] The CIA's complicity in narco-trafficking through connections with para-political and insurgent groups in Southeast Asia, South America, and the Middle East has also fueled the U.S. and global heroin and cocaine trades.[32,33]

These scenarios illustrate ways that drugs have been used to achieve the necessary or desired mindset to undertake physically and emotionally stressful missions. As a result of the acts of war carried out over the centuries, millions of civilians and veterans have suffered emotional and physical trauma, turning to alcohol and other drugs to numb the pain.

Figure 2-1 depicts the core issues related to war and drugs and their cyclic framework. Cultivation, trafficking, and trade of narcotics in mass occur predominantly in countries with unstable governments where power vacuums exist. The drug trade relies on the supply-demand of individual traders as well as government entities, and generates wealth among groups who can influence and engage law enforcement, governments, and civilians, leading to instability, power struggles, violence, and war or war-like situations. Wars produce suffering among soldiers, combatants, and civilians.

An examination of how large-scale cultivation, trafficking, and trade of narcotics become feasible in a region illustrates how these regions are susceptible to military conflict. The risk of civil war is greater in low-income economies, and the World Bank recognizes that civil war reflects a failure of development.[34] Civil war creates territories that are outside the authority of recognized governments and become epicenters of criminal activity, often involving the drug trade. As such, narcotics cultivation and trafficking are most prevalent in underdeveloped countries that characteristically have unstable governments and weak law enforcement.

Military incursions and political unrest are in themselves crises that create turmoil, particularly among civilians. The crisis of war creates dangerous opportunities for drug production, sale, distribution and use. Governmental, political, legal, and economic constructs become unstable during a crisis and present the specters of power vacuums, diverted attention of military and law enforcement, and the loss of traditional bases of economic life.

Figure 2-1 Cycle of War and Drugs

PTSD, Suffering, Dislocation, and Rebellion → Narcotics Cultivation, Trafficking, and Trade → Amassing of Wealth through Drug Trade → Narco-wealth–Based Influence, Power, and Corruption → War, Violence, Instability, Power, Struggle → PTSD, Suffering, Dislocation, and Rebellion

As of the writing of this book, the most volatile region in Afghanistan is the southern province of Helmand, which is also the world's largest opium poppy–growing region. The violence in this region originates with the Taliban militants, the drug lords they protect, the insurgents, and the fight against the U.S. and NATO forces trying to reduce opium production in the region. Afghan drug labs, the opium trade, and the insurgency are intertwined; insurgent groups are funded with hundreds of millions of dollars from the drug trade each year.[35]

Mexico, on the other hand, is an example of a country that, though not currently engaged in war with another nation, is experiencing a dramatic increase in drug production and trafficking. Mexico is not engaged in the war in Iraq, Operation Iraqi Freedom (OIF); Afghanistan, Operation Enduring Freedom (OEF); or any other external war. However, Mexico's northern-bordering neighbor, the United States, has been immersed in these wars for more than nine years, which has presented an opportunity for the drug cartels in Mexico.

As will be discussed in later chapters, during the early years of the U.S. engagement with OEF and OIF, the U.S. needed to allocate financial and personnel resources to meet the demands of the OEF and OIF foreign incursions. As a result, support for the War on Drugs along U.S. borders and resources for Mexico's drug interdiction were reduced. Simultaneously, Mexico's rate of drug-related violence, murders, kidnapping, trafficking, and corruption has escalated as drug trafficking has pushed north, while weapons trade has flowed south of the U.S. border. As the diagram of the connection between war and drugs illustrates, drug trafficking generates wealth among groups who can corrupt, influence, and engage government officials and civilians. This has led to the instability, power struggles, violence, and war-like conditions Mexico is experiencing today.

This is not an indictment of the U.S. for the escalation of drug-related violence and activity in Mexico; rather, it is an illustration of the ebb and flow of drug trends and trafficking based on shifts in drug demand, supply, and interdiction resources. The cultivation and trade of any given drug can easily resurface when the focus and pressure turn toward other security measures and/or the introduction or resurgence of other drugs. This dynamic is in part why certain drugs dominate each decade in a given region. For example, in the 1960s and 1970s, marijuana trafficking and use dominated the North American scene, but its use later decreased with growth in cultivation and trade of South American cocaine in the 1980s.

The U.S. counternarcotics efforts in Mexico, Central America, and South America are carried out by non-government contractors under the Department of Defense (DoD). Although the U.S. Drug Enforcement Agency (DEA) still employs and deploys agents to these regions, DoD subcontractors make up a substantive portion of the interdiction efforts.

It is also noteworthy that many of the same corporations with which the U.S. government subcontracts to carry out the drug war are the same corporations that serve as defense contractors for our military. Finances and human resources are not infinite, and the government can only effectively focus and adequately fund their corporate contractors in limited areas. Defense preparation for two foreign wars and border protection against "terrorist threats" needed to take precedence over drug interdiction. Although funding for the drug war declined in the early years of the OIF and OEF, the drug war remains a lucrative business for defense contractors because it is a heavily funded and outsourced specialized mission.

The increasing recognition that the drug trade funds terrorist organizations has revitalized the corporate defense contractor's role in drug-war counternarcotics. Pentagon contracts for fighting terrorists with ties to the drug trade have created a drug-war business in league with major defense-contract corporations, such as Blackwater, Lockheed Martin, Northrop Grumann, and Raytheon. These defense-contract corporations were recently tapped by the DoD for a five-year contract worth up to $15 billion to fight the drug war.[36] The Northrop Grumman website describes their counter-narco-terrorism global support (CNGS) team. In October 2007, Northrop Grumman was "awarded an indefinite delivery/indefinite quantity (IDIQ) contract by the U.S. Department of Defense to provide technology development application for new products and services to defense and federal civilian agencies, state and local authorities, and partner nations engaged in counter-drug and counter-narco-terrorism (CNT) operations."[37]

Simultaneously, the U.S. prison system has become increasingly privatized; some prisons are run by corporations and subsidiaries of defense contractors. Defense contractors are also using federal prison labor (55 percent serving time for drug-related offenses) to build parts for defense contractors (for example, electronic components for the Patriot [PAC-3] guided missiles), which in turn are sold for significant profit.[38,39] The privatization and profit of such prisons is widely viewed as a conflict of interests—imprisoning more people and keeping them in jail for longer periods of time while using prison labor for lucrative contracts.[40,41] The militarization and securitization of the War on Drugs has created an industry that may be invested in perpetuating its own survival.

In 2002, representatives from my local DEA office contacted me and asked whether I would work with them to conduct a public forum to address the rising use of Ecstasy (MDMA) among America's youth. At the time, I was the associate dean of students at Syracuse University, the director of the university's Substance Abuse Prevention and Health Enhancement Office, and very interested in this type of education and risk reduction, so I worked with the DEA to host a regional forum. There were hundreds of people in attendance, and the DEA had arranged for substantial media coverage, but the program completely missed its mark as a drug prevention initiative. It was instead a carefully orchestrated show designed to link the current designer drug trend to terrorism and national security so that the DEA could build its case to receive funding available through national and homeland security under the post-9/11 threat of terrorism.

Through the ages, the cycle of war and drugs relates to suffering, displacement, and PTSD among combatants and civilians. As such, the direct and indirect impacts of war are, for many people, the reasons why they use mind-altering substances. "Soldier's Disease" was the term used to describe the emotional trauma of opium abuse among veterans of the Civil War. Following World War I, veterans who were psychologically affected by the trauma of war were said to suffer from "shell shock." Today, the human response to the physical and emotional stress of war is better known as posttraumatic stress disorder (PTSD). PTSD is a psychological diagnosis that encompasses a number of symptoms, including depression, anxiety, disordered eating, and heavy alcohol and/or other drug use. There is little dispute that PTSD has affected veterans, their families, and civilians for generations. The use of alcohol and other drugs by members of the military to manage the physical and psychological stress of war and subsequent PTSD are accepted but not well-understood facts of war.

We have become acutely aware of living casualties of war from the Vietnam, Afghan, and Iraq wars. PTSD may be a relatively new clinical term, but as an emotional state, it is as old as war. The resonance of the casualties of war is illustrated in Drew Faust's *This Republic of Suffering*, in which Civil War soldiers document how they were "never quite the same after seeing fields of slaughtered bodies destroyed by men just like themselves."[42] Researchers from the Veterans Administration found that the majority (52 percent) of people with PTSD have been diagnosed with alcohol abuse or dependence, and 35 percent have been diagnosed with drug abuse or dependence. The rate of alcohol abuse and dependence among people with PTSD is double that of the general population, and drug addiction and dependence rates are nearly three times that of the general adult population.[43]

The severity of posttraumatic stress among veterans escalates in direct relation to the intimacy and closeness of combat between killer and victim. The face-to-face combat of the Iraq War, the Vietnam War, and the U.S. Civil War stands in contrast to the distance between killers and targets in aviation-dominated fighting and the technical warfare of the 1990 Gulf War. Killing has tremendous potential to transform some survivors into casualties of war who are the emotional equivalent of the living dead. To survive, they have had to deny and numb basic human feelings, at costs that are paid for generations after soldiers return from the battlefield.

Today, chemists are developing drugs that could enable soldiers to kill without guilt and remorse. Researchers are conducting human tests on propranolol to assess its ability to blunt the effects of trauma and the development of PTSD.[44,45] Propranolol is commonly used medically to treat hypertension and to prevent migraine headaches. However, it is also on the list of banned substances for Olympic competition because it blocks the action of adrenaline, thereby helping to control performance anxiety, or "stage fright."

Medical ethicists have described the potential application of propranolol to blunt soldiers' traumatic response to killing and combat as "the morning-after pill for just about anything that produces regret, remorse, pain, or guilt." The use of a drug to block soldiers' emotional response to killing threatens the ethical basis that preserves humanity.[46,47] To consider the argument against the use of drugs such as propranolol in combat settings, one only has to reflect on the ways in which the Nazis used amphetamine-based drugs to create more violent, less compassionate soldiers to carry out heinous acts against humanity during World War II.

PTSD among those directly involved in battle has become better understood in recent years. There is less of an appreciation for the sociological impact of war as reflected in the surge of drug use among civilians during and following wartime. The spiritual collapse of people, coupled with social and economic dislocation, poverty, and the undermining of traditional authority structures and values, has been the basis for the escalation of alcohol and drug use among regions affected by war and among citizens at home, as we have witnessed following the Vietnam War. One only has to reflect on the escalation of illicit drug use among civilians during and following the Vietnam War. The latter years of the 1960s were punctuated by drug use on the home front and among many young soldiers in Vietnam. In the U.S. in the 1960s and 1970s, marijuana and psychedelic drugs such as psilocybin mushrooms and LSD dominated; their use was a key aspect of what became known as the counterculture. In this regard, drug use became a symbolic gesture against government military actions and a means of expressing political dissent.

The escalation of drug use in recent decades is rooted in the policies and practices of the Cold War and became emblematic of political protests against the Vietnam War. At present, there are serious drug problems in the United States and around the world, and certainly not all are related to war. These problems call for meaningful and significant efforts to reduce the demand for drugs as much as, if not more than, their supply. During the decades of the War on Drugs, the demand for mind-altering substances and the use of drugs as weapons of warfare have simultaneously escalated. This is not an indication of cause and effect, but an illustration of the complex political, sociological, psychological, and biological relationship between warfare and drugs.

There is a plethora of commentary on the failings of the War on Drugs. In truth, we do not know how much worse it might be in the absence of the martial approach. The approach has its weaknesses, but to oppose it without careful consideration of the ramifications of alternatives is shortsighted. Currently, the coastal and northern border regions of Mexico are enduring protracted narco-terrorism due to conflict between cartels over dominance in the drug trade. The U.S. and Mexican governments are embroiled in a war against the drug cartels. The warlike strategies against the violent cartels have taken on a different rhetorical perspective under Gil Kerlikowske, the newest director of the U.S. Office of National Drug Control Policy (ONDCP). The present strategy is clearly depicted as a war against the violent cartels and gangs who traffic in narcotics, rather than against the people who use them. In 2009, Kerlikowske described the drug problem in the U.S. as "much more complex than a 40-year-old metaphor for a war on drugs." In his view, drugs should be viewed as "a public health problem where law enforcement is a big, key player."[48] Kerlikowske's statement represents a view that I endorse. However, since the early days of Kerlikowske's tenure at the ONDCP, the national tone has shifted away from drug use as a public-health issue and has reinforced drug use as an existential threat focused on protecting the nation from organized crime and drug trafficking.

Conclusion

The drug war did not begin with prohibition, nor did it begin with the Nixon Administration's declaration of a War on Drugs. However, the current matrix of drugs and war and their escalation in response to one another does appear to derive from the Opium Wars of the mid 1800s. During this period, the Eastern and Western worlds were linked through political and financial dominance based on the narcotics trade. The British funded their military incursions and the expansion of their colonial empire through opium-trade revenues. The French followed this precedent and pressed the sale of opium in Vietnam and its cultivation throughout the Golden Triangle to generate tax revenues for the French government in the early 1900s. Since then, opium and cocaine trafficking has increasingly become the source of funding for para-political, insurgent, and guerilla fighters around the globe.

Wars are fought for many reasons, and it is important to distinguish between wars fought over drugs and wars ostensibly fought for other reasons. Beginning with the Opium Wars and tracing linkages to the current wars in Afghanistan and Iraq, the subsequent chapters in this book examine the roles that wars have played over time in the development of drug use on a macro (global) level, as well as on a micro level of individual addiction and suffering. In addition to international conflicts, civil wars, and the Cold War, we will examine the War on Drugs and the battles against violence associated with drug trafficking.

CHAPTER 3

The Opium Wars

THE KEY STAGES of opium development have been shaped by Western empires from Alexander the Great in 335 BCE through the current crises in the Middle East.[1] This chapter examines the British Opium Wars and the French colonial wars that were fought to promote the sale and trade of opium in the East. The revenues from the Opium Wars funded colonization in Southeast Asia, which set the stage for more than a century of unrest in the East. The Opium Wars also opened the East to trade with the West, along with European and American struggles for power and influence over strategic lands. The West subsequently engaged in a series of conflicts, including the Philippine, Korean, and Vietnam Wars.

Since the Opium Wars, drugs have been used to openly fund governments, colonialism, civil wars, clandestine operations, and insurgent groups. The Opium Wars also marked the proliferation of opium, morphine, and heroin for medical treatment and global expansion of the pharmaceutical industry. In 1898, German-based Bayer Pharmaceuticals synthesized diacetylmorphine (heroin) from morphine, which is synthesized from opium, and successfully marketed it for everything from a cough suppressant to pain management for surgery, under the name Heroin, derived from the German word *heroisch*, meaning heroic and powerful.[2,3,4]

To say that the modern-day drug epidemic has grown out of one country's rapacious addiction to tea and another's acquisitive greed for silver bullion is factual but oversimplified. England is the nation that was addicted to tea, and the tea the English loved was grown in China. However, China would trade only in silver bullion, and the British had a limited supply of silver bullion. To obtain enough silver bullion to purchase tea from China, the British needed to establish a market for something the Chinese would be willing to pay for with their silver bullion. China was not interested in purchasing British textiles or tableware. The Chinese population did, however, have a growing opium addiction, and the Chinese government and its people were very willing to buy opium with silver. The British sought those profits from the sale of opium, which came in the form of silver bullion, to enable them to purchase the tea they desired from China.

In the nineteenth century, the British fought the Chinese to force them to continue the trade of opium. The first Opium War was fought from 1839 to 1842, and a second Opium War was fought from 1856 to 1860. British and American merchant companies began selling opium to China in 1839, after England went to war to fight to keep the Chinese ports open for the sale and trade of opium. This forced trade made opium widely available throughout China, and like many of their countrymen, Chinese troops became increasingly debilitated through their use of opium, making them less formidable and easier for the British to defeat.[5] These wars were symbolic of the tensions between Eastern culture and Western free-market capitalism, a tension that continues to play out to this day.

Over time, the British also became dependent on the enormous profits and streams of revenue from the opium trade. The British and Chinese opium and tea trades were the catalysts of the Opium Wars and gave birth to the East-West capitalist trade. If we follow the succession of events from the Opium Wars, the makings of the world's current free-market capitalist economy, economic crisis, drug trade, addictions, and drug wars become painfully clear.

In his book, *Opium, Empire and the Global Political Economy*, author Carl Trocki proposes the hypothesis that modern-day mass consumption began with drug addiction, and that mass addiction came into being through the trade of drugs as a commodity. To initiate the cycles of production, trade, consumption, and accumulation that characterize capitalism, a profitable product was necessary to "prime the financial pump." In the nineteenth century, opium was the catalyst that primed the consumer market, the financial economy, and capitalist production. Historians and scholars provide ample statistical and narrative evidence that drug trafficking within and between China, India, and neighboring countries played a fundamental role in the development of imperialism in Southern and Eastern Asia.[6,7,8,9]

Social and economic shifts that accompanied the transitions to imperialism presented both crises and opportunities. The dangerous opportunities that presented themselves through the trafficking and use of opium at this time created vulnerability among the addicted and their communities and provided opportunities for colonial imperialism.

Opium had been available in China for thousands of years and had traditionally been eaten. Eating opium releases relatively low levels of opiates; therefore the impact on the central nervous system is weak and slow because the route of ingestion through the mouth and digestive system is slow and inefficient. Eating a plant-based substance such as opium or chewing coca leaves (which releases low levels of cocaine) weakens the impact of a drug on the central nervous system; therefore, this method rarely led to abuse and addiction due to the inability to consume significant levels of the psychoactive substance.

This changed when the Portuguese and Dutch introduced the practice of opium smoking to China in the 1500s. Smoking is the most direct route of administration, leading to the release of stronger levels of opiates and higher rates of addiction. By the early 1800s, the rate of addiction in China was reportedly as high as 27 percent of their adult male population.[10,11]

This succession of events resulted in the greatest development of colonial-era drug production, resulting in repercussions to this day. Present-day opium production in the Middle East and South Asia is said to be the culmination of 400 years of Western opium patronage.[12]

The Opium Wars did not introduce the use of the drug to the Chinese or the region. However, the wars did mark a significant change in the scale of international drug trafficking, for which China bore the brunt. For centuries, opium had been used for medicinal purposes in China. Around the seventeenth century, it began to be used recreationally, as an indulgence by the Chinese upper class, who had discovered its euphoric effects.[13]

Until a century prior to the Opium Wars, recreational use of opium had been limited primarily to the aristocracy; however, once it began infiltrating the general population, opium was banned in China. Although it was officially banned in 1729, corrupt government officials in the Canton region continued to informally sanction the illicit trade of opium in China. The British were able to pay off some Chinese officials, which provided them with access to their ports. Despite a century-long "ban," by 1830 approximately 1,330,000 pounds (or 10,000 chests) of opium were imported annually from India alone.[14] (In the 1700s and 1800s, quantities of opium were measured in terms of chests; one chest was equal to approximately 133 pounds of opium). Leading up to the first Opium War, opium imports escalated, and by 1833 opium imports had tripled and increased to 4,000,000 pounds (or 30,000 chests) per year.[15] By 1835, there were an estimated two million opium addicts concentrated in the Canton region of China. Figure 3-1 documents the growth in opium imports to China as a result of the Opium Wars.

Figure 3-1 Opium Wars and Annual China Opium Imports (Tons)

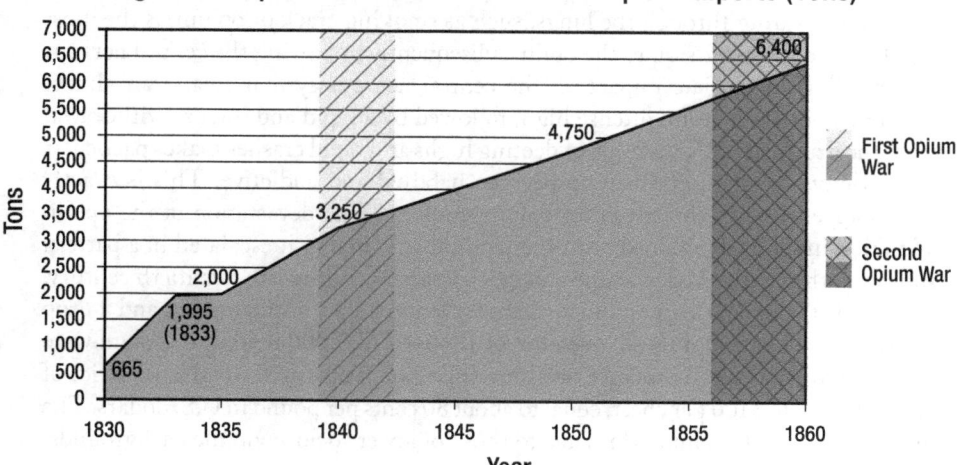

The Emergence of Addiction as an Epidemic

With the advent of the Opium Wars, the British flooded China with opium from India, a British colony. By the mid-nineteenth century, opium was widely available, and its price had dropped precipitously, making it accessible to the poor and the affluent alike. This influx and availability of opium fostered addiction among people of every socioeconomic faction in China. Opium infusion into China's population followed a pattern common today, in which recreational drugs are initiated and socially accepted among the wealthy upper class, only to become more widely available and used among middle and lower socioeconomic classes, at which point the drug usually becomes illegal, restricted, and unaccepted. By 1900, there was widespread opium addiction at all levels of Chinese society, from the Imperial Palace to the street pauper.[16]

Opium eventually claimed the lives of emperors and empresses, and the Chinese government was in collapse. Addiction among the ruling class, government, and emperors in China had a direct impact on the country's ability to defend itself and function. China's economy, government services, and standards of living all declined as a direct result of the escalating opium addiction.[17]

The influx of opium signaled foreign encroachment into Asia. The money bought off officials, fostered corruption, and weakened China. In 1838, a new imperial commander arrived in the Canton region, and he began to crack down on the foreign drug trade and on the Chinese engaged in trafficking. The crackdown resulted in the closure of many ports of trade to the British, serving as a catalyst for the first Opium War.

At the same time as supplies of opium flooded the country, the Chinese developed new, more addictive methods of opium ingestion. Rather than eating opium, they began smoking opium mixed with tobacco. This is significant because psychoactive drugs that are orally ingested, by swallowing or eating, are absorbed into the bloodstream and therefore reach the brain much more slowly than when they are inhaled as smoke into the lungs.

Inhaling a drug through the lungs, such as smoking crack or opium, is the most rapid route of transmission to the brain, subsequently impacting the central nervous system. This immediate impact on the central nervous system creates an almost instantaneous short-term, intense high, followed by a rapid and intense withdrawal from the drug's effect. This cycle of fleeting highs and rapid crashes makes particular psychoactive drugs more likely to become habitual and addictive. This is exactly what happened with the advent of opium smoking. The devastation of the opium addiction in China combined with the method of smoking it escalated in a pattern similar to that of the U.S. cocaine and crack epidemic of the late twentieth century.

The British increase in opium availability led to a glut in the market and a drop in price. In a single month—November of 1840—1,600,000 pounds of opium were delivered to the Chusan province of China. The glut of opium resulted in the price of opium falling to $100 per chest, equal to about 80 cents per pound in U.S. dollars. The drop in price made opium affordable to those of lower socioeconomic backgrounds, luring new buyers and addicts.

In 1840, a British missionary opened an addiction treatment center in Chusan that treated 1,600 opiate addicts between November and December of 1840.[18] The explosion of addiction among the "commoners" in China appears to have been the catalyst for a public-health approach to addiction.

For the time period, the French displayed a relatively sophisticated and scientific knowledge of the health impact of substance abuse and addiction in China. They reported that Chinese who smoked eight pipes of opium per day had a life expectancy of approximately six years from the start of their opium use, whereas casual users could be expected to live up to 20 years.[19]

By the end of the second Opium War, the Peking region rescinded the opium ban in an effort to generate revenue by taxing the opium imports.[20] (Similarly, California proposed the legalized sale and trade of marijuana for tax revenue in 2010.) By the 1870s, all levels of the Chinese government benefited from and came to rely on the revenue from the opium importation and transit taxes. Through this mechanism, opium contributed to the development of a market economy, particularly in the interior provinces of China. This reliance on opium taxation fostered resistance to efforts to reduce the importation, trafficking, and use of opium.[21] Governments in China and Southeast Asia had become addicted to the revenue generated through opium taxation. They had also become reliant on the opium-poppy cash crops and the low-wage labor they employed in their cultivation. The government of Malaysia colluded with Chinese businessmen operating tin mines with manual laborers form China and India. The Chinese businessmen and the Malaysian government controlled the "coolie laborers" by providing cheap opium.[22]

Global Narcotics Trade and Addiction

Not all of the opium traded during the Opium Wars went to China. An estimated 40,000 pounds (300 chests) of opium were sent to England annually. Opium addiction greatly affected the working class of England's industrial cities. Reportedly, many of England's working poor would go to the "backdoor pharmacy" on payday to purchase their weekly doses of opium for pennies per packet. More than a century and a half later, the British Isles are still plagued by heroin addiction. [23]

Around 1840, opium addiction was also hitting hard in the United States. During a medical temperance meeting held in New York City in 1840, a physician, Dr. Mc-Gowan, presented statistics noting that there were between 3,000 and 5,000 persons in New York City who used opium habitually.[24] At the time, this represented roughly 1.5 percent of the population in New York, which was estimated at 312,700.[25] The rate of heroin addiction has remained high in the greater New York metropolitan area, and in Great Britain as well.

Evidence of the global concern about the opium trade and addiction can be found in publications from this period. The following excerpt from the poem titled "Opium," by William Tappan, was written and published in a Boston paper, the *Liberator*, on April 10, 1840. This poem provides insight into the ways in which religion, politics, and commerce were entangled to achieve the desired capitalist outcomes by any means necessary. There is documentation of both humanitarian and Christian missionaries in China providing compassionate aid, but their roles were confusing to the Chinese, because some missionaries were complicit in the opium trade, as illustrated in this Chinese statement of protest echoed in Tappan's poem:

> Why do Christians bring us opium, and bring it directly in defiance of our laws? That vile drug has poisoned my son, ruined my brother, and well nigh led me to beggar my wife and children; you cannot wish me well, your religion cannot be better than mine. Go first and persuade your own countrymen to relinquish this nefarious traffic, and then I will listen to your instructions on the subject of Christianity.[26]

In addition, the East India Company was footnoted in the publication of this poem as having "employed all the resources of science, wealth, and unlimited power, to force it to its [the East India Company's] present height [monopolistic success]; and they have prostituted the means of government to an unlawful end."

England was not the only country engaging in opium trafficking. The French fought alongside Britain in the Second Opium War, and other countries followed Britain's lead, forcing China into unequal trade conditions.[27] Several American trade companies rationalized their involvement in narco-trafficking by differentiating their roles, claiming that they were not engaged in the production or selling of opium, just transportation.[28]

The prosperous opium trade was the foundation for the development of family fortunes of American merchants and political dynasties, with recognizable names such as Delano (grandfather of President Franklin Delano Roosevelt), Forbes (descendent Steve Forbes ran for president in 1996 and 2000), Low, Peabody, Perkins, and Russell (Russell was founder of the Skull and Bones secret society of Yale in 1823).[29,30] Opium was a boon to the mercantile capitalist classes because it created pools of capital that fed the banking/financial systems, transportation, and information infrastructures in the U.S.

The Opium Wars involved and impacted Asia, particularly Southeast Asia. Britain was involved in several colonial wars that drained their money, so they used the opium trade to fund their colonialist expansion. Over a period of 62 years (1824–1886), Britain battled and conquered Burma, eventually incorporating the country into its Indian Empire. Burma was administered as a province of India until 1937, when it became a separate, self-governing colony; in 1948, Burma attained independence from the Commonwealth of India (today Burma is known as Myanmar).[31] Burma's current role in opium production is particularly relevant to this historical analysis of the Opium Wars because of its history with the British Empire during the wars.

In the twenty-first century, the "Golden Triangle" in Burma remains the world's second-largest producer of illicit opium, with an estimated production in 2005 of 380 metric tons and cultivation of 40,000 hectares annually. A hectare is a metric unit of area used to gauge agricultural cultivation and production; one hectare is equal to 2.471 acres.

Opium production in the Golden Triangle region has been increasing since 2001. In 2005, there was a 12 percent increase in production and cultivation from the previous year. The Central Intelligence Agency (CIA) attributes the increase in opium production to the Burmese government's reluctance to take on major narco-trafficking groups, coupled with the lack of serious commitment against money laundering. Inasmuch as the drugs are exported, this region is also its own best customer, with people consuming significant amounts of heroin in addition to methamphetamine. As a result, Burma is currently under Financial Action Task Force countermeasures due to continued failure to address its inadequate money-laundering controls.[32] Here, we see again the link between narco-trafficking, money, and corruption that destabilizes countries and regions.

Conclusion

Prior to the nineteenth century, there is little evidence that drug-related problems, including addiction, significantly impacted social well-being, even in cultures where opium, coca, and marijuana had long been cultivated.[33] Around the mid-nineteenth century, the abuse of opium and its derivative, morphine, begin to appear as documented public-health problems in China, Britain, and the United States. Following the U.S. Civil War, morphine and opiate abuse became known as the Soldier's Disease because of the high rates of addiction among Civil War veterans.

By the turn of the century, opiate use had escalated worldwide; in fact, a century ago it was six times higher than it is today when equitably measured as a percentage of the total population. In Asia, the rate of opium addiction in 1908 was nearly 14 times higher than it is today.[34]

Heroin, which is derived from morphine, which in turn is derived from opium, is still the primary drug used to measure addiction and trafficking globally. In the U.S., there are an estimated 2.9 million lifetime heroin users and 663,000 past-year users, accounting for approximately 0.4% of the U.S. population.[35,36,37] Despite the low percentage of the population, these numbers contribute substantially to the proportion of the world's public-health problems, including addiction, HIV, and heroin-related crime and violence.

Over the past century and a half, several new political and economic orders developed in Asia in connection to the opium trade: European colonial states of Southeast Asia, including French colonialism in Vietnam, Laos, and Cambodia; England's colonialism in India and Burma; Dutch control of Indochina; and Spanish colonization of the Philippines. The economies of the southeast region of Asia were opened to and brought under influence of the West. China's domestic economy was opened to the West, and Southeast Asian economies were transformed into commodity-producing regimes focused on exporting to industrialized European and Western countries. At the same time India's opium cultivation and production was brought under Western control. The opium trade rearranged the economic structure and pushed the world down the path of mass consumption fueled by mass production and trade, which characterize our "modern" economic system. [38]

As with most wars, there are economic destabilization and shifts in social order. The Opium Wars marked one of the most significant shifts in global economics, global trade, and the advent of modern free-market capitalism. The Chinese government was destabilized by corruption, drug trafficking, and addiction among the ruling class as well as the poor. These conditions coupled with severe drought in China set the stage for the Taiping Rebellion of the 1850s that devastated China. This phase of the Chinese Diaspora also marked the advent of Chinese emigration to North America, Mexico, and Latin America. By 1860, there were approximately 35,000 Chinese living in the United States; by 1880, the population had increased threefold to 106,000.[39]

During this wave of western immigration, thousands of Chinese also settled in Mexico, where there were growing opportunities for work building railroad infrastructure. Some Chinese brought with them the knowledge and resources to cultivate opium and began to grow it in the mountainous Sinaloa region of Mexico. The robust ability of the poppy plant (*Papaver somniferum*) to grow in rough terrain has enabled opium to consistently provide entrepreneurial and imperial revenue, which has transformed the socio-economies of its producers and consumers.[40] Many of the mountainous regions that are not conducive to farming for food have proven to be suitable for cultivating opium, as we will explore in later chapters on Afghanistan and Mexico. To this day, there are evident connections between the materialistic consumer and the drug trade.

CHAPTER 4

Drugs and the U.S. Civil War

IVIL WARS ARE AMONG the most brutal wars fought; the American Civil War
was no exception. On April 12, 1861, the Confederacy attacked Fort Sumter,
an American military base/installation in South Carolina, marking the start
of the brutal Civil War that would last through 1865. The Confederacy was made up
of 11 southern states that supported the continuation of slavery and secession from
the United States, whereas the Union referred to the federal government and the 23
states that supported a union of states and abolition of slavery. As with all civil wars,
the fighting occurred in the homeland, affecting both civilians and soldiers and ac-
cruing significant costs for the war when measured in terms of casualties (620,000
dead and more than 420,000 wounded), physical destruction, and emotional toll.[1]

The Civil War soldiers and the civilians providing battlefield care for the fallen
found it necessary to view themselves as machines carrying out their battlefield
functions without feeling. The number of casualties escalated rapidly, and over
time the dead and dying were physically and emotionally handled like cattle at a
slaughterhouse. Such psychological numbing was a means of survival to escape the
horrors of war. In response to this type of emotional numbing, soldiers were issued
written warnings to "guard against unfeeling" and were cautioned that "by familiarity
with scenes of violence and death, soldiers often become apparently indifferent to
suffering and anguish." Soldiers who survived battle were equated with the living
dead, which made "survivors casualties of war."[2] These emotional casualties of war
are the foundation of the multigenerational growth in the use of alcohol and other
drugs that families, communities, and countries experience in the aftermath of war.

Alcohol and other drugs have long been used to prepare soldiers for battle and
to relieve the physical and emotional aftermath of war. Alcohol was the single most
prescribed substance during the Civil War. It was used outright, in addition to serving as the primary ingredient in tinctures and suspension mediums for other drugs.
Alcohol was used to relieve the debilitation that accompanied "grave accidents where

the [body] tissues are crushed." In Michael Flannery's book *Civil War Pharmacy: A History of Drugs, Drug Supply and Provision, and Therapeutics for the Union and Confederacy*, he points out that many of the grave accidents may have been the result of the proliferation of alcohol and the use of liquor as a virtual panacea.[3] Whiskey, sherry, and brandy were standards on the medical supply lists for each regiment. A sample list from the assistant surgeon at Fort Monroe, Virginia, listed 400 bottles of castor oil, 600 bottles of brandy, and 600 bottles of sherry for immediate use. Often the amount delivered was missing significant quantities of alcohol and other drugs from what was listed on the invoice.[4]

The pitiful suffering of war is most profound for civilians in the regions where the war is fought. Civil wars pit fellow countrymen/women against each other, leaving deep scars. Historical analysis of the American Civil War illustrates how addiction to medication prescribed to relieve physical suffering (for example, morphine) develops when the drug also provides relief from psychological suffering and emotional anguish many soldiers face following war.

The nature of killing in combat yields emotional wounds, and the psychological and social scars are further complicated in civil wars. Researchers have documented that not all soldiers are capable of killing even when under fire; there are shooters and non-shooters. Regardless of whether they enlisted on their own or were drafted, few are able to take a life when faced with this challenge. This dynamic is particularly evident upon examination of the rate of non-firing among the soldiers in the Civil War, which has been calculated and estimated at 80 percent.[5] The rate of non-firing was determined through analysis of the loaded and unfired muskets, particularly those that were loaded repeatedly and never fired. Even among those who are less able to kill, many have had to take a life to save their own. For these soldiers, the emotional scars are likely deeper, and the ghosts of war more vivid.

The Union and Confederate soldiers of the American Civil War were considered to be the best-trained and best-equipped soldiers of their time. They were repetitiously trained to muzzle-load muskets with gunpowder and bullets in rapid succession to fire up to five times per minute. Historians and researchers note that each soldier was issued a standard of 40 rounds of ammunition. Yet there were documented reports of some soldiers firing 200 to 400 rounds, while others never fired. This occurred because very few men actually fired at the enemy, and those unable or unwilling gave their ammunition to those who would fire it.

Here we see that despite being trained to function automatically, muzzle-load, and fire five rounds per minute, the preconceptions and delusions of combat were shattered, and for many, their humanity came to the fore. Those who did not flee but could not bring themselves to shoot loaded and passed weapons (limited fighting) to the few willing to shoot (active fighting). Others fired over the heads of the enemy (posturing); some fell to the ground and played injured or dead (inactive retreat).[6]

One Civil War veteran describing the Battle of Antietam reported that men were falling down in place and running back into the cornfield rather than engaging in the battle and killing their combatant countrymen. Further evidence of the fact that very few soldiers are capable of shooting and killing is documented in the records and artifacts. Many recovered weapons from the Civil War were found to have been loaded multiple times but not fired, indicating that these soldiers repeatedly loaded but never fired their guns. After the Battle of Gettysburg, 27,574 muskets were recovered, and some 24,000 were loaded; 50 percent (~12,000) from both sides and all regiments had been loaded multiple times but not fired.

Researchers meticulously calculated the feasibility of weapon malfunctions and human error, and they concluded that most soldiers were not trying to kill the enemy. The conclusion of these factors illustrates what we have now come to understand as a pattern of war engagement—not everyone is capable of killing. The close hand-combat was very traumatic for those who reluctantly killed as well as those who witnessed the slaughter in close combat.[7]

Although the terminology of post-traumatic stress disorder (PTSD) emerged following the Vietnam conflict, the recognition that traumatic events can lead to psychological, physical, and biological manifestations was articulated during the Civil War. A PTSD-like disorder was referred to as "war syndrome," or "Da Costa's Syndrome," after the American internist Jacob Mendez Da Costa of the military hospital in Philadelphia.[8] The study of this type of war syndrome was prompted by the pervasiveness of a collection of vague physical symptoms that had no consistent sign of physiologic origin or disease and that occurred in patients who appeared to be in relatively good general health. Da Costa studied soldiers and civilians who had been referred to him for a syndrome that he called "irritable heart," characterized by shortness of breath, palpitations, sharp or burning chest pain, fatigue, headache, diarrhea, dizziness, and disturbed sleep. This collection of symptoms is consistent with what we now recognize as PTSD, chronic fatigue syndrome, and other illnesses stemming from exposure to chronic and uncontrollable stress and trauma.[9]

The bloody battles of the Civil War were fought in our own backyards, and although this war predated televised coverage, thousands of civilians watched the battles from the sidelines like spectators at a soccer match. Exposure to this type of carnage affected civilians and soldiers alike. Citizens of the northern Union and southern Confederacy expressed concern about the implications of exposure to such brutality and the emotional numbing and detachment stemming from desensitization, the results of which are brutally illustrated in Drew Faust's *This Suffering Republic: Death and the American Civil War.*[10]

The medical resources and skills were crude enough that significant injuries to limbs at the battlefield generally resulted in amputation of the limb onsite to avoid gangrene. Painful amputation was managed with heavy doses of morphine and alcohol. Limbs were removed onsite with hacksaws and piled in wagons to be dumped elsewhere; the following photograph shows the limbs and human remains of Civil War soldiers.

The victors of the battlefield removed the bodies of the dead (Figure 4-1) because they controlled the site. During this process, the survivors had to come face to face with the pain they had inflicted on their fellow countrymen. While removing the remains of the dead, survivors became aware of the fact that directly or indirectly,

Figure 4-1 Body parts of Civil War soldiers are piled on a cart following battle.

Courtesy of New York State Historical Society

they had brought this suffering on their fellow human beings. The horrific task of burying hundreds of corpses and body parts became the responsibility of civilians as well as soldiers. The physical and emotional handling of bodies for removal and burial was described as similar to the treatment of vegetables and animals.

The Battle of Antietam was particularly gruesome for Union soldiers who arrived to remove the remains of Confederates four days after they had been killed. Officers bought liquor for their men to drink before they buried the rotting corpses, because they "believed they would be able to carry out their orders only if they were drunk."[11] This statement is a discerning acknowledgement of the need and desire to emotionally shield oneself from the horror, pain, and suffering of war, particularly when it is fought in one's homeland.

Through the world opium trade, fostered by the Opium Wars, opiate narcotics had become readily available to soldiers, civilians, and the medical community. The sap drawn from the poppy seedpod produces raw opium, which is further processed to create morphine. As noted in the previous chapter on the Opium Wars, opiates were widely available in the U.S. in the mid 1800s. Morphine was first synthesized from opium in 1803, and this medical discovery was followed by the development of the hypodermic syringe in 1853.[12,13] Injecting morphine produced a more rapid, potent effect because it entered directly into the bloodstream. Previously, morphine was orally ingested in pill form, and it took considerably longer to enter the bloodstream and subsequently affect the brain and central nervous system.

The use of opium to subdue physical pain is evident in medical and historical literature. During the American Revolutionary War, opium was cultivated in several colonial territories to meet the medical needs of American soldiers.[14] Opium was hailed as a wonder drug during the Civil War period, and the Confederate states proposed cultivation of the opium poppy as a cash crop with enormous profit potential. An 1862 Confederate newspaper article noted that, "The poppy may become one of the most profitable crops.... Certainly, it is an object worthy of public encouragement, as the annual amount of opium imported into the United States is valued at upward of $407,000."[15] In 1870, the U.S. Surgeon General wrote the following about opium: "[T]his medicine merits first place among these remedies. It was used almost universally in all cases of severe wounds, and was particularly useful in penetrating wounds of the chest, in quieting the nervous system, and indirectly in moderating hemorrhage."[16]

Civil War physicians frequently dispensed opiates, and opiate-based medications continued to be heavily dispensed following the Civil War. Just after 1865, the Union Army was issued 10,000,000 opium pills, more than 284,0000 ounces of opiate preparations (such as laudanum and paregoric), and some 30,000 ounces of morphine.[17]

An unintended secondary effect of opiate use was the psychological relief it brought to those who used it. The need for pain relief and the desire for psychological relief can be appreciated in the following excerpt illustrating the interpersonal violence, brutal nature of the injuries, and proliferation of morphine in the Civil War battlefield.

"In 1862 (sic) the Civil War broke out.... [Soldiers] would fire point blank at the enemy and these young men were presented to their field surgeons with terrible shrapnel wounds ... along with terrible pain.

"About all the field surgeon could do was use the two new invented tools that had been presented to him ... the hypodermic needle and syringe, along with Morphine Sulfate.... They injected the young wounded veterans with huge amounts of Morphine daily (every four hours) to kill their pain.... It was necessary for the surgeons to do full-quarter amputations—literally take the arms and legs off right at the start of the body, usually to stop infectious gangrene.

"In 1865 there were an estimated 400,000 young War veterans addicted to Morphine.... The returning veteran could be ... identified because he had a leather thong around his neck and a leather bag (with) Morphine Sulfate tablets, along with a syringe and a needle issued to the soldier on his discharge." [18]

Here again, we have documentation of the convergence of alcohol, other drugs, and war. During the Civil War, alcohol and opiates were appealing and available means of numbing oneself emotionally and physically. Opium was among the most popular and widely dispensed drug in the 1860s; it was prescribed for a wide range of ailments, ranging from diarrhea to pain.[19] Soldiers were issued morphine kits for pain management, and injured soldiers were provided with morphine supply kits upon discharge to enable them to manage their physical pain at home.

Morphine was used to treat injuries and relieve the pain of amputation and injury among soldiers; opiate addiction followed and emerged as a significant public-health problem in America in the latter part of the nineteenth century. Following the Civil War, morphine addiction was known as the Soldier's Disease.[20,21]

The liberal use of morphine to ease the suffering of wounded soldiers during the Civil War is believed by many to have laid the foundation for the evolution of modern-day drug addiction in the United States.[22,23] Soldiers were issued a satchel with morphine tablets upon discharge. In hindsight, there is little wonder how addiction could have developed following the war. Today, we recognize the addictive nature of prescription narcotics as among the most prevalent and significant addictive substances, surpassed only by alcohol, nicotine, and cannabis.

The lack of public-health education and awareness about the addictive potential of morphine was further complicated by the lack of medical knowledge regarding the physiology of addiction. To be counted and documented, morphine addiction needed to be understood as a medical diagnosis. At the time, addiction was a newly emerging health problem, and as a result, the number of addicted Civil War veterans was not well documented; estimates range from 45,000[24] to 400,000.[25] Therefore, there have been those who dispute the fact that opiate (morphine) addiction in the U.S. increased in part because of the Civil War.[26]

Illustrating the lack of understanding in the medical and pharmaceutical fields is the fact that alcohol, opium, and morphine were categorized as stimulant drugs.[27] These drugs are central nervous system depressants, not stimulants. Moreover, when heroin was first developed, it was used to treat morphine addiction, which only furthered drug addiction.

Conclusion

During the Civil War, tens of thousands of people were exposed to morphine to treat their war-related injuries, and many soldiers became morphine addicts. Addiction was an emerging phenomenon, and reliable statistics on addiction were not kept in a consistent manner at this time. Physicians were ill-prepared to treat the emerging epidemic of addiction, and it was actually thought that heroin would be an effective treatment for morphine addiction when it was first developed in 1898 in Germany. In reality, opium can be processed into morphine and heroin. It was soon learned that using one opiate to treat addiction to another opiate was ineffectual. Heroin was, and remains, one of the most physically addictive drugs.

The Civil War permanently changed the American pharmacy and pharmaceutical industry. It created an unprecedented need for economy-of-scale, mass-produced medications, particularly pain management drugs such as morphine. In 1860, there were 84 pharmaceutical and chemical manufacturers in the U.S.; by 1870, there were nearly 300. Most of the opium was imported from Turkey; however, some opium poppies were grown in North and South Carolina, Vermont, and California, in an effort to meet the demand for morphine.

Concomitant with the national growth of pharmaceutical industries was the mass production of alcohol for consumption and as a medicinal solvent.[28] The Union and Confederates relied on the private sector to meet the demands for a large-scale supply of alcohol and other drugs. Savvy businessmen in the alcohol and pharmaceutical industries made their fortunes with lucrative army contracts that supplied the armies of a divided nation.[29]

The changes the Civil War brought to the pharmaceutical industry, including the patent medicine trade, contributed to the development of drug addiction. Following the war, addiction to opiates and other narcotics was referred to as Army Disease, Soldier's Sickness, and Soldiers' Disease.

Addiction in the South was referred to as a "hidden epidemic," which developed in part due to an unregulated patent medicine industry. It is notable that there is evidence that in the South, there were higher rates of addiction among women than men, and that many Civil War veterans who developed drug problems following the war had no record of addiction during their tour of duty. This suggests that the use of opiates was to relieve psychological pain, particularly among women.

It is also noted that drug use was a problem before the start of the Civil War, and narcotics were being consumed at alarming rates prior to 1861.[30] The combination of these factors underscores that routes to addiction can be multifaceted, including physical, social, and psychological elements. The following quote from a 1928 publication by the American Social Health Association illustrates the connection between opiate abuse in the U.S. and the Civil War: "What effect the war of the American Revolution and that of 1812 had upon its [opium's] spread, we have not seen indicated in any record we have consulted, but that the Civil War gave it a considerable impetus seems definitely established."[31]

Following the Civil War and up until World War I, opiate use in the U.S. became widespread and difficult to contain. There were two primary patterns of opiate use during this time. One type of opium user used (sometimes abused) it therapeutically and legally; they were typically white, middle-class, middle-aged, and mostly women. This type of use was of moderate concern and carried little moral stigma. A secondary type of opium use that emerged was recreational opium smoking, primarily among Chinese. This type of use was highly stigmatized, linked to crime, and led to the ban on smoking opium imports in 1887. By 1896, U.S. opium imports had peaked and began diminishing. In the 1890s, the first state anti-morphine laws appeared.[32]

CHAPTER 5

French Connections and
the Corsican Brothers

W HAT DO NAPOLEON BONAPARTE and cannabis have in common? It was
Napoleon's army that first introduced the use of cannabis (hashish and
marijuana) to France and then to the West. In the early 1800s, Napoleon's
army was introduced to cannabis in Egypt while en route to Asia. During the push
east, the army encountered new cultures and traditions and assimilated the most
notable elements into French culture; among these treasures was cannabis.

The culture of subjugated regions influences the "mother land" just as the coloniz-
ing country influences the regions it acquires. Travel to foreign lands was expensive,
difficult, and time-consuming; therefore, it was limited to the wealthy, their ser-
vants and laborers, and their military security. International trade and colonization
results in both countries acquiring new cultural practices from each other that are
introduced as new and novel among the aristocracy, thereafter disseminating across
social strata. Together these factors contribute to historical trends of drug diffusion.
As we saw with the use of opium in China, the introduction of cannabis to France
followed this pattern and was popular among avant-garde artists and writers in Paris
who developed their own cannabis rituals and established hash-smoking cafes, such
as Le Club des Hashischins.

Similarly, opium smoking in France was introduced by French expatriates returning
home from their Indochinese colonies. By the early 1900s, opium dens proliferated
French port cities, such as Toulon, Marseille, and Hyères.[1] To this day, Marseille
remains a significant point of narcotics transshipment between the East and West.

From the mid to late 1800s the East, particularly Imperial China, was opened to
the West through the Opium Wars and Britain's forced opium trade with China.
With the gates to the East open, the West rapidly began to compete for colonization
in Asia, Southeast Asia, and the Asia-Pacific region. Colonization and the military

might required to take over another country are costly propositions. Britain relied on the money from the opium trade to fund the expansion of the British Empire and to recover the costs of war for their broad political and colonial interests. Not surprisingly, following the Opium Wars, the rate of opium addiction, and therefore the demand for the drug, spread like wildfire throughout Asia.

Building on the British model of drug-funded imperialism, the French colonized West Africa, French Equatorial Africa, Southeast Asia, the Caribbean, and Canada. Like the British, the French relied heavily on revenues from their opium trade to fund their political and colonial interests, particularly in the Southeast Asian region. The first major French military intervention in Southeast Asia was in the mid 1800s under Napoleon III. By 1897, their empire had come to be known as the French Indochinese Union (French Indochina), encompassing Laos, Cambodia, and the Tonkin, Annam, and Cochinchina regions of Vietnam. Although French and Portuguese missionaries had been active in the region since the early 1700s, their scope of colonization remained modest until the French became active in opium trafficking. With the seemingly endless stream of revenue derived from their post–Opium War monopolization of opium sales to Vietnam, French colonialism rapidly expanded.

Most colonial governments had begun to distance themselves from opium dealing by auctioning "opium farms" and franchises to the highest bidder, often a consortium of influential Chinese who managed the opium dens and complex opium markets. In 1881, however, the French administration in Saigon established the Opium Reige, which was a direct governmental opium marketing monopoly. The Reige model proved very profitable and was replicated in the Dutch Indies, Siam, and British Burma. To counter criticism, the Reige "monopoly" model was publicized as a drug-control measure to reduce "native" opium use. Conversely, opium sales and use spread to new regions while per-capita use doubled in Malay states.[2]

Drug Expansion and Economic Contraction

Prior to World War I, Germany served as the premier global supplier of pharmaceutical narcotics, including heroin, morphine, and cocaine. However, during World War I, France and their allied countries realized they had inadequate control over their own supplies of these drugs needed for pain management. France turned to their Indochinese colonies as important sources of opium for refinement into heroin and morphine. As a result, new trade routes and networks were established to move substantive quantities of opium from Indochina into France.

Disruption of licit opium trade routes resulted in shortages of opium for medical and recreational illicit use. To simply meet the medical needs, illicit smuggling increased, and once the door was open for illicit trafficking, it quickly expanded to meet the needs of licit and illicit markets. What made them more attractive is that the illicit drugs were less expensive because they were not saddled with government taxes. Relatively inexpensive opiates and cocaine became widespread and were more readily available than alcohol in some regions.

During World War I, there were limitations on alcohol production and consumption, and pub operating hours were restricted by curfews. Together, these factors made uncontrolled drugs enticing alternatives to alcohol. In conjunction with the social and emotional unrest from the war, a burgeoning illicit drug-use problem was spreading through Western Europe. There were reports of widespread drug abuse among Allied troops stationed in France during 1915. London papers reported that English prostitutes were doping Allied troops and robbing them while the soldiers were on leave in England.[3]

France depended on opium-trade revenues for government financing. The opium trade accounted for a significant portion of government funding for France and the expanding number of French colonies. In the decades following World War I and the U.S. stock-market crash in 1929, the global economy was affected by a severe financial depression. Income and spending declined dramatically, as did trade and tax revenues. To compensate for the loss in taxes and trade, the French government increased revenues by stepping up the opium trade and exploiting their colonial monopoly in French Indochina. In addition to the opium grown in Indochina, France imported more than 60 tons of opium from Turkey and Iran into Vietnam, a move that yielded 15 percent of all of the tax revenues for the French empire.[4]

Not unlike the cultural dynamics of the Opium Wars in the mid 1800s, the French opium monopoly and heavy trafficking into Indochina came to be viewed by the Vietnamese as French exploitation and drug-facilitated oppression. During their century of colonial rule in Vietnam, the French exploited the land, forced the sale of opium, and put many of the Vietnamese people into indentured servitude. These conditions set the stage for a communist revolution, uprising against French colonialism, and the eventual collapse of French Indochina.

Rates of corruption and addiction in Vietnam were epidemic in the 1930s, with more than 2,500 opium dens in Indochina by the start of World War II.[5,6] Opium cultivation and heavy trade in Vietnam resulted in addiction rates of 20 percent that affected one and all. Government officials addicted to opium were not only ineffective in their work, but they were also highly susceptible to corruption. The high rates of addiction and government corruption would eventually contribute to the downfall of French Indochina and create a firm foundation for the advent of communist rule in North Vietnam. Efforts to combat the spread of communism in the region in turn led to the Vietnam War.

During World War II, opium trade routes from India and Persia were cut off, greatly limiting French trade and Indochina's access to opium. This not only eliminated opium revenue, but also initiated an epic level of drug withdrawal in the region. The French believed they needed to establish self-sufficient opium cultivation.

To enable the French opium monopoly to continue to yield profits, France turned to the Hmong of Laos and the Tonkin people of northwest Indochina in 1940 and asked them to expand their opium production from small cultivated plots for personal and local use into vast agricultural cultivation for trade. The French identified influential tribal leaders to broker their opium trade with the Hmong farmers, forging a cooperative system that repressed untaxed, independent, clandestine opium cultivation and smuggling through the expansion of Hmong opium production, thereby strengthening the economic viability of the Hmong people and the French government. Historically, the region was dominated by local tribal opium market structures that were reinforced by armed insurgents who supported smugglers and Hmong opium farmers. French colonial officials in Indochina were directed by the French government to expand poppy—and therefore, opium and heroin—production. This government plan is well documented in French government telegraph communications instructing colonial officials to encourage poppy cultivation, survey the areas of cultivation to measure the surface yield, and repress clandestine trafficking.[7]

Under this French policy, opium production in the region increased 800 percent, from 7.5 tons in 1940 to 60.6 tons in 1944.[8] Much of the opium produced went to meet the demands of Indochina's addicts, while some was diverted to meet the medical needs of French troops. The remaining opium trade surplus, which increased 150 percent, filled the coffers of France and its colonies.

In exchange for American post–World War II reconstruction funds, France promised to suppress their opium trade in Indochina.[9] The French government allegedly continued to sell opium to maintain and cure existing heroin and opium addicts by selling opium to addicts as maintenance therapy. However, French colonial authorities continued to sell opium to shore up their budgets. In 1947, opium sales generated one third of French Indochina's budget.[10]

The French supported the political aspirations of the Hmong and Tonkin tribal leaders who cooperated with their poppy-cultivation operation. The poppy-cultivation areas were also strategically located along major communication routes that would become crucial during the Vietnam War. The relationship between French officials and tribal leaders seemed to benefit both sides in the short run. The French made political commitments to these tribal groups that ultimately resulted in the demise of French colonial rule in Indochina and the rise of communist interests, which opened the door for the unrest that would eventually fuel the war in Vietnam.

Espionage, Opium, and Organized Crime

The First Indochina War (also known as the French Indochina War and the Anti-French Resistance War) began in 1946 and culminated in the defeat of the French in 1954 at the Battle of Dien Bien Phu. The final period of French colonialism after World War II resulted in a divided North (communist) and South Vietnam.[11,12]

From 1946 until the defeat of the French at Dien Bien Phu in 1954, French military intelligence financed their covert operations through the protection and control of opium trafficking in Laos and northern Vietnam. French paratroopers fighting alongside hill tribes collected the opium, and French aircraft would fly it down to Saigon. The Sino-Vietnamese mafia that was the instrument of French intelligence would then distribute the opium. Everything from the central bank accounts to the profit-sharing of the opium trade was controlled by French military intelligence.

To combat French oppression based on indentured servitude and the sale of opium, Ho Chi Minh began to empower the Vietnamese under nationalist communist reform, and in 1954 Vietnamese forces defeated the French at Dien Bien Phu. Following defeat of the French, it was agreed through the Geneva Convention that North and South Vietnam would remain divided until free elections could be held to determine which government would lead a unified Vietnam. Most Vietnamese supported Ho Chi Minh because of his nationalist and communist stance. Knowing this, South Vietnam's President Ngo Dinh Diem refused to hold elections, and the country remained divided until the end of the Vietnam War in 1975.

The involvement of the French, and later the CIA (as we will see in Chapters 7 and 9), in the support of opium trafficking in Laos and Cambodia led to the establishment of new markets and new routes of communication, commerce, and drug trade that remain a feature of the Southeast Asian economy to this day. Noted historian Dr. Alfred McCoy conducted an investigative interview with Police Colonel Smith Boonlikit in Bangkok, Thailand, on September 21, 1971. During the interview, Colonel Boonlikit allowed McCoy to read and copy reports from U.S. Customs, the U.S. Bureau of Narcotics, and Interpol that related to French Corsican syndicates in Southeast Asia. These papers clearly documented the role of colonists, primarily Corsican gangsters, who remained in Laos after French military withdrawal in 1954 and established small charter airlines, which collectively became known as "Air Opium" and operated from 1955 to 1965.

Ostensibly formed to provide otherwise unavailable transportation for businessmen and diplomats, the airlines actually served to restore Laos's link to the drug markets of South Vietnam that had vanished with the departure of the French air force in 1954. "Air Opium" was forced out of business in 1965, when Laotian General Ouane Rattikone monopolized and assumed leadership of the Laotian opium trade. The Corsican syndicates remained connected and later served as the link between heroin laboratories in Laos and America-based distributors when Golden Triangle laboratories began producing No. 4 heroin in the early 1970s that would flood Western markets.[13]

According to Maurice Belleux, former head of the French Service de Documentation Extérieure et de Contre-Espionnage (SDECE, the French equivalent of the CIA), following the First Indochina War, the CIA took over French drug trafficking assets and engaged in similar complicit trafficking practices.[14] Building on these networks, the CIA worked with regional tribal leaders in Southeast Asia by assisting in the transshipment of opium. This provided money for clandestine operations to support the anti-communist mission of the CIA, which operated in the region as an often rogue arm of the U.S. government.

Fearing the spread of communism, the U.S. used the CIA to support Ngo Dinh Diem's Republic of South Vietnam following the defeat of the French. The CIA's central mission was containment of the spread of communism, and they fueled the U.S. involvement in the region through their complicit actions that supported the Kuomintang (KMT), Hmong, and Laotian opium trafficking. The drug trafficking generated funds that supported the Vietnamese hill tribes in opposition to communist

North Vietnam. Opium and heroin trafficking enabled them to conduct operations without the need for congressional approval or oversight.

Ho Chi Minh was concerned that the U.S. was yet another foreign power that would exploit Vietnam, and by 1960, Ho Chi Minh's government began the first phase of what developed into a war with the United States and South Vietnam, known as the Vietnam War.

The opium traders in the Golden Triangle needed international connections to traffic their heroin to Europe, North America, and the rest of the world. They established connections with the French Corsican syndicate in the port city of Marseille, France, operating much like the Sicilian mafia in Italy and the U.S.

Each of these syndicates has used underworld drug trafficking to wield power and influence. The Corsicans were involved in covert government and paramilitary operations and favored whomever served their needs and interests at a given point in time. During World War II, the Corsicans were used by the Nazi Gestapo to spy on the communist underground in Marseille. The CIA and their predecessor organization, the Office of Strategic Services (OSS), were involved with the Italian mafia and the Cosa Nostra in Sicily and southern Italy. Senior administrators for the CIA have testified that American intelligence became involved with the mafia warlords and drug lords "not for drug purposes and not for personal gain but to achieve a higher ideological goal" of defeating communism.[15]

In the years following World War II, the CIA was established to combat the spread of communism around the world. Among the CIA's initial clandestine operations was to pay the Corsicans to break the port strike led by the French Communist Party in the Marseille ports. The alliance with the CIA was critical in enabling the Corsicans to establish a position powerful enough to launch Marseille as the Western hemisphere's heroin capital following World War II.[16]

The alliance was beneficial for American intelligence because the Corsicans had critical information and were capable of breaking the strike, fragmenting the French communist groups. The OSS and later the CIA became tightly involved with the Corsican brotherhood through their efforts to combat the communist parties in France. The fact that the Corsicans were notorious heroin manufacturers and criminals was more than redeemed by their ability to get things done. [17,18]

By the late 1940s, the Corsicans had established a direct heroin trafficking route between Marseille and New York City—the "French Connection." The Corsican and Sicilian syndicates processed raw opium trafficked from Turkey, Laos, Afghanistan, and India, turning it into heroin and distributing it throughout Europe and across the Atlantic to mafia contacts in New York City. Under the Corsican network, by the 1960s Marseille was a global heroin capital and the new destination of opium produced in the Southeast Asian networks established in French Indochina.

Corsica is a French island boasting a hybrid French-Italian culture. A Corsican named Bonaventure Francisci, living in Laos, was among the top heroin brokers in Southeast Asia. Francisci brokered heroin trades directly with Ngo Dhin Nhu, the brother of South Vietnam's president Ngo Dhin Diem, until the assassinations of both Nhu and Diem in 1963. Their arrest and assassination was in connection with a CIA-backed coup d'etat. The CIA agent Lucien Conein, himself of Corsican origin, was stationed in Saigon and involved in the 1963 coup that led to Ngo Dhin Diem's assassination. As part of his CIA intelligence work, Conein maintained ties to Corsican gangsters in Southeast Asia and Marseilles. He was eventually appointed by the Nixon Administration to the White House team focused on the drug war in Southeast Asia.

Despite documented concerns raised by U.S. officials, it wasn't until 1972 that effective action was taken to break the Corsican-American drug trade. That year, U.S. and French law-enforcement agencies successfully busted the French Connection.[19] The result was a heroin shortage, particularly along the east coast of the U.S. The shortage was readily filled by the ingenious use of rogue U.S. military connections to smuggle heroin from Southeast Asia, and soon thereafter by Afghan heroin.

Opération Moustique—Operation Mosquito

Count Alexandre de Marenches, head of France's secret foreign intelligence service (the DGSE), worked with senior advisors in the Reagan Administration to strategize the use of drugs as tools of war in their shared anti-communist and anti-Soviet efforts during the Soviet-Afghan War. At de Marenches' suggestion, the U.S. government proposed the use of subtle drug warfare tactics against the Soviets to the mujahideen, Afghan Muslim guerrilla warriors engaged in jihad.[20] Replicating the tactics of the North Vietnamese, the mujahideen used raw opium and heroin as a tool of war against their Soviet enemies. The Vietcong had used marijuana, raw opium, and heroin to weaken their enemies by making the drugs readily available to soldiers.

In what was codenamed "Operation Mosquito," France and the U.S. worked together to encourage opium-growing mujahideen guerillas to weaken their Russian opponents by flooding Soviet Afghan bases with hashish and heroin. U.S. General Vernon Walters had been the U.S. defense attaché in Paris prior to being appointed deputy director of the CIA. De Marenches and General Walters had become close friends and allies during Walters' time in France.

In early 1981, during the initial days of the Reagan administration, de Marenches proposed a Franco-American joint venture to counter the Soviet communist threat in Afghanistan through anti-communist propaganda and the supply of illicit drugs to Russian soldiers.[21] France backed out of formal involvement in Operation Mosquito, but in 1981 President Reagan approved a covert program to weaken Soviet soldiers in Afghanistan by addicting them to drugs. The initiative was successful, as the proliferation of opium, heroin, and hash in Afghanistan greatly impacted the Soviet troops, the majority of whom were using these drugs regularly inside the Democratic Republic of Afghanistan.[22]

Conclusion

France, like other European colonial powers, funded much of its empire expansion through the taxation of the cultivation and sale of opium-based drugs. The profits the French government garnered from taxation of opium and heroin sales were substantial enough to fund a great deal of the development and infrastructure for their colonies, most notably French Indochina. As substantial as the narcotic-based tax funds were, they were dwarfed by the profits realized by those directly involved in the processing and trafficking of heroin. Once the narcotic-based revenue streams were realized, they were not easily controlled by the French, and became sources of funding for colonial-opposition forces in Vietnam, Laos, and Cambodia. From that point forward the Golden Triangle became the nexus of narco-funding, which is covered extensively in Chapters 7 and 9, on the Cold War and the Vietnam War, respectively.

CHAPTER 6

High Hitler

World War II

NOT ONLY HAS WAR influenced the use of alcohol and other drugs throughout history, leaders under the influence of stimulants, depressants, and hallucinogens have greatly affected the directions of their countries and the outcome of wars. Inebriated and addicted leadership intensified the fog of war. This was particularly evident in the events leading up to and throughout World War II. Alcohol and other drug abuse was rampant from the highest levels of government and military leadership to the lowest-ranking soldiers. Alcohol, amphetamines, and morphine were used regularly as agents to facilitate acts of war and to shield users from war's aftermath. The pervasive use of amphetamines among Nazis, Kamikaze pilots, and Allied forces are well documented.[1,2]

The alcoholic leadership of Winston Churchill, Joseph Stalin, and others of their time has been less examined. We often focus on illicit drug use and its impact; however, the damage caused by legal drug use reveals human behavior at its ugliest and most frightening. Joseph Stalin was a raging alcoholic. Eyewitnesses to Stalin's alcoholic rages included Nikita Khrushchev, Charles de Gaulle, and Winston Churchill. Stalin's alcohol-induced megalomania, some historians claim, played a role in his murderous rampage, in which he instigated the killing of an estimated 25 million of his countrymen.[3] It is reported that Stalin was on an alcoholic bender during the first two weeks of the German invasion of Russia. Unable to function in a drunken stupor, Stalin was notably absent during this critical initial phase of the German invasion and provided little to no command. During his alcoholic bender, Stalin's direct reports did not dare to question his capacity or try to assume command out of fear of his erratic behavior and murderous impulses.

Drug Development

Ephedrine, the active ingredient in amphetamines and methamphetamine, was first synthesized in Germany in 1887 for medical uses, including increasing blood pressure, opening nasal and bronchial passages, and stimulating the central nervous system. Ephedrine- and amphetamine-based products were marketed as a safe cure-all to the public at large. Methamphetamine in crystallized form, today known as crystal meth, was developed by Japanese scientist Akira Ogata in 1919. By the 1940s, methamphetamines had become a widely available wonder drug, used for the treatment of asthma, depression, obesity, epilepsy, and even opiate addiction.

Developed by the German-based Temmler pharmaceutical company, the methamphetamine-based drug Pervitin was first introduced to the market in 1938. Shortly thereafter, Isophan, a similar stimulant drug, was developed and introduced by the German-based Knoll pharmaceutical company. These drugs instantly became popular among German civilians.

Drugs in the amphetamine family are categorized as central nervous system stimulants, and they are highly addictive. Dependency develops quickly, triggering psychosis and distorted thinking. Amphetamines and cocaine are potent psychomotor stimulants that induce exhilarating feelings of power, strength, energy, false self-confidence, mental focus, and short-term euphoria, while reducing the need for food or sleep. These qualities make them ideal for situations requiring high performance and productivity, including, unfortunately, war. Persons using these drugs experience a period of extreme exhilaration and energy followed by intense psychological depression and physical fatigue, because they deplete the neural stores of dopamine in the pain and pleasure centers of the brain. More than almost any other type of drug, cocaine and methamphetamine are associated with violence, anti-social behavior, and psychosis. Use over extended periods results in psychological distortion and physical stress.

Both the Allied and Axis forces used amphetamines and methamphetamines for performance enhancement during the Second World War. Stimulant drugs were used to help increase industrial and military efficiency among civilians working the assembly lines on the home front and for soldiers on the war front.[4,5] American, British, German, and Japanese troops were given stimulants to stay alert, to stimulate energy, to sharpen concentration, and to accelerate the capacity of both mind and body.

On the American home front, a persistent marketing campaign urged men and women to increase production of materials, equipment, and weaponry for the troops fighting in Europe and the Pacific. Throughout the war, the United States War Production Board conducted a pervasive campaign urging workers to produce more and work harder. The campaign included posters announcing, "He's a 'fighting fool'—give him the best you've got! More production!"; "She's a swell plane—give us more! More production!"; and "Give it your personal attention, will you? More production!"

At the same time, the U.S. Office of War Food Administration, the Office of Price Administration, and the Office of War Information ran marketing campaigns urging Americans to "Do with less, so they'll have enough!" Civilian food rationing was implemented, and civilians were encouraged to reduce consumption of sugar and meat. Simultaneously, social marketing warned that, "There's danger when people tire too easily; when minds are slow to think; when bodies can't fight disease."[6]

To meet the divergent objectives of more production with less food intake while avoiding the danger of fatigue and slow thinking, one of the logical solutions seemed to be the use of commercially available amphetamines. Amphetamine-based drugs, such as Benzedrine and Methedrine, became the working person's helper, and use of these potent stimulants increased dramatically.[7]

Human Experiments

Throughout World War II, drugs were used as tools of warfare against the enemy, tested on prisoners, and used by soldiers for performance enhancement.[8] Publicly, Hitler was against drug use, specifically condemning the use of cocaine, a popular society drug in Germany until the 1930s. Under the auspices of public-health promotion, the Nazi Party preached abstinence from alcohol and other drugs, at the same time as they pumped their soldiers full of amphetamines, morphine, cocaine, and alcohol.

Performance enhancement and gaining a competitive edge were the primary motivators for developing, testing, and using drugs. The potential military benefits of stimulants such as Pervitin were brought to the attention of Dr. Otto Ranke, a physician and director of the Institute for General and Defense Physiology at Berlin's Academy of Military Medicine.[9] Researchers concluded that Pervitin could help the German military win the war because it increased users' willingness to take risks while reducing hunger, thirst, pain sensitivity, and the need for sleep. Ranke anticipated that Pervitin could facilitate nearly unlimited endurance on the war front. Initially, Pervitin was given to military drivers during the invasion of Poland, and then it was deceitfully distributed to troops fighting on all fronts, without their knowledge or consent.

At the Dachau concentration camp, Nazi doctors attempted to conduct mind-control experiments by giving mescaline (a potent hallucinogen from the peyote and San Pedro cactus) to French and Jewish prisoners.[10,11] The Nazis administered mescaline to 30 prisoners to see whether it was possible to impose one's will on a person under the influence of such a hallucinogen. The Nazis determined that it was not possible to control another person's mind in this way.[12] In fact, they found that hallucinogens made it extremely difficult to get a person to follow even the simplest of directions, and eventually they terminated the research.

In the waning years of the war, Nazi Germany was growing desperate for soldiers, and they wanted to find ways to chemically extend the capacity of the military they had. In early 1944, then Vice-Admiral Hellmuth Heye asked German scientists to develop a drug that could extend the limits of troops and enable them to continue fighting beyond a period considered normal, while at the same time boosting their self-confidence. Soon thereafter, pharmacologist Gerhard Orzechowski developed and presented Heye with a pill, code-named D-IX, that contained cocaine, methamphetamine, and a morphine-based painkiller.

Researcher Wolf Kemper, who uncovered the project, described D-IX as a super-drug designed to redefine the limits of human endurance. It was first tested on Jewish prisoners at Sachsenhausen, a Nazi concentration camp in Oranienburg, Germany. Jewish prisoners were given the experimental drug and forced to march up to 50 miles (75km) without resting, carrying 50-pound (20kg) packs. Nazi physicians who observed the prisoners' performance on D-IX were so enthusiastic about the results that they planned to supply all German troops with the pills. The results were promising, and it was later tested on German Naval submarine crewmembers. However, the war ended before D-IX could be put into mass production.

Nazi physicians even experimented on themselves with drugs. Dr. Franz von Wertheim, a medical officer stationed near the Western Wall, wrote the following in his diary entry dated May 10, 1940: "To help pass the time, we doctors experimented on ourselves. We would begin the day by drinking a water glass of cognac and taking two injections of morphine. We found cocaine to be useful at midday ... as a result, we were not always fully in command of our senses." By 1945, the rate of morphine addiction among military doctors had increased 400 percent from the beginning of the war.

Speedkrieg

In preparation for the war, Germany amassed millions of amphetamine tablets to facilitate superhuman performance among their pilots, soldiers, and sailors. Soldiers burned through their drug stockpiles during the Blitzkrieg, and by mid-year 1940, more than 35 million tablets of Pervitin and Isophan had been distributed to the German army (Heer) and air force (Luftwaffe). The Nazis surged across Europe at lightning speed, fueled by methamphetamines, and soldiers were high on Pervitin when they steamrolled into Poland and France. Soldiers burned through their drug stockpiles during the Blitzkrieg. There are reports of soldiers, freezing in sub-zero temperatures, exhausted, and having collapsed in the snow, then taking Pervitin and within 30 minutes feeling better, becoming alert, and marching in order. [13] Although stimulant drugs were used pervasively by both Allied and Axis forces, the Nazis and the Japanese military were the most notorious for using stimulants to create violent, less compassionate soldiers. The use of amphetamines and other drugs by Nazi military leaders, including Hitler, kept them alert and greatly fueled their aggression, megalomania, and paranoia.[14] The U.S. military was little different; they distributed an estimated 200 million amphetamine pills to U.S. soldiers during World War II. Little was publicized about the potential risks and long-term effects of amphetamine and methamphetamine use; their benefit as a short-term solution was thought to outweigh their potential risks.

The Imperial Japanese armed forces were also administered significant amounts of methamphetamines. For special operations such as Kamikaze flights, pilots were given a type of methamphetamine known as Philopon, which was methamphetamine mixed with green tea powder, pressed into tablet form, and stamped with the crest of the emperor.[15]

Despite doctors' warnings about their side effects, amphetamines were part of every first-aid kit and were disseminated as part of the standard medical protocol for soldiers suffering from exhaustion.[16]

Alcohol

In addition to the proliferation of stimulant drugs, the Nazi Party liberally dispensed alcohol and opiates to the troops as long as they believed drugging and intoxicating their military would help them defeat the Allies. The German army did not monitor the side effects of the drugs, their addictive potential, or possible deterioration of moral standards as a result of their use.[17]

Toward the end of the war, Germany relied on younger and younger soldiers, and more of them relied on alcohol and other drugs for courage, coping, and endurance. Understanding the emotional desperation of the troops, Walther Kittel, a general in the Nazi medical corps, wrote in reference to alcohol that "only a fanatic would refuse to give a soldier something that can help him relax and enjoy life after he has faced the horrors of battle, or would reprimand him for enjoying a friendly drink or two with his comrades." Officers would distribute alcohol to their troops as a reward, and schnapps was routinely sold in military commissaries, a policy that also had the beneficial side effect of returning the soldiers' pay to the military. "The military command turned a blind eye to alcohol consumption, as long as it didn't lead to public drunkenness among the troops." Public drunkenness and alcohol-related misbehavior were punishable by "a humiliating death."

Commander-in-chief of the German military, General Walther von Brauchitsch, expressed concern that his troops were committing "the most serious infractions" of morality and discipline because of "alcohol abuse." Most notably, as a result of heavy alcohol use, soldiers were fighting, getting into serious accidents, mistreating their subordinates, and lashing out against superior officers, in addition to committing "crimes involving unnatural sexual acts." The general believed that alcohol was jeopardizing "discipline within the military." According to an internal statistic compiled by the chief of the German medical corps, 705 military deaths between September 1939 and April 1944 were linked directly to alcohol. The actual figure was likely much higher, because suicides, traffic accidents, and accidents involving weapons were frequently caused by alcohol use but not included in the official statistic.

Alcohol was popular with troops on all sides during World War II. The prevalence of alcohol, particularly bootleg alcohol, resulted in many injuries and otherwise preventable deaths. When beer, wine, or liquor could not be found, American troops improvised and resorted to desperate measures, such as making cocktails with juice and Aqua Velva aftershave (which contained pure alcohol).

Methyl alcohol, which was used as a solvent, a fuel, and an antifreeze, posed a particularly grave danger to troops in World War II and was listed as the leading factor in deaths resulting from the inadvertent ingestion of poisons among German soldiers during the war. Among the German military, the number of cases in which soldiers became blind or even died after consuming methyl alcohol began to increase after alcohol use was prohibited. In 1942, a German officer stationed in Norway was executed by firing squad for selling methyl alcohol, which was reportedly 98 percent pure, for production of liquor. Several soldiers became ill, two died, and some were reportedly blinded. The execution of bootleggers was publicized to deter soldiers from making potentially lethal drinking alcohol, and it was hoped that this would deter soldiers from drinking. However, soldiers apparently felt that anything that could help them escape the horrors of war was worth the risk.

High Hitler and Addiction Among the Reich

Hitler reportedly had a litany of illnesses, including asthma, Parkinson's disease, syphilis, and gastrointestinal problems that required constant medical supervision by his personal physician. Despite his public opposition to alcohol and drug use, the Führer received regular injections of amphetamines and a potent solution of 10 percent cocaine from his private physician, Dr. Theo Morell. [18,19] In addition, a partial list of the unorthodox medications Hitler took on a regular basis includes topical cocaine, testosterone, and a compound of strychnine and atropine. It is reported that the Nazis also put methamphetamine-based Pervitin in chocolate bars called Shokokloa, which Hitler kept stocked in his office.[20] Medical historians have questioned whether the Führer's medical problems were the result of his excessive drug regimen, though his drug use undoubtedly affected his behavior.[21,22,23]

Neither Dr. Morell nor anyone else in Hitler's circle dared deny him his medical or drug requests, including the stimulant Pervitin. There were accusations that Morell was responsible for Hitler's addiction to drugs. Yet many among the Nazi elite were drug addicted, often for decades, before meeting Morrell. Dr. Morrell fulfilled a physician's role similar to those of present-day physicians involved with celebrities' prescription-drug addictions and overdose cases.[24]

Morell gave Hitler regular intravenous amphetamine and opioid injections.[25] Although Hitler's psychotic behavior has been attributed to a number of psychiatric symptoms and diagnoses, researchers have concluded that there was "one basic cause of Hitler's psychiatric disability, amphetamine toxicity, and no other diagnosis."[26] Hitler's chronic amphetamine use would have increased his paranoia and impaired his judgment, particularly in the presence of other mental-health issues.[27] Autopsy revealed that Hitler suffered from cardiovascular deterioration that, although attributed to Parkinson's Disease, is consistent with the strain induced by regular use of the stimulants he was taking.

Hermann Göring (also known as Goering), the commander of Germany's air force, the Luftwaffe, was Hitler's second in command and designated successor.

In addition to being one of the most powerful members of the Nazi Party, Göring was a morphine addict, battling his opiate addiction for more than 20 years, right up until his imprisonment at Nuremberg.[28] In 1925, he had to be restrained in a straightjacket and forcibly admitted to Langbro, an asylum notorious for its violent inmates. Hermann Göring's addiction was so profound that he is cited as a case study in *Substance Abuse: A Comprehensive Textbook*, as someone who was able to function efficiently despite his addiction to drugs, and for his co-occurring addictive behavior of hoarding material possessions.[29]

Addiction

Following World War I, there was an "outbreak of morphinism" (addiction to morphine) among veterans. Morphinism includes not only the physical addiction to the drug, but also the psychological deterioration and criminal behavior that often accompanies such addiction. To prevent a repeat of the post–WWI social, psychological, and physical impact of morphine addiction, Germany's military medical command implemented a strict and comprehensive treatment protocol. All German soldiers who became addicted as a result of military injury and medical treatment were documented and reported to a central medical board. Registered morphine addicts would be provided with medical monitoring and either granted regulated access to medical morphine or admitted to a drug rehabilitation center. The Nazi architect of this protocol, psychiatrist Dr. Wuth, predicted that "in this manner morphine addicts will be recorded and monitored, and the entire group will be prevented from becoming criminal."

Nazi medical officers were instructed to admit alcoholics and drug addicts to German treatment facilities. Within these facilities, the government medical officers had the advantage of being able to control and institutionalize addicts indefinitely. Once incarcerated in an addiction treatment facility, addicts were evaluated under the provisions of the "Law for the Prevention of Offspring with Hereditary Diseases," which also subjected people with alcohol and other drug addiction to forced sterilization and even euthanasia.

Despite general knowledge of the risks involved, morphine addiction became widespread among the wounded and medical personnel during the course of the war. Medical personnel had ready access to morphine and would often self-administer the drug for psychological numbing. Four times as many military doctors were addicted to morphine by 1945 as at the beginning of the war.

The Nazi leadership was more lenient with those who became addicted to drugs as a result of the war than they were with those who became alcohol dependent. This was apparently due to their concern over being sued for damages, because the Nazis were responsible for dispensing the addictive drugs in the first place. Addiction to opiate-based pain medication, such as morphine, was not the Nazis' only drug problem. Their prolific use of amphetamines led to stimulant addiction of epidemic proportions among their ranks. Military physicians quickly began to observe evidence of physical tolerance and dependence developing among soldiers, who needed ever-increasing amounts of the stimulant to attain even modest effects. Despite the chronic flow of amphetamines to the war front, letters home from soldiers often included requests for additional supplies of Pervitin.[30]

German medical officers issued written warnings that "every medical officer must be aware that Pervitin is a highly differentiated and powerful stimulant, a tool that enables him, at any time, to actively and effectively help certain individuals within his range of influence achieve above-average performance." Even with growing concern about the rapid buildup of tolerance and the addictive potential of the drugs, the subsequent issuance of "Guidelines for Detecting and Combating Fatigue" recommended the same dosing levels issued at the start of the war: "Two tablets taken once eliminate the need to sleep for three to eight hours, and two doses of two tablets each are normally effective for 24 hours."

Following World War II, amphetamine use spread through Japan, Europe, and North America. Amphetamines became readily available and were widely marketed as a safe euphoriant, to enhance mental concentration and alertness, to alleviate depression, to combat fatigue, and for weight loss. There was also a significant increase in abuse of prescription drugs, including opiate-based medications, among physicians, nurses, and the chronically ill in the decades following World War II.[31] Veterans returned home with an appetite for stimulants, and the demand for methamphetamine grew with the burgeoning postwar suburban sprawl. Methamphetamines, sold under a host of brand names collectively known as "mother's helper," enabled a generation of women to redirect from the wartime workforce back into isolated domesticity.[32] By 1949, amphetamine use required a doctor's prescription, typically given throughout the 1950s and 1960s to fight depression and for weight loss.

When vast military stocks of methamphetamine in pill form were released to the market following the war's end, its abuse became pervasive, and Japan was particularly hard hit. Allied forces dumped the stockpiles in Japan, where methamphetamine abuse and addiction flourished amid the devastation of war and atomic bombing. Likewise, the release of German supplies into the market tremendously impacted Japan, which suffered significant rates of opium and methamphetamine addiction following World War II. At one point, 24 different types of medication containing methamphetamines or amphetamines existed on the open market in Japan. Methamphetamine-related deaths in Japan led to the Stimulant Control Law of 1951, and by 1954 Japan had initiated a campaign to eradicate methamphetamine.[33]

The Nazi love affair with methamphetamine has had major repercussions in the present day as well. The surge in availability of methamphetamine and home-based meth labs in the Midwest of the United States can be traced back to a single individual, Bob Paillet, who claimed that in the early 1990s he found Nazi documents stamped with a swastika in the Missouri State University library, describing how to make methamphetamine without an open heat source, from the readily available chemicals ephedrine, anhydrous ammonia (farm fertilizer), and lithium. Paillet used the "Nazi dope" recipe to irrevocably transform the scale of crystal-methamphetamine production and distribution in the U.S., transforming the nature of addiction and the culture of rural America in the process.[34,35]

Conclusion

The paranoid and psychotic mindset of commanders under the influence of stimulant drugs enabled the Nazi collective to carry out heinous acts of violence against humanity. The drugs cannot be blamed for their behavior, but it is noted that alcohol and other drug use was particularly heavy among Nazi physicians and others engaged in mass killings. In turn, millions of civilians and veterans suffered emotional and physical trauma and turned to alcohol and other drugs to numb the pain.

Trauma and post-traumatic stress disorder (PTSD) from the Second World War have affected veterans, their families, and civilians for generations. PTSD among World War II veterans is not well documented and has been underreported because recognition and acknowledgment of its relation to military personnel has been relatively recent. One of the common ways veterans have tried to cope with PTSD is through the heavy use of alcohol. Rates of alcoholism are significantly correlated with the severity of combat-related stress, particularly among those veterans who suffered wartime head injuries.[36] Researchers have documented cases in which onset of PTSD in World War II veterans has been delayed for more than 30 years. The symptoms emerged in association with later-life stresses, such as bereavement, social isolation, and chronic medical illness.[37]

It is imperative that we recognize that the trauma does not end when the war is over. For many survivors, the post-traumatic stress continues to escalate for decades. One such example is the case of World War II veteran Grover Cleveland Chapman from Greenville, South Carolina. Like many veterans, his post-traumatic stress symptoms became most apparent decades after the war. With each stage of life's transitions, he became increasingly debilitated by PTSD, and when he sought services through the Veterans Administration, he was repeatedly denied PTSD benefits by the Department of Veterans Affairs. In April 2008, his final appeal for PTSD treatment was denied. In a last gasp of desperation, Grover Cleveland Chapman took a cab to the Greenville Veterans Outpatient Clinic, sat down in front of the facility, pulled out a loaded .38 caliber revolver, put it to his head, and pulled the trigger. He was 89 years old.[38]

In response to this high-profile case and the ever-increasing number of OEF and OIF veterans with PTSD, the U.S. Department of Veterans Affairs and the U.S. government have recognized the lifelong battle with substance abuse, trauma, and depression that so many veterans and service members face. The Veterans Benefit Program Improvement Act of 2010 put forth legislation that revised and improved the procedures that service members and veterans must go through to receive mental-health and disability benefits.

CHAPTER 7

The Cold War Was Hot
for the Drug Trade

There was a direct conflict between the Cold War and the Drug War.
Alfred McCoy, professor of Southeast Asian History,
University of Wisconsin–Madison,
and author of *The Politics of Heroin*

FOLLOWING WORLD WAR II, American forces fanned out across Europe, under what was known as the U.S. Naval Technical Mission, in pursuit of scientific data, industrial materials, and intellectual property that could be salvaged from the fall of Nazi Germany. The Central Intelligence Group (the predecessor to the CIA) was modeled after the Office of Strategic Services (OSS), which served as the principal intelligence organization during World War II and engaged in intelligence collection, analysis, and covert actions.

Through the U.S. Naval Technical Mission, with oversight from the Central Intelligence Group, America "imported" more than 600 key Nazi scientists under the guise of Project Paperclip. In an effort to capitalize on the potential strategic use of mind-control experiments conducted by Nazis during World War II, the Central Intelligence Group brought scientists who had been involved in Nazi war crimes to the U.S. Among the scientists recruited by the Central Intelligence Group to emigrate to the U.S. were numerous physicians who designed and carried out crimes against humanity. Most notable was Dr. Hubertus Strughold, the German scientist whose chief subordinates were directly involved in atrocities and unethical medical research on humans, including mescaline (hallucinogen from the peyote cactus) studies at Dachau concentration camp. Their drug experiments were motivated by their pursuit of a competitive edge for the Luftwaffe. Despite well-documented evidence and numerous allegations that Dr. Strughold sanctioned Nazi medical torture experiments during World War II, he was permitted to settle in Texas and became an important figure for America's space program.[1]

The Central Intelligence Group (CIG) transferred the Nazi labs to the U.S. and funded research replicating the Dachau experiments.[2] The CIG saw potential in the use of hallucinogens such as LSD as tools for espionage to disrupt thought processes and control the minds of spies and enemies.

Concomitant with the end of World War II was the beginning of the Cold War, which would last until 1991. The objective of the Cold War was to contain and prevent the spread of communism, particularly in relation to Soviet power. Allied countries such as Great Britain, Canada, and the U.S. did not engage in direct military conflict with the Soviet Union, but rather engaged in serial covert operations, proxy wars, espionage, arms races, cultural rivalry, and technical competition. However, the period included two significant "hot" wars to prevent the spread of communism, first in Korea (1950 to 1953) and later in Vietnam (1964 to 1975).

Birth of the CIA

Created through executive order of Congress on July 25, 1947, under the Truman Administration, the Central Intelligence Agency (CIA) was among the most influential entities in both official and unsanctioned efforts to combat communism throughout the Cold War. The original mission of the CIA was to coordinate intelligence (through the use of espionage and covert operations) for issues of "common concern."

During the CIA's early years of operation, a number of their covert operations did not go well due to lack of human and financial resources.[3] Following on the heels of World War II and modeled after the OSS, the CIA operated beyond public scrutiny and with only cursory Congressional review. Lack of oversight and the secrecy of their missions were paramount to the CIA, which depended on access to funds and personnel that did not require disclosure to the U.S. Congress. The CIA developed self-funding enterprises for some of its international covert operations, most of which were clandestine. Their most profitable and reliable streams of funding came from alliances with warlords and drug lords.

When the CIA began operation, the global opium trade was at its lowest point since the peak of the Opium Wars a century earlier. This decline was due in large part to the trade restrictions imposed during World War II. This trend would soon be reversed, as witnessed by the revival of an illicit narcotics trade due in part to the conduct of U.S. foreign policy and the CIA's covert action arm.[4]

During the Cold War, geopolitical changes and political instability in Southeast and Southwest Asia were conducive to the regional expansion and promotion of the drug trade, particularly in the Golden Triangle, encompassing Laos, Thailand, and Burma (Myanmar). Throughout the 1950s and 1960s, imbalances in drug cultivation and disruption of trade routes occurred during times of political unrest and military incursions. The Korean War, for example, caused a disruption in trafficking and access to trade routes for opium, limiting Western nations' access to the product. In response, the United States and Europe turned to Pakistan, an area known as West Bengal at the time, asking for an increase in opium cultivation.[5] As a result, both licit and illicit opium production increased in Pakistan, with the greatest concentration of cultivation in border regions near Afghanistan. This increase in opium cultivation would continue, creating the epicenter of the new opium empire, the Golden Crescent in Central Asia near the Middle East.[6]

The Iron Curtain and the Golden Triangle

The Iron Curtain defined the boundaries of communist control during the Cold War. Nearly 4,000 miles of it fell along the opium-producing rugged highlands stretching from Turkey to Thailand and encompassing the southern borders of the Soviet Union and communist China. During the decades of the Cold War, the CIA mounted substantial covert operations along the Soviet and Chinese borders, making the Asian opium zone one of the most significant territories of the Cold War. The CIA and allied organizations established alliances with individuals and groups that were opposed, in some way, to pro-communist forces in their region. The CIA engaged hill tribes and ethnic warlords along this strategic front in covert operations that were independently funded by the regions' opium trade.

Revenue from the drug trade also provided the CIA with autonomy, because it enabled them to conduct furtive operations without Congressional oversight. For instance, in the early 1950s, the CIA began recruiting tribal warlords, most of whom we know today to be drug lords, for operations against communist China in northeastern Burma. Among the drug lords who were CIA assets were Generalissimo Chiang Kai-Shek, director-general of the Kuomintang (KMT); Gulbuddin Hekmatyar, leader of Afghan mujahideen; and General Manuel Noriega, former president of Panama.[7,8]

President Harry Truman's involvement in China and Southeast Asia is believed to have played a substantial, however indirect, role in the creation of the Burmese opium kings. When the threat of communism expanded to Southeast Asia, the CIA became involved with the KMT in Burma. Although known drug runners, the KMT were useful allies in resisting the drift toward communism. Protected by the CIA, the Burmese military under the dictatorship of Chiang Kai-Shek, leader of the KMT, turned Burma into the world's top producer of high-grade opium. Figure 7-1 illustrates the increasing rate of opium production prior to World War II and through the Vietnam War. By 1971, opium production in Burma had increased to 1,200 tons annually; this was 150 times the 1930 level of eight tons.[9]

Chiang Kai-Shek's rise in power was closely linked to Tu Yueh-sheng, leader of the infamous international heroin-trafficking Green Circle Gang. In the latter part of the 1930s, Tu Yueh-sheng had begun trafficking heroin into San Francisco and Seattle. CIA planes knowingly transported arms and raw opium between the Burmese bases of Chiang Kai-Shek's KMT and Bangkok, where the drugs were sold to General Phao Siyanan, head of Thailand's police.[10]

Figure 7-1 Burma Opium Production and CIA Regional Involvement

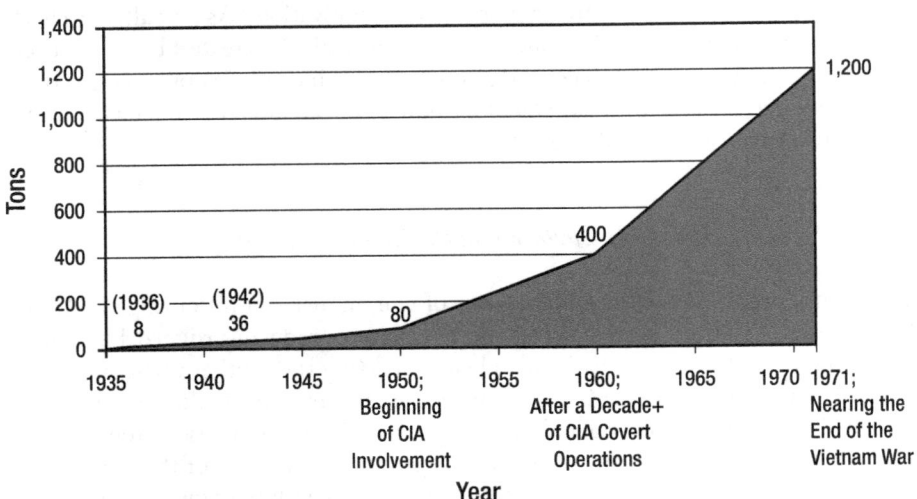

Trafficking of opium provided Chiang Kai-Shek and the Burmese military with substantial revenue streams to build their anti-communist government and military defense. At the start of the CIA's covert involvement in Burma in the late 1940s, opium production in the Burmese region was about 80 tons per year. By 1960, it had increased to 400 tons per year, and near the end of the Vietnam War, opium production reached 1,200 tons annually. This exponential growth occurred in part through the CIA's support of the KMT warlords and their drug trade. The CIA allowed the KMT to transport their opium through Civil Air Transport (CAT), which later became known as Air America.[11]

The highland mountain regions along the Iron Curtain are not conducive to most agricultural crops; however, opium poppies grow well in this type of inhospitable climate. Income from opium thus provided mountain-dwelling highlanders with an occupation that reduced their need for social and economic interaction with ethnic groups from the lowlands. This dynamic of ethnic isolation was particularly evident in the Thai and Burmese regions of Southeast Asia from the 1940s through the 1990s, Laos from 1965 to 1975, and Afghanistan from the 1980s through today. This socio-economic insularity perpetuated cultural differences, including the languages used in commerce, education, and politics.[12] Through the opium trade, the hill tribes and the CIA were both able to amass enough wealth to remain financially independent, isolated, and largely ungovernable.

Some of the very people who are the best sources of information and who are capable of accomplishing things also happened to be the criminal element.[13] To achieve its mission, the CIA needed to ally itself with powerful local groups who were coincidentally most often warlords, drug lords, and tribal leaders; as a result, the CIA became enmeshed in the Southeast Asian drug trade.

To fight the groups sympathetic to communism, the warlords and tribal leaders needed weapons. Buying weaponry required significant amounts of money, and in these regions opium served as the main currency and hence the major source of power for the people with whom the CIA was involved. The CIA also provided protection, transportation, and commercial contacts that facilitated the movement and marketing of narcotics on a global scale.

CIA complicity in most cases did not involve direct participation in the opium and heroin trades. Rather, it was their tolerance and calculated ignorance of the local allies that established the CIA's culpability. These facts were corroborated by the CIA's own internal investigations.[14,15] The intelligence and supplemental forces gleaned from CIA covert missions were their top priorities.[16]

Concomitant with the close of the Vietnam War, opium production in Burma and the rest of the Golden Triangle declined precipitously. Opium production in Laos alone plummeted by 85 percent during the decade following the end of the Vietnam War.[17] Figure 7-2 depicts the rise and fall of opium production in Laos with the timing of the Vietnam War. Although the reduction in opium production was attributed in part to drought conditions in Laos, the decline in the need for military funding, coupled with the relocation of opium cultivation to the Golden Crescent, accounted for the most significant decline. The increase in cultivation in the Golden Crescent, the mountainous region along the Pakistan and Afghanistan border, coincided with the Afghan Islamic resistance movement beginning in 1973. This was also the site of the next major military campaign for the enlargement of Soviet territory. The cultivation of opium and hash in the region funded Afghanistan's defense against the Soviets in the Soviet-Afghan War, which lasted from 1979 to 1989.

Figure 7-2 Laos Opium Production Prior to and Following the Vietnam War

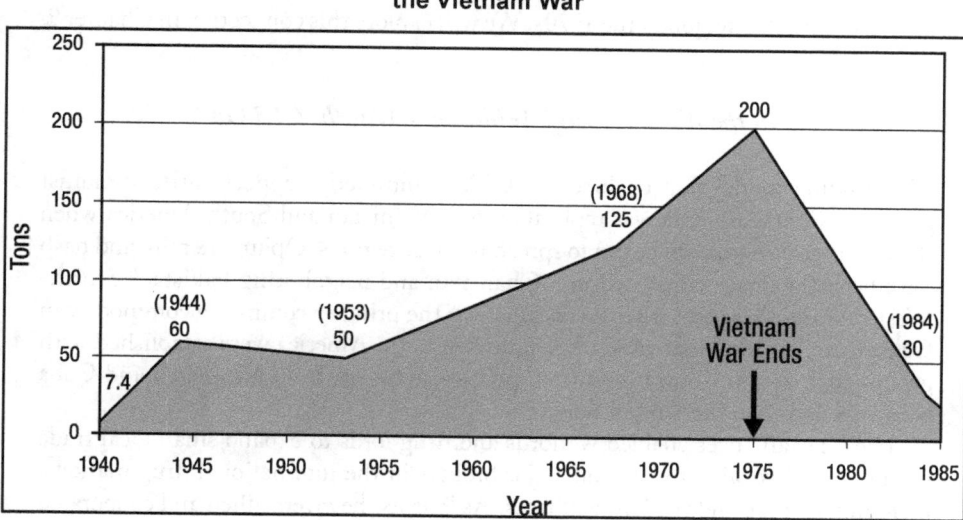

It is not only the countries where the drugs are sent and sold that are affected; the rates of addiction increase in source countries and regions with narcotics cultivation and trafficking. Laotian communities that cultivated opium poppy as a cash crop had the country's highest crude rates of addiction (7–9.8 addicts per 100 people). By contrast, Laotian communities involved in opium commerce but not cultivation had slightly lower rates (4–5.5 per 100 people), and communities where neither opium production nor commerce was present had the lowest rates of addiction (1.8–2.3 per 100 people).[18]

The geopolitical influence on the diffusion of drug use and trafficking cannot be overstated. The confluence of access routes, people in desperate situations, and a lawless climate fuels drug cultivation, trafficking, and use. A decade after American military intervention, Southeast Asia had become the leading source of the world's opium, supplying 70 percent of illicit opium-based drugs, including America's escalating heroin market.[19]

Opium smoking was not uncommon among KMT soldiers and Yao villagers in the small villages near Mae Salong, but it was limited to local cultivation and use.[20] However, after a road was built by a U.S. Navy Seabee construction team linking Mae Salong with major highways under the auspices of the U.S. Agency for International Development's Accelerated Rural Development (USAID ARD), KMT opium and heroin trafficking exploded, and the KMT became a formidable international narcotics force.

The growth of the KMT's opium-trafficking network was also supported through funding from USAID, and two C-47s from Air America were used by the KMT to start their own private airline in 1967, Xieng Khouang Air Transport. As it turned out, USAID ARD was a counter-insurgency program that was designed to provide the Thai army with access to rugged mountainous regions in times of rebellion and the ability to transport heavy military equipment. The road was a boon for the KMT and its influence on international narcotics trafficking.[21] The KMT was the source for drug kingpin Frank Lucas's notorious heroin trade in the greater New York metropolitan region in the 1970s. We will explore this connection in Chapter 9.

In the War on Drugs, Which Side Was the CIA On?

The funding model that enabled the CIA to indirectly support anti-communist groups in Southeast Asia was replicated in Afghanistan and South America when the threat of communism began to spread in those regions. Opium, heroin, and hash have been the drugs cultivated in Afghanistan and neighboring Pakistan's North-West Frontier Province, whereas cocaine was the primary commerce commodity in Central and South America. CIA alliances in Latin America were established with groups such as the Contras and with political refugees from Nicaragua and Cuba who were living in the United States.

The CIA alliances enabled warlords and drug lords to expand small local trade in opium and cocaine to become major brokers in the international drug markets, including Europe and the United States. As long as they were allied and cooperated with the CIA, the drug lords were protected from investigation by local law enforcement, Interpol, and even the U.S. Drug Enforcement Agency (DEA). This enabled drug lords to release periodic surges of heroin from Asia and carefully timed releases of cocaine from Latin America, generating mass revenue when needed.

On July 12, 1988, John Lawn, head of the DEA, testified that Lieutenant Colonel Oliver North had intentionally and prematurely leaked a DEA undercover operation, jeopardizing agents' lives, for political advantage in an upcoming Congressional vote on aid to the Contras.[22] The Contras' practice replicated the strategies used in Southeast Asia of self-funding for paramilitary communist-opposition groups through drugs-for-arms sales. Once the lucrative contacts were established in South America, the practice took on a life of its own, and trafficking in both drugs and guns throughout the region proliferated at a fevered pitch. During the Cold War, the swells in drug supplies in source countries, the United States, Canada, and Europe followed the waves of U.S. covert operations in Southeast Asia, Afghanistan, and Latin America.[23]

These covert actions throughout the Cold War simultaneously undermined America's War on Drugs. President Nixon's metaphor of "war" elevated drug trafficking to a matter of national security and spawned several federal agencies that would become the DEA. This transferred responsibility for dealing with the drug problem from state and local governments, where the emphasis was on treatment of drug abuse as a community health problem, to nationally coordinated security agencies reporting directly to the president. However, Nixon's War on Drugs did have a positive impact on disrupting the flow of heroin from Asia into the U.S.

During Gerald Ford's presidency, information came to light through the Church Committee Hearings regarding the Department of Defense and the CIA's long history of testing of psychedelic drugs on some of their own agents and U.S. civilians without their knowledge.[24] In light of these findings, President Jimmy Carter banned funding and support of major CIA covert operations. This ban was in effect from 1976 to 1978 and resulted in removing many of the protections for drug lords.

However, under the Reagan and H.W. Bush administrations, covert CIA operations returned to and surpassed their pre-Carter levels. In 1981, George H.W. Bush, former director of the CIA, became vice president of the United States under President Ronald Reagan. During the last decade of the Cold War era, the U.S. was governed by the Reagan Doctrine, which was the foreign policy devised by President Ronald Reagan's administration and which continued under the administration of President George H.W. Bush. Under the Reagan Doctrine, the U.S. provided covert and overt aid to resistance movements and right-wing guerilla groups to oppose communism, particularly involving the Soviet invasion of Afghanistan and Soviet-backed encroachment in Latin America and regions of Africa and Asia. U.S. government officials were again complicit in the trafficking of cocaine in North and South America to provide billions of dollars in weaponry to support Afghan resistance to the Soviets. Moreover, the CIA and their allies provided leaders of the Afghan mujahideen, such as Gulbuddin Hekmatyar, immunity for their narcotics trade because it helped fund their insurgency and purchase of munitions. As we will see in Chapter 12, these alliances have significant impacts today.[25]

The Contras, the Crips, and the Cocaine Epidemic

In their efforts to support anti-communist groups in Latin America while simultane-ously engaging in covert support of Afghans fighting the Soviet invasion, the CIA was complicit in the trafficking of cocaine, much of which ended up in the United States. Revelations of the Latin American involvement by the CIA and U.S. govern-ment officials, notably Lieutenant Colonel Oliver North, would become known as the Iran-Contra Affair.

As in Vietnam, the CIA felt that it needed to find methods of self-funding that would enable it to conduct covert operations that did not require Congressional fund-ing and hence oversight. During the 1980s, the CIA, with the knowledge of select senior White House administrators, facilitated funding for their covert operations and the support of the Contras through the international sale of guns and munitions and the protected transportation of drugs. Specifically, the sale of arms to Iran by the U.S. helped the CIA fund the Contras' fight against the Sandinistas in Nicaragua. Nicaraguan exiles who also enjoyed CIA protection were living in San Francisco, Los Angeles, and Miami, which resulted in the establishment of large-scale drug rings in these cities in the early to mid 1980s.

From an epidemiological perspective, the U.S. involvement in Nicaragua was the catalyst for the crack epidemic in the U.S. The degree of CIA involvement and complicity in the cocaine and crack epidemics that would consume the U.S. is a hotly debated issue. Although the evidence does not reveal that the CIA had direct involve-ment in trafficking of cocaine, court documents and Congressional hearings show active engagement of exiled Nicaraguan Contras (living in the U.S. under government protection) in the South American–North American cocaine and crack trade.[26,27,28]

The Middle East/South America/CIA connection is illuminated in the Iran-Contra Affair through its televised 1987 Congressional hearings. Oliver North's personal records and notebooks were reviewed as evidence regarding the sanctioned and covert role of U.S. weapons and drug trafficking with the Nicaraguan Contras and Iran. One of the more damning pieces of evidence was a page in Oliver North's notebook in his own handwriting, which referenced the use of CIA airplanes to transport "paste" from Colombia. The "paste" refers to coca paste, the semi-refined product of coca leaves that is then processed into powder cocaine.[29] The following is a transcribed partial listing of entries in Oliver North's diaries. He makes direct reference to drug-related funding of Contra operations and knowledge of narcotics trafficking by associates:

July 9, 1984: Call Michel re Narco Issue—RIG at 1000 Tomorrow—DEA Miami— Pilot went talked to Vaughn—wanted A/C to go to Bolivia to p/u paste—want A/C to p/u 1500 kilos—Bud to meet w/ Group

July 17, 1984: Call to Frank M—Bud Mullins Re—leak on DEA piece—Carlton Turner, Call from Johnstone—McManus, LA Times-says/NSC source claims W.H. has pictures of Borge loading cocaine in Nic.

July 12, 1985: $14 million to finance came from drugs[30]

The Senate Foreign Relations Committee's Subcommittee on Terrorism, Narcotics, and International Operations initiated hearings under the leadership of Senator John Kerry and found substantial evidence of drug smuggling on the part of Contra pilots and supporters. The Committee concluded that, "US officials involved in Latin America failed to address the drug issue for fear of jeopardizing the war efforts against Nicaragua."[31] After methodically investigating the evidence that led to the establishment of the Iran-Contra hearings, Senator John Kerry stated, "Our borders are inundated with more narcotics than in any time ever before. It seems as though stopping drug trafficking in the United States has been a secondary U.S. foreign policy objective, sacrificed repeatedly for other political and institutional goals, such as changing the government of Nicaragua, supporting the government of Panama, using drug-running organizations as intelligence assets, and protecting military and intelligence sources from possible compromise through involvement in drug trafficking."[32]

The efforts to overthrow the Marxist Sandinista regime in Nicaragua established the roots of the crack epidemic, as U.S.-based Nicaraguan exiles set up cocaine and crack rings in South Central Los Angeles. The Nicaraguan exiles established ties to street gangs, primarily the Bloods and the Crips, who in turn manufactured crack cocaine. Profits from the drug trade by Nicaraguan exiles, such as Danilo Blandon, went back to the Contra army, which had been created by the CIA for the purpose of sabotaging the Sandinista revolution that had ousted Nicaraguan dictator Anastasio Somoza in 1979. Somoza was liked by the U.S. and had sent his military officers to the U.S. for training.

The extent of the drug trafficking directly linked to the Nicaraguan exiles and the Contra army was not elucidated in the public hearings of the Iran-Contra affair in 1987, but emerged a decade later in journalist Gary Webb's three-part series, "The Dark Alliance," which ran in the *San Jose Mercury News* on August 18, 19, and 20, 1996. Excerpts from the first article in the series capture the essence of the sociocultural and human impact of the Cold War policies and the rogue arm of the CIA: "For the better part of a decade, a San Francisco Bay Area drug ring sold tons of cocaine to the Crips and Bloods street gangs of Los Angeles and funneled millions in drug profits to a Latin American guerrilla army run by the U.S. Central Intelligence Agency.... This drug network opened the first pipeline between Colombia's cocaine cartels and the black neighborhoods of Los Angeles, a city now known as the 'crack' capital of the world."[33]

When the CIA's involvement in the flow of cocaine into the U.S. came to light through Webb's meticulous reporting, California senators Barbara Boxer and Maxine Waters called for and held a town hall forum in South Central Los Angeles. In addition to the 5,000 outraged residents who rallied at the town meeting, attendees included John Deutch, then director of the CIA. Deutch vehemently denied CIA involvement in the flood of cocaine into Southern California. However, Mike Ruppert, a former narcotics officer with the Los Angeles Police Department (LAPD), spoke openly about the LAPD's complicity in the CIA's sponsorship of the cocaine trade, which was flooding California—and Los Angeles, in particular—with drugs. All of this was broadcast live by CNN from Locke High School in the L.A. community of Watts on November 15, 1996. Ruppert informed Deutch of three major CIA operations—Amadeus, Pegasus, and Watchtower—in which CIA agents recruited LAPD officers to protect their interests in drug trafficking.[34]

Notable among the Contras was Norwin Meneses, who in July 1979 was provided safe passage with refugee status to the U.S. despite the fact that he was widely known in Nicaragua as El Rey de las Drogas (the King of Drugs). The DEA had been keeping files on Meneses since 1974, and his involvement in narcotics was well known to U.S. officials. Meneses was one of many Nicaraguans who settled in the San Francisco Bay Area. He set up cocaine rings in San Francisco and Los Angeles for the purpose of raising funds to support the Contras' fight against the Sandinistas and the new Nicaraguan regime.[35]

Meneses, well connected to limitless supplies of South American cocaine, was working in collaboration with Miami-based Donald Barrios, an exile from Managua, Nicaragua. The third major player in their Nicaraguan émigré triangle was Los Angeles–based Danilo Blandon, also from Managua. Blandon had close ties with the U.S. Department of Commerce and State and was well known by the CIA and the U.S. as a supporter of Somoza. Miami, Los Angeles, and San Francisco would become the hotbeds of cocaine and crack trafficking in the U.S. during the 1980s.

In 1981, during the early days of their drugs-for-munitions subvention ring, they brought 900 kilos of cocaine into the U.S. through Meneses' San Francisco–based operation. In 1981, one kilo of cocaine had a street value of nearly $50,000. With 900 kilos, Meneses' operation would yield nearly $45 million that year. With the support of Blandon and Barrios, their trafficking boomed, and by 1983 they were bringing 5,000 kilos of cocaine into the U.S. via Los Angeles and Miami.

The abundant availability of cocaine resulted in a significant drop in prices and therefore profits. One kilo of cocaine sold for about $25,000 in 1984, half of what the same amount had fetched a few years earlier. The drug cartels responded to the drop in cocaine's value by introducing the highly concentrated and even lower-priced cousin of cocaine—crack. Developed by the cartels, crack cocaine was a cheaper, more addictive drug that could help retain their profit margins with the falling price of cocaine. Crack cocaine is created on stovetops in kitchens using cocaine, baking soda, and water. Mixing ingredients into the cocaine extends its volume, so that more can be sold at lower prices. This made cocaine in the form of crack a cheap drug accessible to anyone with a few dollars.

Crack is inhaled as smoke and therefore creates a rapid intense high that peaks and dissipates faster than cocaine, which is inhaled nasally. Crack's instantaneous effect on the user results in rapid addiction. Consequently, crack flooded the inner city and became the financial underpinning of gangs. The crack epidemic particularly affected women in the inner cities and devastated family systems. It caused intergenerational trauma, the effects of which are still being felt.

The crack trade was dominated by the Bloods and Crips with roots in Los Angeles. One of the most infamous dealers and member of the Crips was "Freeway" Ricky Ross, whose primary cocaine supply was linked to the CIA asset Danilo Blandon.[36,37]

Blandon was introduced to Ross and supplied him with cocaine, which Ross cooked into crack. Blandon in turn took the profits from the cocaine sales and funded the Contras in Nicaragua. Ross was buying bulk cocaine directly from Blandon for $10,000 less per kilo than the going rate. Court records indicate that Ross's operation was buying 100 kilos of cocaine per week at the peak of their trade.[38] With this type of discount and mass purchasing power, Ross gained an edge in the market similar to the advantage Frank Lucas had in the New York metropolitan heroin market through his direct purchasing routes from the KMT in the Golden Triangle.

Figure 7-3 shows the percentage of the U.S. population by age group using cocaine from 1979 to 2000. The data is from the National Household Survey on Drug Abuse collected in 1979, 1982, 1985, 1988, and each year from 1990 to 2000.[39] The rate of use was highest during the late '70s and early '80s. During this time period, Nicaraguan exiles were known to have been trafficking cocaine into the U.S. to raise money for the Contras, while the Sandinistas were also allegedly engaged in drug trafficking to raise funds in opposition to the Contras. The source of the cocaine was Colombia, where the drug cartels were bolstered by the leadership of Pablo Escobar, who arranged to transport cocaine through Panama with the support of Panamanian General Manuel Noriega.[40] This is also the time period when the CIA was given legal exemption from having to report known drug activity among CIA assets.

Blandon and his associates bought weapons and surveillance equipment from former Laguna Beach police detective Ronald Lister, who had worked as an informant for the DEA and the FBI. It is alleged that Lister also had ties to the CIA in the 1980s, related to some work he was involved with in Central America. Lister provided

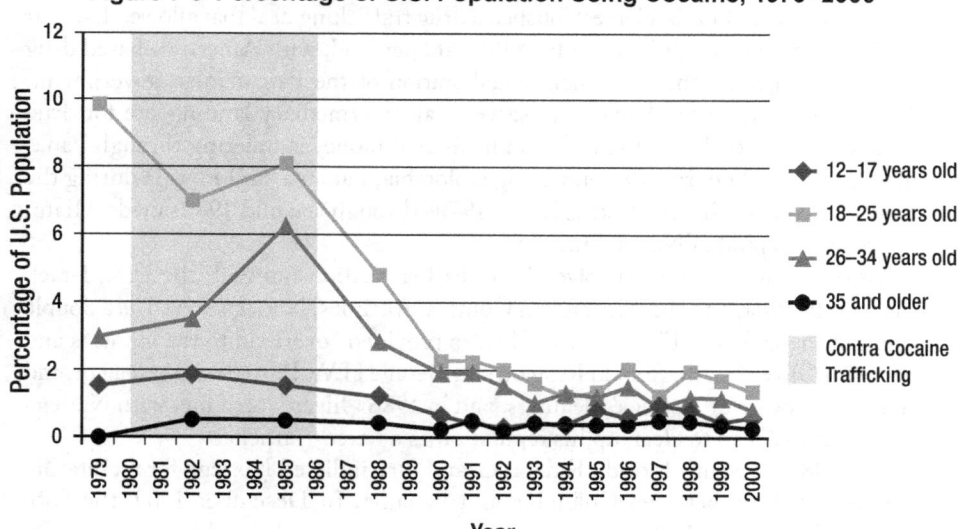

Figure 7-3 Percentage of U.S. Population Using Cocaine, 1979–2000

weapons demonstrations for Contra supporters living in Southern California.[41] As we will see in the following chapter, Laguna Beach had been a key site in the psychedelic drug movement in the 1960s and 1970s.

Not confining his arms deals to the Contras, Blandon sold "Freeway" Ricky Ross surveillance equipment, semiautomatic rifles, Uzis, and submachine guns to help Ross and his associates protect their drugs, money, and territory. Ross in turn armed his associates and sold munitions that fostered the bloody gang wars of the 1980s in Los Angles; such gang wars have since spread throughout the U.S., taking hold in medium-sized cities as well as larger metropolitan areas.

Concurrently, cocaine was flooding Miami, which saw an average of two cocaine overdoses per week in 1981, whereas in the preceding years two or fewer per year had been the norm. For an indication of the flow of money and drugs into southern Florida at this time, we need only look at the fact that more than $6 billion was deposited in Miami banks during the early 1980s. During this same time, comparably sized U.S. cities had annual bank deposits of $12 million, whereas in Miami the annual bank deposits averaged $600 million.

Federal banks benefited as well, and in the mid 1980s, the Federal Reserve Bank in Miami had significantly more in reserve than all other Federal Reserve Banks in the U.S. combined. The money flowing in South Florida rotted the morality of police, city officials, and several mayors who were indicted and convicted of corruption linked to drug money.[42]

General Manuel Noriega

Certainly not all of the cocaine coming into the U.S. was linked to the Nicaraguan exiles. In 1982, Panamanian General Manuel Noriega and Colombia's Medellin Cartel kingpin Pablo Escobar established a drug trafficking deal that allowed Escobar to ship cocaine through Panama for $100,000 per load, with American-based drug traffickers enjoying the convenient collaboration of the Panamanian government. Noriega also permitted Panama to serve as an intermediary landing site for drug flights from Colombia to the U.S. and facilitated money laundering through Panamanian banks. The triangle connecting Colombia, Panama, and Florida during the early phase of cocaine trafficking in the 1970s through the mid 1980s made Miami the cocaine capital of North America.

Noriega had also been involved in an earlier relationship with the U.S., Israel, the Middle East, and the Nicaraguan Contras. At times, Noriega served as a double agent of the U.S. and Fidel Castro. He also provided covert aid to the Contras and met with Oliver North, Ronald Reagan, and George H.W. Bush. North, Reagan, and Bush were aware of Noriega's dealings, and in 1986 Oliver North met with Noriega to discuss his need to clean up his reputation as a narco-trafficker.

In 1988, the South Florida Federal Grand Jury indicted Noriega for facilitating narco-trafficking between Colombia and Panama. In December 1989, the U.S. invaded Panama with the intent of capturing Noriega to bring him to justice for trafficking cocaine bound for the U.S. The U.S. military invaded Panama near the Vatican (Nunciatura) Embassy, where Noriega was known to be hiding. The U.S. military's unusual tactics included blaring rock music from massive speakers to drive Noriega from the embassy. During this highly televised, reality TV–style invasion, the U.S. military went after what was believed to be Noriega's sizable cocaine stash, which turned out to be tamales. Nonetheless, there was concrete evidence of Noriega's complicity in money laundering and the trafficking of drugs into the U.S. Eventually, Noriega was captured, brought to trial in the U.S., and imprisoned.

Whereas there is limited evidence of federal officials' and the CIA's direct involvement in drug trafficking, there are strong indications of tacit approval or complicity with respect to their assets who were known drug traffickers. In 1999, a CIA report developed under the direction of Inspector General Frederick Hitz refuted charges that CIA officials knew that their Nicaraguan allies were dealing drugs. However, the report did conclude that the CIA did not bother to look into allegations about narcotics dealing and that there was little or no direction given to CIA operatives when confronted by the rampant trafficking of drugs in Central America during the 1980s.[43] The Hitz report states, "At best, these incidents represent negligence on the part of U.S. government officials responsible for providing support to the Contras.... At worst, it was a matter of turning a blind eye to the activities of companies who use legitimate activities as a cover for their narcotics trafficking." The report also states that the CIA made conscious use of major traffickers as agents, contractors, and assets.[44]

In February 2000, the House of Representatives' Permanent Select Committee on Intelligence held additional hearings to examine the role of U.S. government agents in drug trafficking. The Committee Report on the Central Intelligence Agency's Alleged Involvement in Crack Cocaine Trafficking in the Los Angeles Area concluded, after years of internal investigation and Congressional hearings, that covert support for the Nicaraguan Contras in the 1980s undermined the U.S. War on Drugs. The DEA's efforts to prosecute major drug traffickers were routinely dismissed on national-security grounds, because the same traffickers were CIA assets. As director of the CIA in 1976, George H.W. Bush defended these practices and cover-ups because they were legal under a 1954 agreement between the CIA and the U.S. Department of Justice. This agreement gave the CIA the right to block prosecutions in the name of national security and to prohibit disclosure of secret operations. The created *de facto* immunity from prosecution for CIA assets trafficking drugs.

Throughout the 1980s, while President Ronald Reagan and his wife Nancy were championing the "Just Say No" campaign as part of the War on Drugs, the Reagan administration was enabling narco-financing for the Contras in Nicaragua. By the mid 1980s, the Reagan administration was deeply involved in covert operations and support of the Contras as part of U.S. Cold War anti-communist/anti-Marxist efforts. Reagan linked the Cold War and the War on Drugs, stating, "The link between the governments of such Soviet allies as Cuba and Nicaragua and international narcotics trafficking and terrorism is becoming increasingly clear.... These two ends—narcotics trafficking and terrorism—represent the most insidious and dangerous threats to the hemisphere today."[45]

Nonetheless, the objectives of the War on Drugs were consistently subordinated to anti-communist policy interests.[46] Reagan's fear that Congress would restrict or cut off funding for the Contras led to the development of covert sources of funding and arms trading. North, former staff of the National Security Council, created the National Security Enterprise to funnel arms and equipment to the Contras while funding these activities through transshipments of cocaine into the U.S. The Contra network created by North and other senior officials attracted drug traffickers in need of cover and U.S. market access for their operations.[47]

Few people have grasped the impact that the U.S. Cold War practices and policies have had on the development of the cocaine and crack epidemics. Government complicity was enabled in part by citizens who did not want to believe their government could be involved intentionally in dishonest actions. There have been allegations that the CIA has employed agents strategically at key papers, such as the *Washington Post*, to serve not just as informants, but more importantly as strategic counterpoints who can discredit journalists reporting on topics they do not want in the public realm. This appears to be what happened with Gary Webb's series "Dark Alliance." Webb was vehemently discredited by journalists at *The New York Times*, *Los Angeles Times*, and *The Washington Post*, to the point that he took his own life on December 10, 2004.

U.S. intelligence agencies have admittedly recruited reporters, and intelligence operatives have fraudulently used journalism credentials. In its investigation of U.S. foreign and military intelligence operations, the Senate Select Committee on Intelligence, chaired by Frank Church, found that more than 50 American journalists had worked clandestinely as CIA agents during the Cold War era. The extent of the CIA's infiltration of journalism and its influence on what is reported and what is subverted is not fully known and is still in practice.[48] CIA agents have often posed as journalists to gain access and protection while operating around the world. While most reporters paid no attention to the topic, Doug Valentine published a book exposing the CIA's role, and Peter Kornbluh of the National Security Archives kept the records alive and available for researchers and reporters. Today these records are openly available online.[49,50]

American journalists were slow to report on the role of the CIA in tacit support of cocaine trafficking to support funding for the Contras. There was journalistic complicity in their lack of reporting the CIA's involvement in cocaine trafficking, documentation of which came to light readily once journalistic scrutiny was applied.

Colombia and FARC

On July 13, 2000, President Bill Clinton signed into law Plan Colombia, a $1.3 billion counter-narcotics and counter-terrorism package consisting mainly of military assistance. Plan Colombia was designed to reduce Colombian cocaine production and break the narco-funding of leftist peasant guerrillas known as the Fuerzas Armadas Revolucionarias de Colombia, or FARC. A decade later, the expenditures have risen to $7.3 billion dollars, and although many of the original goals and timelines, such as cutting cocaine production by 50 percent by the year 2005, were not met, there has been some progress. The FARC has been seriously weakened and is operating at half the strength it possessed in 2000, while criminality and violence have steadily decreased. The Colombian state has been strengthened—particularly the military, which has nearly doubled in size since the implementation of Plan Colombia. But progress has come at a significant cost in terms of human suffering: An estimated 14,000 civilians and some 21,000 fighters from all sides of the drug war died in the narco-based fighting between 2000 and 2010.

While today the Colombian government conducts aggressive coca eradication operations, the Peruvian and Bolivian governments have thus far been reluctant to eradicate coca cultivation in certain key growing areas. In Colombia, efforts were made to eradicate coca cultivation through aerial spraying of herbicides over 130,000 hectares; however, due to aggressive replanting on the part of coca growers, Colombia remains a key producer. The large coca plantations have decreased, while increasing numbers of peasants continue to cultivate smaller coca crops.

The CIA reported that 551 metric tons of export-quality cocaine (85 percent pure) were seized or destroyed in 2005. This reflected an increase of 26 percent in Colombia's coca production from the previous year, with 144,000 hectares of coca plants. Cocaine production in Colombia has continued to increase to 167,000 hectares of coca cultivation in 2007.[51] Still, according to the United Nations Office on Drugs and Crime (UNODC) report for 2010, overall coca production in Colombia declined by 58 percent between 2000 and 2009.[52] Despite the aggressive War on Drugs, Colombia remains the world's leading producer, cultivator, and supplier of coca and coca derivatives to the North American market and is playing an increasing role in European markets. Some South American countries have responded to the drug war in Colombia with increased coca cultivation, including Peru (38 percent increase) and Bolivia (112 percent increase) during the first decade of this century.[53]

On February 12, 2003, an airplane flying reconnaissance missions as part of the eradication of Colombia's coca plantations crash-landed in FARC territory. The plane was carrying passengers later revealed to be a Colombian sergeant and four American DEA subcontractors. The Colombian sergeant, Luis Alcides Cruz, and one of the Americans, Thomas Janis, were shot by FARC rebels, and the three other Americans, Thomas Howes, Keith Stansell, and Marc Gonsalves, were taken captive. The three American hostages were accused by FARC of being CIA spies. The hostages were used as bargaining leverage to negotiate a prisoner exchange of hundreds of FARC rebels with the Colombian government.

The revelation in 2008 that the U.S. hostages were DEA agents and U.S. defense subcontractors pointed out the U.S. government's increasing reliance on the outsourcing of drug enforcement and interdiction efforts through defense contractors.[54] Such outsourcing addressed staffing shortages while distancing the government from responsibility for the actions of private contractors.

In December 2004, Attorney General John Ashcroft, the FBI, and the DEA extradited Juvenal Ovidio Ricardo Palmera Pineda, a.k.a. Simón Trinidad, a high-ranking member (Estado Mayor Central) of FARC, to the U.S. to face charges of terrorism and narcotics trafficking stemming from the FARC abduction of the American subcontractors. Ashcroft linked narcotics and terrorism in this statement: "The Trinidad case highlights the convergence of two of the top priorities of the Department of Justice: the prevention of terrorism and the reduction of the flow of illegal and deadly narcotics into this country."[55] Assistant Attorney General Christopher Wray also conveyed the nexus of these issues in this quote from the Department of Justice press release regarding the indictment: "The FARC is a dangerous organization of terrorists, drug traffickers, kidnappers and murderers." Since 1997, FARC has been designated by the U.S. State Department as a foreign terrorist organization.

A federal grand jury returned a narcotics indictment in March 2004, charging that Trinidad controlled and directed FARC drug-trafficking activities by issuing orders regarding the acquisition, transportation, and sale of cocaine by various fronts of the FARC and the movement of drug money. The indictment alleges that Trinidad managed and controlled money for the FARC that was used by the organization to conduct cocaine-trafficking activities. The indictment alleges that Trinidad announced to local coca growers the price the FARC would pay them for each kilogram of cocaine base and advised them that the quality of their cocaine base was "inferior" and "needed to be improved."[56] The indictment further alleged that Trinidad met with and received money from, or supplied money to, other FARC drug traffickers, that he attended drug-trafficking meetings, and that he spoke of sending cocaine to the United States.[57]

Trinidad was convicted in July 2007 on kidnapping and hostage charges, but the jury deadlocked on the terrorism and narcotics charges. In a separate trial, FARC rebels Anayibe Rojas Valderrama (a.k.a. Sonia), Antonio Celis, and Juan Diego Giraldo were prosecuted on drug charges and convicted of exporting cocaine to the U.S. and of manufacturing or distributing cocaine with the knowledge or intention that it would be imported into the U.S. to finance the FARC rebels.[58] In the trial against Sonia, testimony was presented claiming that over a two-year period, Sonia traveled by riverboat on a biweekly basis up and down the Rio Caguan, buying hundreds of tons of cocaine, much of which was to be exported to the U.S. This returned hundreds of millions of dollars to the impoverished economy. Although the Colombian military controlled the river at that time, Valdez and Sonia purportedly made hundreds of enormous drug deals in a regular pattern.

The 2004 narcotics indictment called for the forfeiture of all FARC assets derived from the alleged violations, and the terrorism indictment called for the forfeiture of all FARC assets, foreign and domestic, as provided in the U.S. Patriot Act. This was a clear effort to weaken the FARC's efforts to advance communism in the region and establish a Marxist state in the FARC-controlled safe zone situated between two of Colombia's largest coca-cultivation areas. In return for cash payments and weapons, FARC insurgents protected cocaine laboratories and drug-trafficking activities and controlled local cocaine-based markets in southern Colombia.

The impact of the cocaine trade can be felt in every corner of the western hemisphere. Colombian drug lords have taken advantage of political instability and poverty in Haiti to establish Port-au-Prince as one of the key transit points for cocaine in the Caribbean. In a report from the U.S. State Department, cocaine traffickers shipped 75 tons of cocaine through Haiti in 2000, equaling 15 percent of the cocaine consumed in the U.S. in 2000. This represented nearly a 25 percent increase in cocaine transshipment through Haiti from the previous year.[59] The significant poverty level, political instability, and geographical closeness of Haiti make it a vulnerable target for Colombia's cocaine cartel.[60] One can only imagine what the impact of the 2010 earthquake in Haiti may be with regard to its vulnerability in the chain of narcotics trafficking. Likewise, Colombian cartels have targeted politically unstable and war-torn regions in western Africa for transshipment of cocaine to Europe.[61]

Collapse of the Soviet Union and the End of the Cold War

Drug cultivation, trafficking, and use escalated in the Americas, Europe, and Southeast Asia from the 1960s through the end of the Cold War. Throughout the Cold War, the Soviets claimed that socialist societies did not experience drug abuse. They portrayed this as an important marker of their purported superiority over capitalist countries in the West. The degree to which alcohol and other drugs were used within the Soviet Union is hard to quantify, because the Soviets did not allow independent inspections and external investigation of domestic drug production, manufacturing, or treatment facilities, nor did they maintain data for pertinent national-health indicators, such as cirrhosis prevalence.[62]

Since the collapse of the Soviet Union, there is abundant data on the escalating rates of alcohol and other drug abuse in many former Eastern Bloc countries. Substance abuse and addiction are most prevalent in the countries that are economically unstable and have high unemployment rates, lending credence to the Soviet assertion that the etiology of addiction is rooted largely in social factors. In contrast, the western Cold War enforcement position was based on the assumption that individual deficiencies are the root cause.[63] Russia has data to support the link between an open economy and addiction and the contention that rising rates of addiction are the underbelly of globalization. In 1991, at the end of the Cold War, capitalism and heroin alike were practically nonexistent in Soviet Russia. However, by 2001, conservative estimates reported that Russia had 3 million addicts, a twelvefold increase from the previous decade.[64]

The collapse of the Soviet Union was due in large part to the financial drain and strain of the Soviet-Afghan War. With the dissolution of the Soviet Union and the disintegration of post–Cold War states, former Soviet Union military wares were being sold on the international market and readily acquired by narcotics traffickers. There was massive wholesale distribution and trafficking of weaponry, from Kalashnikov rifles to MIG aircraft and Soviet submarines. As a result the world became awash in advanced weaponry and expertise, which has subsequently supported the proliferation of drug cartels and terrorist organizations. These organizations have proliferated in concert with the expansion of multinational markets, the globalization of terror, escalating drug markets, and mounting insecurity. Vacuums of stability created by conflict and absence of governance in areas such as the Balkans, Afghanistan, Colombia, and certain African countries offer ready-made areas for terrorist training and recruitment activity, while smuggling and drug trafficking routes are often exploited by terrorists to support operations worldwide.[65]

During the Cold War, the U.S. was happy to accept Russian immigrants and defectors. Many Russians were earnestly looking for freedom and the legitimate opportunities available in America. However, there were also many Russian criminal elements that spread to cities throughout the U.S. New York City first began attracting Russian mobsters in the 1970s. Unlike this earlier wave of Russians criminals, those who immigrated after the 1991 breakup of the Soviet Union were reportedly more hardened, violent, and adept at working with international criminals.[66]

The growth of the cocaine market in Eastern Europe and the former Soviet Union led criminal groups from the former Soviet republics to become partners in crime with the South American drug cartels. In 1997, several Soviet mini-submarines loaded with cocaine from Colombia were confiscated in the Caribbean port of Santa Marta.[67] That same year, Ludwig "Tarzan" Fainberg, a South Florida–based organized crime figure from the former Soviet Union, and two Cuban immigrants working as middlemen for Colombian drug cartels tried to buy a submarine from the former Soviet Union for $5.5 million to transport cocaine from Colombia to the United States and Canada. Fainberg had begun buying Soviet military transport equipment within a year after the collapse of the Soviet Union, purchasing Russian helicopters for Colombian drug traffickers in 1992.[68]

After the end of the Cold War, stockpiles of munitions and equipment supplied by the Soviets and the United States remained among the paramilitary groups and countries backed by one of these two superpowers. Soviet submarines and equipment were sold off and co-opted and have become increasingly used by drug cartels. In 2010, grenades made in the U.S. that had been sent to Central America during the Cold War surfaced amidst the cartel violence in Mexico. The grenades have been sold to criminal syndicates and cartels who have terrorized Mexico, detonating them amidst civilians and targeting law enforcement.[69]

In 2000, police near Bogotá, Colombia, found Russian documents alongside a partially completed submarine vessel that was to be used to transport up to 200 tons of cocaine in a single shipment. The documents indicated that the Russian mafia or Russian scientists and technicians were involved in the construction or reconstruction of a submarine prototype based on former Soviet Union military plans. Not unlike the way in which former Nazi scientists were acquired by the U.S. and their allies following World War II, former Soviet engineers, scientists, and military personnel were sought for their skills and expertise.

Certainly not all of their skills have been put to use with government oversight. Many availed themselves to international criminal syndicates, the most lucrative of which traffic in illegal weapons and narcotics. The United Nations estimates the global illicit drug trade to be worth as much as the international tourist trade, which is billions of dollars per year.[70] Many of the mafia, cartels, and drugs syndicates have the organizational reach of multinational businesses, and they have thrived in an era of globalization, banking deregulation, and free-trade agreements.

Conclusion

The end of the Cold War has altered the focus of national security for both the Soviets and the U.S. Within Russia's National Security Strategy (NSS) for 2020, there is considerable focus on drug addiction and narco-trafficking. With the world's longest border and their proximity to Asia, Russia encompasses an important drug- and human-trafficking transit route into Europe. Their post–Cold War security strategy recognizes alcoholism and drug addiction as epidemic and important threats to Russian society.[71]

The post–Cold War national security threats to the United States are also drug-related, as evidenced by the drug-related violence in neighboring Mexico and the narco-funded terrorists in Afghanistan. Reverberations from CIA covert actions and policies that were complicit in the drug trade present internal threats to our nation's security. Alliances with drug lords and criminal enterprises established models of funding para-military and political networks that the U.S. cannot rein in. The following chapter will focus on the CIA and the Department of Defense's decades of psychedelic drug testing and development in their search for Cold War mind-control drugs.

CHAPTER 8

Project Bluebird and MK-ULTRA

Most people occasionally stumble over the truth, but pick themselves up and continue on as if nothing had ever happened.

Winston Churchill

All truth passes through three stages. First, it is ridiculed. Second, it is violently opposed. Third, it is accepted as being self-evident.

Arthur Schopenhauer

THE DEPARTMENT OF DEFENSE and the CIA's clandestine drug-testing activities are among the many legacies of the Cold War. Since the CIA's inception in 1947, they, along with the Department of Defense, were very focused on developing mind-control techniques, including the creation of "truth drugs" to aid in the interrogation of captured enemy operatives and to assess the trustworthiness of CIA contacts. They also sought to develop drugs that could serve as non-lethal incapacitants and could disorient masses of people. When the Korean War did not result in the use of nuclear weapons, they felt it was best to focus on developing drugs as weapons to control and temporarily incapacitate people.

The CIA's relationship with drugs stretched from alliances with drug lords and criminal drug smugglers to research and the application of mind-altering drugs. The British and U.S. governments' LSD mind-control experiments of the 1950s and 1960s are well documented in film footage and written records made public in recent decades. These government agencies primarily experimented on people without their consent; subjects included military personnel, CIA agents, American servicemen, prisoners, the mentally ill, children, and patients at the Addiction Research Center in Kentucky.

The use of hallucinogens such as ergot (a grain fungus prevalent in Eastern Europe), mescaline, and LSD (lysergic acid) held promise as a means to screen recruits and to disarm the psychological defenses of enemy spies and prisoners of war (POWs). The hope of U.S. and British intelligence services was that the use of hallucinogens would result in disclosure of classified information and would reveal true personal intent. This all began during the post–World War II intelligence sweep of Europe, when the Office of Strategic Services (OSS) and the Central Intelligence Group (CIG) found evidence that the Nazis had been conducting mind-control experiments on their prisoners, and there was widespread concern that the Soviets had acquired this knowledge and would use it for biochemical espionage or warfare in their efforts to spread communism.[1,2]

The sense of urgency to develop mind-control drugs was sparked by the fear that the Soviets had obtained the knowledge from Nazi scientists and would use it as a Cold War weapon; the fear was further amplified in response to the Korean War (1950–1953). Several U.S. troops who had been captured and held as POWs in North Korea were believed to have been drugged and brainwashed by the pro-communist North Korean forces. A number of senior government officials feared that the Soviets, North Koreans, and Chinese would be able to use drugs and mind-control techniques to infiltrate democratic nations and gain control of the people. Consequently, during the Korean War, the U.S. also conducted mind-control experiments on some North Korean POWs under the initial phases of Project Bluebird, a longstanding CIA operation. The North Korean POWs were given substantial alternating doses of barbiturates (depressants) and amphetamines (stimulants) and then interrogated.[3]

In the decades following the Korean War, the U.S. Department of Defense and the CIA conducted more than 150 mind-control research programs with U.S. soldiers, CIA agents, and myriad involuntary civilian subjects, enemy troops, and prisoners. Among the drug-weaponry ventures of the CIA and Department of Defense were efforts to create synthetic tetrahydrocannabinol, or THC (the active ingredient in marijuana), cocktails of Nembutal (a sedative hypnotic), Dexedrine (an amphetamine-based stimulant), and Seconal (a sedative hypnotic), in addition to performing human experiments with LSD and hypnosis. The most notorious CIA-directed mind-control psychedelic drug experiments were conducted under the code name Project Bluebird, which would later be renamed Project Artichoke, MK-NAOMI, and MK-ULTRA. The details of these experiments were kept secret and veiled from Congress through circuitous funding often funneled through the Department of Defense, specifically the Navy. The prefix MK was code for work conducted by CIA Technical Services.[4]

One of the longest sustained programs of research, development, and testing of hallucinogens ran from 1955 through 1972 at the U.S. Army arsenal in Edgewood, Maryland. It took the researchers 17 years to conclude that the effects of LSD and marijuana were too unpredictable and made the user too mellow to be useful weapons in the Cold War. The Edgewood program did result in the development of one interesting hallucinogenic weapon, artillery rounds filled with powdered quinuclidinyl benzilate (BZ), an extremely disorienting drug that produced confusion and a sleep-like state that can leave people impaired for days. The BZ bombs were reportedly used on a limited basis in Vietnam. The Army reportedly stockpiled 50 tons of BZ, enough to incapacitate the world populous. The BZ bombs were stored in an arsenal in Arkansas and later destroyed.[5,6,7]

The British armed forces also experimented with mind control and non-lethal methods of incapacitating enemy forces. In 1964, the British Armed Forces intentionally dosed a group of British Royal Marines with LSD. The LSD was placed in their drinking water and given to them prior to the start of one of their training exercises in Proton Down, England. The experiment was filmed so that the effects of the drug could be documented and used for training purposes to enable the British to predict the potential effect of the drug on enemy forces. Footage of this can now be viewed at the Imperial War Museum's online exhibit of British experiences in the Cold War.[8]

The misuse of power that took place during the Cold War, coupled with anti-communism paranoia, enabled the CIA and the research arm of the Department of Defense to commit human rights violations, such as drugging civilians with powerful hallucinogens without their knowledge or consent.[9] Projects such as MK-ULTRA were initiated because, as CIA Director of Intelligence Stansfield Turner stated in 1977, the agency was charged with learning state-of-the-art behavioral modification at a time when the U.S. government was concerned about the inexplicable behavior of persons behind the Iron Curtain and American prisoners of war who had been subjected to so-called brainwashing.[10]

Evidence that the CIA engaged in drug-related mind-control experiments is presented in documents that have been made public. One such document is a memorandum to the members of the Advisory Committee on Human Radiation Experiments, dated June 27, 1994. The subject of the memo, "Methodological Review of Agency Data Collection Efforts: Initial Report on the Central Intelligence Agency Document Search," is the CIA's Project MK-ULTRA.[11] MK-ULTRA is referenced in the aforementioned memorandum in connection to the CIA's use of radiation on human subjects. Information on human radiation experiments was inadvertently discovered during research on CIA records of mind-control drug experiments that had come to light in the Church Committee hearings and investigations into medical abuse and drug testing chaired by Senator Edward Kennedy in the 1970s. The following quotes give credence to what otherwise sounds like an implausible conspiracy theory.

"In the 1950s and 60s, the CIA engaged in an extensive program of human experimentation, using drugs, psychological, and other means, in search of techniques to control human behavior for counterintelligence and covert action purposes.... Project MK-ULTRA was a program concerned with research and development of chemical, biological, and radiological materials capable of employment in clandestine operations to control human behavior.... MK-ULTRA was the subject of extensive internal, congressional, and outside investigations in the 1970s. In 1973, the CIA purposefully destroyed most of the MK-ULTRA files concerning its research and testing on human behavior. In 1977, the agency uncovered additional MK-ULTRA files in the budget and fiscal records that were not indexed under the name MK-ULTRA. These documents detailed over 150 subprojects that the CIA funded in this area."[12]

One of the subprojects is referenced in the June 9, 1953, memorandum (see Figure 8-1) written by CIA agent Dr. Sidney Gottlieb, chief of the Chemical Division of

Figure 8-1 MK-ULTRA Subproject 8 Memorandum from Dr. Sidney Gottlieb[1]

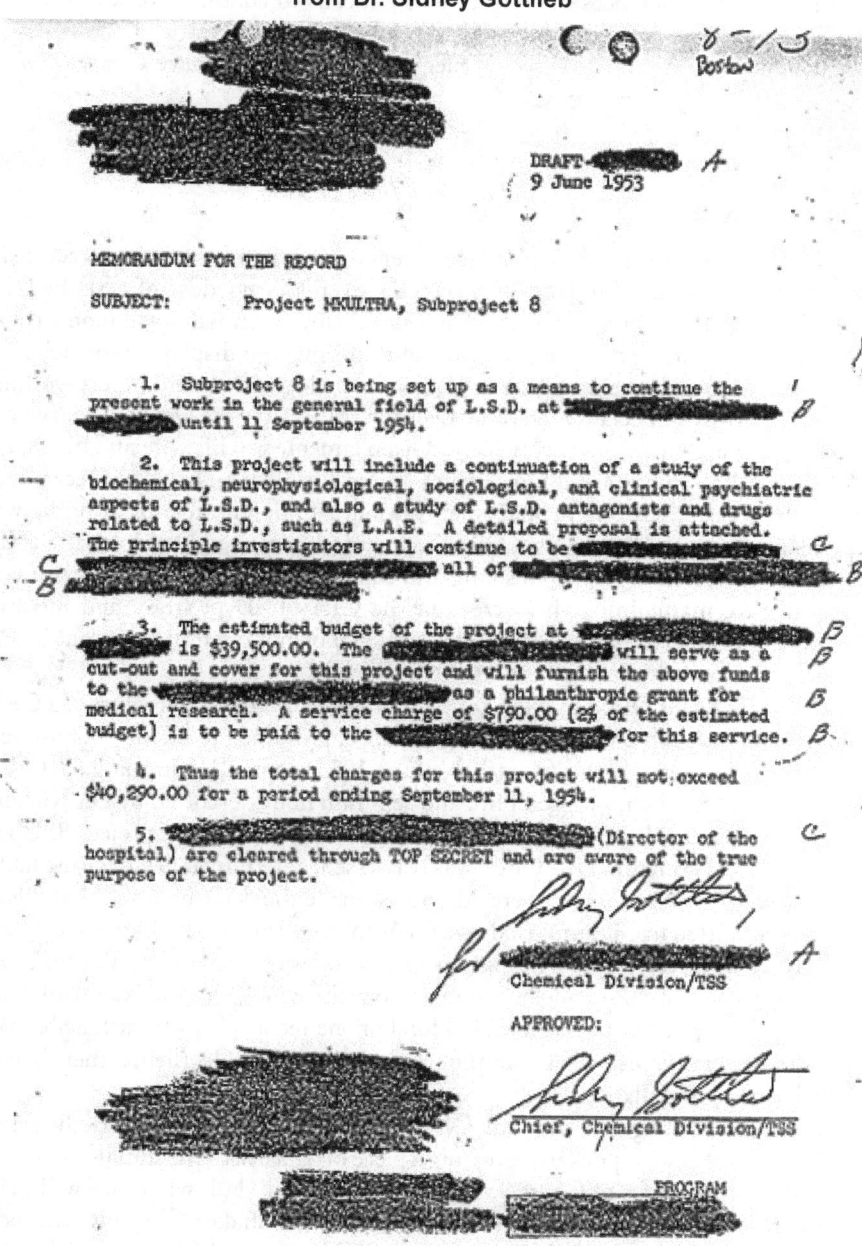

1. United States Senate. "Human Drug Testing by the CIA, 1977: Hearings Before the Select Committee on Intelligence and the Subcommittee on Health and Scientific Research of the Committee on Human Resources." August 3, 1977. 95th Congress 1st Session. Washington, DC: U.S. Govt. Print. Off., 1977. Print. Appendix C 109.

the CIA's Technical Services Staff and director of numerous MK-ULTRA projects. Gottlieb's memo references Subproject 8 as a means to continue work in the bio-chemical, neurophysiological, sociological, and clinical psychiatric effects of LSD. Gottlieb further notes the "top secret" clearance for those who have *knowledge of the true purpose of this project*.[13]

The Acid Tests

On November 19, 1953, a group of CIA agents and military scientists meeting at Deer Creek Lodge in Maryland were secretly given a heavy dose of LSD by CIA agent Dr. Sidney Gottlieb. Frank Olson, an Army scientist, was among those drugged that night; he became psychotic and continued to display erratic behavior in the days following the drugging. Olson was a biological warfare expert working in the U.S. Army's Special Operations Division (SOD) at Fort Detrick, Maryland. Upon returning home from the incident, Olson lamented to his wife and his super-visor that he had embarrassed himself and "made a terrible mistake" at Deer Creek Lodge. Thereafter, Olson's mental state continued to be unstable. Fearing he was experiencing a mental breakdown, Olson's supervisor contacted Dr. Gottlieb's office to arrange for psychological counseling and support. However, Gottlieb's primary concerns were maintaining the secrecy of the CIA's LSD program and his own self-preservation, because he had violated protocol by not obtaining consent before dosing the agents with LSD.

Dr. Gottlieb sent Olson to New York City to see Dr. Harold Abramson, a CIA-funded LSD researcher with top-secret clearance, presumed to be the doctor refer-enced in the last paragraph of Gottlieb's June 1953 memo. Abramson gave Olson Nembutal and bourbon, assessed him, and sent him home, escorted by Dr. Richard Lashbrook, Gottlieb's deputy and colleague on MK-ULTRA Subproject 8. Upon returning to Washington, DC, Olson was reassessed, determined to still be unstable, and flown back to New York, where Abramson made the determination that Olson should be admitted to Chestnut Lodge, a CIA-approved and trusted psychiatric asy-lum in Rockville, Maryland. The night before Olson was to fly back to Washington, he allegedly committed suicide by jumping from the window of the New York City hotel room he shared with Lashbrook. Hotel phone records show that Lashbrook's first call after Frank Olson went out the window was to Dr. Gottlieb, rather than to the police or an ambulance.[15,16]

During the investigation of Frank Olson's death, the police had reportedly asked Lashbrook to empty his pockets, revealing a piece of paper with the initials G.W. and M.H., believed to refer to George White, alias Morgan Hall, whom we will meet later in this chapter. Through Abramson, LSD began to make its way into the local community. Abramson had given some of the CIA-procured LSD to anthropolo-gist Gregory Bateson, who in turn gave some to his friend, Allen Ginsberg, a beat poet who opposed militarism and materialism and who would later write the poem "CIA Dope Calypso."

The cover-up would not unravel for decades, until Olson's adult children began to push the investigation after reading an article in *The Washington Post* that recounted findings from the Rockefeller Commission describing the death of a man who had jumped from a hotel window after having been secretly given LSD by the CIA. President Gerald Ford personally met with and apologized to the Olson family on July 21, 1975.[17]

The revelations of Olson's potential murder raised awareness of the need for political and ethical reform at the highest levels, and President Ford subsequently established the Rockefeller Commission to report on charges relating to the CIA's domestic activities (see Figure 8-2). Subsequently, Dr. Sidney Gottlieb and Dr. Richard Lashbrook were subpoenaed and testified in September 1977 before a Senate subcommittee investigating the MK-ULTRA research. Gottlieb was protected from admonishment by his close allies, two former OSS agents, CIA Director Allen Dulles and Deputy Director for Plans Richard Helms. Dulles was complicit in the agency's misdeeds, having personally approved Helms's proposal to develop biological and chemical agents for covert use.[18,19]

LSD in Pont-Saint-Esprit

Recently, evidence has come to light that the CIA, in an effort to test the effects of hallucinogens on civilian populations, went so far as to drug a small French community. In his 2009 book *A Terrible Mistake: The Murder of Frank Olson and the CIA's Secret Cold War Experiments,* journalist Hank Albarelli presents well-documented claims that the CIA and the U.S. Army's Special Operations Division (SOD) were responsible for intentionally drugging/poisoning the small French town of Pont-Saint-Esprit with hallucinogens.

During the height of the Cold War, on August 16, 1951, some 300 residents of Pont-Saint-Esprit suffered from what was initially thought to be widespread food poisoning. Beyond the symptoms of nausea, vomiting, and headaches, hundreds of residents of Pont-Saint-Esprit experienced horrifying hallucinations. Some engaged in self-injurious behavior, others committed suicide, and many temporarily went insane. By the time it was over, there were at least seven deaths, 46 people were detained in asylums, and many others were unable to ever hold a job or lead normal lives again.

According to transcripts of a conversation between the Swiss pharmaceutical company Sandoz (which invented LSD in 1938) and the CIA, Sandoz supplied the CIA with the hallucinogen that was allegedly used in the Pont-Saint-Esprit incident. The transcripts reveal that the CIA devised a plan to contaminate the food supply of a community with LSD and test the results.[20] There is still some dispute as to whether the hallucinogen the CIA allegedly used to lace bread, in what became known as the "cursed bread" incident, was lysergic acid (LSD) or the ergot fungus. The Sandoz transcripts that Albarelli discovered state that the chemical used at Pont-Saint-Esprit was diethylamide, the "D" in LSD.[21]

Figure 8-2 A Justice Department Report on the Rockefeller Commission

Justice Department Report

The Rockefeller Report states on p. 226:

"In the late 1940's, the CIA began to study
the properties of certain behavior-influencing
drugs (such as LSD) and how such drugs might
be put to intelligence use. This interest was
prompted by reports that the Soviet Union was
experimenting with such drugs and by speculation
that the confessions introduced during trials
in the Soviet Union and other Soviet Bloc
countries during the late 1940's might have
been elicited by the use of drugs or hypnosis.
Great concern over Soviet and North Korean
techniques in 'brainwashing" continued to be
manifested into the early 1950's. "

Dr. Frank A. Olson, a bio-chemist, was a civilian

employee of the Army working at Fort Detrick in a

cooperative effort with the CIA. On November 19, 1953,

at one of the periodic meetings of Ft. Detrick and CIA

personnel, a dosage of LSD was placed by CIA personnel

in drinks consumed by Dr. Olson and others, all of whom

were members of the group. Prior to receiving the LSD,

Dr. Olson had participated in discussions where the

testing of such substances on unsuspecting subjects was

agreed to in principle. However, neither Dr. Olson,

nor any of the others was made aware that they had been

given LSD until about 20 minutes after the fact.

Albarelli unearthed these documents while researching the involvement of the
CIA in the alleged murder of Frank Olson in 1953. Albarelli asserts that Olson
had been involved in the Pont-Saint-Esprit incident and was drugged so the CIA
could interrogate him concerning their suspicions that he had discussed the Pont-
Saint-Esprit incident with people outside the operation. As we now know, shortly

thereafter Olson "committed suicide" by "jumping" from a window at the Statler Hotel in New York City.[22]

Skeptics have questioned whether the incident at Pont-Saint-Esprit involved the CIA and LSD, or whether it was simply a case of food poisoning caused by flour tainted by the ergot fungus.[23,24] However, the theory of CIA involvement has gained traction and is perceived as plausible because of the CIA's historical involvement with LSD and other drug testing on human subjects, the historical OSS and CIA networks in France, and CIA complicity in drug trafficking during the Cold War. A historical review of government documents providing evidence of the CIA's testing of LSD on individuals and groups by putting the drug in their water; their attempts with air-dispersal methods at a party in one of their safe houses in San Francisco; the US Department of Defense's testing of chemical agents placed in cereal, wheat, and rice; and the agency's activities in this region of France make the incident at Pont-Saint-Esprit plausible.

The drugging of a small community to study the effects on its citizens seems viable given the fact that Olson and his CIA colleagues were in France at the time of the incident and similar stunts had been tried: Dr. Gottlieb spiked the CIA's punchbowls with LSD at their 1954 Christmas party; in 1950, a CIA contractor conducted aerosol-spray tests of LSD in the New York City subways; and a CIA memo surfaced that outlined a potential plan for putting LSD into a city's water supply to observe people's behavior.[25,26] Moreover, the Pont-Saint-Esprit incident was inadvertently discovered in the process of searching for information about Frank Olson's death; the author did not set out to prove such a point. Following the release of Albarelli's book, the French intelligence agency, Directorate-General for External Security (DGSE), contacted the U.S. State Department to inquire about possible U.S. government complicity in the 1951 incident.

Dr. Sidney Gottlieb directed LSD research and mind-control experiments throughout the United States, with substantial operations in San Francisco and New York City, and at McGill University in Montreal, Canada. Gottlieb reviewed OSS records from World War II to search for a suitable candidate the CIA could hire as a contract worker (and as such, technically outside the governance structures of the CIA) for rogue operations such as conducting drug testing on unsuspecting civilians. In reviewing OSS files, Gottlieb came across information about Federal Bureau of Narcotics agent Colonel George H. White, alias Morgan Hall, who had worked in the OSS organizing the testing of marijuana as a truth serum on unsuspecting subjects during World War II. Impressed by White's experience in narcotics and his record with the OSS, Gottlieb hired White to run covert drug-testing operations in the U.S. for the CIA.

The CIA had a number of "safe houses" in New York and San Francisco. These safe-house projects were part of the CIA's MK-ULTRA project to identify drugs that could be used to manipulate human behavior and gain a Cold War espionage advantage over the Soviets. Diaries of CIA operative George White, alias Morgan Hall, provided documentation and detailed accounts with names, dates, and locations of safe houses in San Francisco (225 Chestnut St., Telegraph Hill) and New

York (81 Bedford Street, Greenwich Village). One infamous project was Operation Midnight Climax, which used drug-addicted prostitutes, who were paid with money or drugs, to give LSD and other powerful drugs to unsuspecting customers while being secretly observed and recorded by CIA agents using microphones disguised as wall outlets, hooked up to tape recorders and monitored by agents in a "listening post" adjacent to the safe-house apartment.[27] White's diaries document his meetings to discuss drugs and safe houses with Harry J. Anslinger (White's former boss and head of the Federal Bureau of Narcotics), Gottlieb, and Lashbrook.

Anslinger's presence is significant because until his retirement in 1964, he championed drug prohibition and was a particularly vocal opponent of marijuana. Anslinger's critics note that he inflated the dangers of psychedelics such as marijuana as a means of enhancing the importance of his position in national and international politics and to enable him to amass resources for the Bureau of Prohibition and the Federal Bureau of Narcotics. The more identifiable the enemy (marijuana, addicts, peace activists, hippies), the more resources he could amass for the Federal Bureau of Narcotics, the predecessor to the U.S. Drug Enforcement Agency (DEA).

The DEA evaluates substances and classifies drugs into five schedules according to their abuse potential, addictive nature, and whether they have accepted medical use. The highest-risk drugs are categorized as Schedule I, and the lowest as Schedule V.[28] Although LSD, marijuana, mescaline, psilocybin, and psilocin are currently listed as Schedule I drugs, medical research has found each of these drugs to be far less addictive and less risky than legal drugs, such as alcohol and tobacco.[29] Despite scientific evidence documenting effective medical use of cannabis for glaucoma and wasting disease, and the controlled use of psychedelics to treat a range of mental-health conditions, they remain Schedule I drugs.[30,31] Interestingly, cocaine, methamphetamine, and opium are only classified as Schedule II drugs, suggesting that the hallucinogenic drugs have been highly politicized in their classification. This is not to say that these drugs are without risk. However, it does illustrate the political nature of drug classification and the legal status of particular drugs.

During the Church Committee Senate hearings into the domestic activities of the CIA, it was revealed that CIA agents conducted numerous experiments that involved drugging civilians in the San Francisco area. Philip Goldman, former MK-ULTRA agent, testified that among the activities they carried out were an LSD air-dispersal "bug bomb," billy clubs that shot tear gas, drug-laced swizzle sticks that melted away in drinks, and a hypodermic needle that shot drugs into corked wine bottles. Goldman stated that most of the devices were turned over for field testing to George White (Morgan Hall), who conducted operations for both the Bureau of Narcotics and Dangerous Drugs and the CIA. Goldman testified that he presumed White, who had since died, tested the devices in San Francisco bars.[32]

Through MK-ULTRA, the CIA and the Department of Defense had amassed stockpiles of LSD. Fearing the potential sale of LSD to the Soviets and Chinese, the CIA tried to buy all of the LSD produced by the Swiss-based Sandoz pharmaceutical company. Although Sandoz would not turn it all over to the U.S., it agreed to sell the agency 100 grams of LSD per week, a significant amount considering pure LSD is dosed in micrograms. Meanwhile, the CIA underwrote the domestic research and development of LSD through Indiana-based Eli Lilly pharmaceuticals. In 1954, they succeeded, and Gottlieb noted that they could now acquire LSD in tonnage quantities, enough to incapacitate large populations and armies. The CIA operatives wanted to test the effects of hallucinogens, such as marijuana and LSD, on humans, and they regularly used groups of people they deemed disposable, notably drug addicts, prisoners, ethnic minorities, and prostitutes.

The use of psychedelics drugs from 1960 through the early 1970s was heavily concentrated in San Francisco, New York City, and Boston, cities where universities conducting federally funded research on psychedelics were located. In San Francisco and New York, there were also CIA safe houses where LSD was tested on unsuspecting civilians.[33] At the time, the public was unaware of the government's role in the development and testing of LSD as a Cold War weapon.

Researchers in the early 1970s noted that the phenomenon of LSD use was unique because of the stark "differences in distribution according to geographic location, social class, age, sex, and education." Inquisitively, they mused, "the majority of the reports of LSD use seemed to come from college campuses and towns which have college campuses. Greatest density seems to be in California, followed by New York, Chicago, Boston and to a lesser degree Washington."[34] One study published in 1966 estimated that 40 percent or more of the students at Stanford University had taken hallucinogens, whereas Senator Robert Kennedy reported that only one percent of the overall U.S. college population had taken LSD that year.[35]

The fact that the San Francisco area was the region of the country with the most significant LSD use in the 1960s is not coincidental. The stark contrast in availability and use of LSD in and around San Francisco compared to other regions of the country came about through federally funded research on psychotomimetic drugs, LSD in particular, that was conducted at Stanford University in connection with Menlo Park Veterans Administration Hospital.[36] The study recruited college students to voluntarily test LSD and other psychotomimetic drugs. Among those recruited in 1959 was Ken Kesey, a Stanford University student and future author of *One Flew Over the Cuckoo's Nest*. Kesey so enjoyed the experience that he sought employment at the Menlo Park Veterans Administration Hospital, where he could gain ready access to an array of psychedelics, including LSD, mescaline, psilocybin, cocaine, Dimethyltryptamine (DMT, Ditrant), and IT-290 (αMT).

A substantial amount of the psychedelic drugs were procured in this manner from the research sites near Stanford University and University of California at Berkeley, and they made their way into the San Francisco Bay Area community. Ken Kesey mimicked the behavior of Dr. Gottlieb, lacing punch bowls at Grateful Dead concerts with LSD and then filming people who were unaware that they were tripping on acid. Kesey became one of the most notorious proponents of LSD in the 1960s; once LSD became illegal in 1966, Kesey became a wanted felon and fled to Mexico as a fugitive for his role in dispensing LSD.[37]

Like Ken Kesey, Timothy Leary played a significant leadership role in the psychedelic era of the '60s. Leary, a professor in behavioral psychology, had created a personality test called "The Leary," which was used by the CIA to screen prospective employees. Following an exposé on "magic mushrooms" that appeared in a 1957 issue of *Life* magazine, Leary became interested in the potential use of such drugs and traveled to Mexico, where he experimented with psilocybin mushrooms. Upon his return to Harvard, Leary began conducting research with psilocybin, which he was able to procure for free through Sandoz Laboratories, where Dr. Albert Hoffman had successfully synthesized the drug. At the same time Leary was conducting his research at Harvard, the CIA had procured some of Hoffman's synthesized psilocybin and was testing it on patients at the Addiction Research Center in Kentucky.

Through his research and personal interest in psychedelics, Leary connected with a broad group of colleagues and students at Harvard and MIT who had been turned on to LSD or "acid" through the CIA-backed LSD research that had long been conducted in Boston. Leary gained such status in the "acid counterculture" that he even ran for governor of California against Ronald Reagan in 1969, and he joined the Beatles to record the antiwar classic "Give Peace a Chance."[38]

Certainly, not all of the LSD in the San Francisco area came from CIA and Department of Defense supplies, but there is no question that the actions of these agencies turned on the key leaders of the acid movement in the 1960s, Leary and Kesey. Somehow, the proprietary formula for LSD made its way into the public domain, which enabled bathtub chemists to manufacture the drug. The Mafia was said to be behind a well-organized network manufacturing and distributing LSD in San Francisco. Their arrival on the scene in 1967 coincided with the growth of the anti-war movement, and it was alleged that the CIA had helped the Mafia set up their network to keep the anti-war protestors incapacitated. During this time, Stanley Owsley and the Brotherhood of Eternal Love were also manufacturing significant amounts of LSD, disseminating millions of tabs of acid in the latter part of the '60s.

Establishing the Afghan Hash Connection

In addition to LSD, hash and marijuana became symbolic of the countercultural rejection of the government's involvement in Vietnam, and these drugs were pervasive throughout the anti-war movement. In 1966, Stanley Owsley and the Brotherhood of Eternal Love established themselves as a "religious organization/church" whose stated purpose was to "bring the world a greater awareness of God through the teachings of Jesus Christ, Buddha, Ramakrishna, Babaji, Paramahansa Yogananda, Mahatma Gandhi, and all true prophets and apostles of God, and to spread the love and wisdom of these great teachers to all men irrespective of race, color or circumstances."[39] This was a lofty and laudable goal, with the caveat that the Brotherhood's ceremonial sacrament was the illegal drug LSD.

The Brotherhood of Eternal Love not only facilitated the distribution of some one million hits of Orange Sunshine acid, they also established a direct trade route for trafficking hash between Kandahar, Afghanistan, and California. Members of the Brotherhood would fly to Germany and purchase an iconic Volkswagen van, drive it to Kandahar, purchase a large quantity of hashish to stash inside the van, and ship it back to California. While visiting the Brotherhood in Laguna Beach in 1970, Timothy Leary was arrested for possession of marijuana. He escaped from prison with the help of the Brotherhood and made his way to Kabul, Afghanistan, where he enjoyed the proliferation of hash until his arrest by U.S. agents in 1973.[40] Like the hippies in the Haight-Ashbury area, the Brotherhood of Eternal Love imploded when cocaine (a stimulant) arrived on the scene, turning several members into coke addicts and perverting the idealism of the group's spiritual origins.[41]

Conclusion

Cold War psychedelic drug development and testing, coupled with the social anxiety over communism and rapid changes in the world, created a fertile environment for the proliferation of drug use. Psychedelic drugs were pursued by scientists and government officials for their potential to control enemy combatants and elements within society if need be. However, their experimentation on college students and vulnerable or marginalized communities backfired and became the foundation of an existential revolutionary social complex welded to the anti-war and peace promotion movements of the 1960s and 1970s. CIA scientists spent decades exploring the covert potential of psychedelic drugs as weapons of Cold War espionage, and in the process the youthful counterculture co-opted the very drugs the CIA intended to use to interrogate and control people.

Testing mind-altering drugs such as LSD, psilocybin, and marijuana on college students and unwitting citizens across the country enabled those who were given the drugs to see the world in a unique and different way, one that made the government's anti-communist actions transparently hypocritical. In the name of democracy and freedom, the CIA and the Department of Defense were trying to develop drugs and techniques that could control people, and they did so without the consent of or regard for American citizens they deemed unworthy of such rights. This viewpoint is noted in the government's own words, quoted here, as they appear in testimony before the Select Subcommittee on Intelligence and the Subcommittee on Health and Scientific Research regarding Project MK-ULTRA in August 1977:

> The research and development program, and particularly the covert testing programs, resulted in massive abridgments of the rights of American citizens, sometimes with tragic consequences. The deaths of two Americans can be attributed to these programs; other participants in the testing programs may still suffer from the residual effects. While some controlled testing of these substances might be defended, the nature of the tests, their scale, and the fact that they were continued for years after the danger of surreptitious administration of LSD to

unwitting individuals was known, demonstrate a fundamental disregard for the value of human life.[42]

The pervasive federally funded LSD research in San Francisco is key to understanding how these drugs came to be so prevalent in the region. As more and more people experienced the effects of the psychedelic drugs, their view of the world order was irrevocably changed. In the course of these experiments, a number of intelligent and charismatic individuals were turned on to the drugs; they subsequently tuned in to a peaceable existence and rejected the emerging character of the government throughout the Cold War. The visibility and honesty of this aspect of the peace movement engaged increasing numbers of vocal followers who were open about their disapproval of government hypocritical actions.

The government viewed the anti-war movement as un-American counterculture and a sociopolitical threat that had co-opted and exploited their Cold War secret weapon—psychedelic drugs. During the course of the Vietnam War, drug use became tantamount to the anti-war movement. If you weren't in support of the war, you were said to be in support of socialism and communism, and individuals and groups who were involved in the peace movement were routinely investigated under the House Committee on Un-American Activities (HCUA or HUAC).[43]

CHAPTER 9

The Vietnam War and
the Blowback at Home

*Drugs were a gift to soldiers who were knee deep in horror every day and saw the most
repugnant things you could imagine.*

Richard Belzer, *The Drug Years*

N O WAR ILLUSTRATES THE CONNECTION between war and drugs more than
the Vietnam War. In the decades leading up to this conflict, the CIA had
conducted the Cold War in a way that prioritized suppression of communism
over any concerns regarding the availability and use of drugs. Since the early 1950s,
the CIA had worked with the Kuomintang (KMT) and regional hill tribes in Laos,
Burma, Vietnam, and Thailand to develop paramilitary operations and enable these
anti-communist groups to flourish, thanks to financial support from their opium and
heroin trades. The CIA's proprietary airline, Air America, and U.S. army trucks were
implicated in the transportation of opium and heroin in the region. Officers in the
South Vietnamese military ran significant drug-trafficking networks inside Vietnam,
and both North and South Vietnamese people made potent, cheap opium, heroin,
and marijuana readily available to U.S. soldiers.[1]

Coupled with the fact that the Vietnam War was unsuccessful, was unpopular,
and relied heavily on the military draft to fill its ranks, it is easy to understand
why unmotivated and often unwilling participants sought refuge in drugs. An
estimated 30 percent of soldiers returned home with significant drug-abuse problems. Stateside, the anti-war protestors openly smoked marijuana and took LSD
to distinguish themselves from the policies of the government and "establishment"
they opposed.

The image on the U.S. gunner in Figure 9-1 was painted by U.S. soldiers
during the Vietnam War to represent the grave nature of war. The number 13

represents the letter "M," the thirteenth letter of the alphabet, and was code for marijuana. Soldiers in Vietnam commonly used M and 13 as their code reference for marijuana.

Figure 9-1 *Nazi Skull 13*

Photo by Aldo Stephen Panzieri

The Counterculture and Protest Through Drug Use

The act of using drugs was politicized by their illegal status, and when millions of people started getting high on marijuana, they realized that it was not the treacherous drug that Harry Anslinger, the U.S. government, and prohibitionists had purported it to be in such notable anti-marijuana film campaigns as *Assassins of Youth* and *Reefer Madness*. Marijuana's illegality was viewed as proof that the government was lying about everything and that their policies were irrational.

The use of psychedelic drugs, such as marijuana and LSD, became synonymous with the peace movement, Vietnam protests, and the counterculture of the 1960s, all of which were investigated by the House Un-American Activities Committee (HUAC).[2] As Americans took to the street to protest the war, the Department of Defense was increasingly tasked with containing civil unrest. Military strategists had proposed the use of psychochemical incapacitants, such as air-dispersed LSD and BZ. Although tested, they were never used to diffuse civilian crowds.

Throughout the late 1960s, recreational drug use became fashionable among young middle-class Americans and epidemic in urban communities. The social stigma previously associated with drugs decreased as their use became mainstream and representative of protest and political unrest. The psychological underpinnings of taking drugs and rebelling against authority were complementary. The experience of taking psychedelics contributed to politically radical and revolutionary consciousness through the shared structural characteristics of political rebellion. Carl Oglesby, former president of Students for a Democratic Society (SDS), described the psychological underpinnings of taking acid and rebelling against authority as complementary "independent prongs of an over-arching transcending rebellion that took in the person and the State at the same time."[3]

The psychedelic movement gained traction through faculty at Harvard University. Timothy Leary wrote extensively about LSD, psilocybin, and marijuana and their prevalent use among students and faculty. Drug use became part of the intellectual community and was very much a part of civic engagement in the form of war and government protests. Taking drugs was a political statement against the establishment, and where there was drug use, there was generally a corresponding level of political activism.[4]

Sociologists, psychologists, and medical professionals studying the rapid growth in LSD use during the 1960s and early 1970s drew varying conclusions about the appeal of the drug. Some felt it was caused by young people's identity crises brought on by shatteringly swift changes in the world and its values, and that taking drugs was an attempt to escape anxiety associated with these changes. The mystique of drugs was also welded to the underlying strains inherently experienced by the most potentially unstable group of any society, the adolescents and young adults. Still others suggested that drug use grew out of a reaction to society's competitiveness and materialism, and the desire by youth to create a society based on love and cooperation.[5] In truth, all of these factors played a role in the escalation of drug use in the 1960s and 1970s, just as they do today.

Drug use on the home front was also rising and manifesting as a counterculture in relation to growing disapproval of U.S. actions in Vietnam. The Vietnam draft raised anxiety and awareness of the potential for any young man not presently attending college to be called to serve and fight in a war he did not support. The horror of the Vietnam War was televised nightly, which provided unprecedented coverage of the reality of war, including the arrival of coffins stateside. The hyper-visibility of the war radicalized people and galvanized active resistance. The culmination of the Cold War; the Vietnam War; and the assassinations of President John F. Kennedy, his brother Senator Robert Kennedy, Martin Luther King Jr., and Malcolm X created a sense of apocalypse. The palpable civil unrest and human brutality cultivated a spiritual collapse that made society susceptible to seeking refuge through psychoactive substances, and the proliferation of drugs readily filled this void. Drug use was more likely to occur among adolescents and young adults who opposed the traditional established order, regardless of gender, socioeconomic status, or religion.[6]

In the 1960s, the anti-war counterculture spawned a drug subculture heavily concentrated in San Francisco's Haight-Ashbury area. For a brief time, the peace movement existed as a utopian social experiment. However, disingenuous people seeking to take advantage moved in and began pushing stimulants and tainted drugs; by the late 1960s, the Haight-Ashbury area had transformed from a culture of peaceful pot-smoking to one of aggressive intravenous methamphetamine-injecting.[7]

As the drug scene diversified in the Haight-Ashbury community, the CIA became increasingly concerned about the counterculture's activities. At the height of this period, Dr. Louis Jolyon (Jolly) West, a psychiatrist with a CIA background in LSD and hypnosis research, rented an apartment in the Haight-Ashbury community to observe the acid scene like a living laboratory. Dr. West was one of several scholar-informants who served to keep the CIA informed of the developments in the "above-ground" LSD scene during the Cold War.[8]

Drugs as Tools of War

Just as rape is used as a technique of war, drugs can be used to pacify or terrify military enemies, including civilians. There is substantially less resistance among stoned or otherwise chemically debilitated people than among the general population. The North Vietnamese knew this, and they strategically used heroin and marijuana as tools of war, making potent drugs readily available to U.S. soldiers. Not only were troops incapacitated while high, but their cognitive functioning was greatly reduced for days or even weeks following the use of heroin, marijuana, and even alcohol.

The soldiers' drug habits had developed through readily available supplies and strategic promotion of potent, cheap marijuana and heroin to servicemen in Southeast Asia. During the Vietnam War, the Vietnamese supplied American troops with narcotics to weaken, disarm, and disorient them. Addiction became a significant problem for the military based in Vietnam. Drug-rehabilitation centers were established in Cua Viet and Saigon to treat servicemen in the theater of war.[9,10] Many soldiers who smoked marijuana and took other drugs in Vietnam would not likely have done so at home in the U.S. However, in Vietnam, the soldiers' fellow servicemen became extremely important friends and substitute family members who greatly influenced each other and collectively established normative behaviors. New soldiers would adhere to the behavior of members of their group. Although there were units with no illicit drug use, some commanders estimated rates of marijuana use at 75 percent within their companies.

The more-senior soldiers would often acculturate new soldiers into their unit by getting them high with hash or marijuana.[11] Marijuana and hash use were relatively easy to detect because of the smell and smoke, which made the soldiers identifiable targets. As news of widespread marijuana use hit the American public, the pressure was on for the military to curtail soldiers' use. The military waged a visible marijuana-suppression campaign, including urine screenings and pervasive inspections; military arrests for marijuana possession reached as many as 1,000 in a single week.[12]

Interestingly, the efforts of the U.S. military command to suppress the use of marijuana among servicemen reportedly contributed to the switch to opium, and opiate-based drugs such as heroin.[13] One of the easiest ways to use opium was in the form of "OJ's," or opium joints. The OJ's were made by taking a tobacco cigarette, loosening and removing some of the tobacco by rolling it between the fingers, and adding opium to the partially emptied cigarette. A vial of about 250 milligrams (mg) of 94 to 96 percent pure heroin would then be added to the cigarette, which was smoked.

Opiates were widely available and inexpensive. In 1967, opium cost about one dollar for a 250 mg vial; a vial of morphine went for five dollars. Servicemen reported scoring heroin from children as young as eight. The selling of drugs to soldiers by the Vietnamese was both a product of the need for financial capital and an ingenious form of drug warfare, incapacitating soldiers. The widespread use of opium and intravenous heroin soon dwarfed the problem of marijuana use among U.S. servicemen in Vietnam.[14] By the end of the Vietnam War, U.S. Army medical doctors reported that between 10 and 15 percent of the servicemen in Vietnam were heroin users; other sources reported that as many as one in four servicemen became addicted to heroin, with an estimated $80 million spent annually on heroin in Vietnam.[15,16,17]

The picture in Figure 9-2 was taken by Air Force Sergeant Aldo Stephen Panzieri in Vietnam, circa 1969. The unidentified U.S. soldier is seen snorting heroin with an M-16 rifle and pump-action shotgun at his side.

Other drugs were available and used by U.S. forces, such as Binoctal, an addictive sedative drug consisting of Amytal and Seconal. Binoctol was available as a prescription and often sold over the counter in Vietnamese pharmacies. Vietnamese children would sell the drug to servicemen for between one and five dollars for 20 tablets. Some soldiers overdosed and died, taking 20 Binoctol tablets at once.[18,19]

Not all drug use was illicit and unsanctioned. As was the practice during World War II, U.S. Air Force and Navy pilots in Vietnam used amphetamines to stay alert for their often-harrowing missions. The pilots were issued amphetamines (speed) and sedatives to alternately keep them alert or induce sleep as needed in response to the timing of their missions. "Go-pills" (speed) and "no-pills" (sedative) are still in use in the military today.

Drug use within the United States grew in response to increased availability through connections with the Golden Triangle region of Southeast Asia. Heroin use readily spread to the U.S. through military transportation routes, allegedly including coffins and body bags carrying U.S. servicemen home for burial.[20] Between 1965 and 1972, heroin use escalated among both troops in Vietnam and civilians stateside. In 1965, there were only 57,000 known heroin addicts in America, the majority in black urban ghettos.[21] Throughout the latter part of the 1960s, drug use among U.S. civilians was escalating, with more than six percent of industrial workers testing positive for heroin.[22] By 1969, heroin addiction had spread to white communities and diversified socioeconomic groups, with a five-fold increase in the number of heroin addicts.[23] In early 1970, reports of heroin overdoses averaged two per month; by the end of 1970, they averaged two per day, and by 1972, there were an estimated 560,000 heroin addicts in the U.S.[24]

These demographics reflect an emerging profile of heroin users as young and relatively affluent. The influx of pure and relatively inexpensive heroin from Southeast Asia required new approaches to supply reduction, including making it more expensive for traffickers to bring their products to market.

**Figure 9-2 Unidentified U.S. Soldier Snorting Heroin
with an M-16 Rifle and a Pump-Action Shotgun at His Side**

Photo by Aldo Stephen Panzieri, circa 1969

Vietnam Veterans and PTSD

The following narrative from a Vietnam veteran illustrates the ghosts of war that psychologically tortured him and many others like him, and the comfort they sought in alcohol or other drugs to quell their memories.

I had killed, I had killed with passion, and I had enjoyed the suffering that I brought to my enemies, for it was payback for what they did to us. Combat memories loomed over me during the day, and the faces of those I had killed haunted me at night. My life became a cycle of suffering, and drinking to relieve the suffering. The cycle focused around drinking, and drinking, and more drinking. My life was not just a heap of broken images but a living hell many times worse than anything I had experienced in Vietnam. I was an alcoholic by my 24th birthday and dangerously on the verge of suicide. Unknown to me at the time, I was not alone in this dilemma. Years later, I discovered that every other person I knew in my unit also had descended into his own version of hell. It took me years of hard work to recover and to enter the social mainstream.[25]

This personal narrative from Daryl Paulson illustrates the psychological pain of post-traumatic stress disorder (PTSD) and addiction, coupled with the secondhand social effects of trauma and substance abuse. Vietnam veterans returned home to an unwelcoming country and found few options in the U.S. Virtually nothing was done to aid veterans and their loved ones who needed assistance in adjusting to their stateside return. Many veterans were treated as outsiders and felt rejected by American society.

In the 2009 film *The Good Soldier*, Will Williams (2nd Battalion, 27th Infantry Wolfhounds U.S. Army, in Vietnam 1962–1970), talks about his horror in Vietnam, his return home, and the rejection he experienced from protestors in the U.S., which drove him to sign up for another tour of duty. He earned a Purple Heart for being wounded in action and the Bronze Star for bravery in Vietnam in 1966 and 1968. However, for decades after returning home from Vietnam, he struggled with alcohol abuse, post-traumatic stress disorder, and poverty. Alcohol abuse and trauma made it difficult to obtain and keep a job, feeding into the cycle of poverty.

Even within the ranks of Vietnam veterans, there was some peer rejection. Hell's Angels, a California-based motorcycle gang with many Vietnam-veteran members, would not allow Latinos to join because of their ethnicity. As a result, the Mongols, a Latino biker gang of disaffected Vietnam veterans, was born. Roger Pinney, the founder of the Mongols, describes himself as suffering from undiagnosed and untreated PTSD following the Vietnam War. Pinney and a number of other Latino veterans reported being treated disrespectfully when they returned to the U.S. In response to the disrespect and rejection by society after returning from Southeast Asia, they formed their own band of brothers, the Mongols gang, in Montebello, California.[26] The Mongols served as family and a niche to rebel against society. Southern California was ruled by the Mongols, and Northern California was ruled by the Hell's Angels. Both groups were heavily involved in drug dealing, arson, extortion, and murder.[27]

As a result of social rejection, coupled with untreated and undiagnosed PTSD, some veterans reverted to what they knew best—weapons and tactics—which escalated street crime and violence, particularly in relation to the drug trade. The rapid rise in the U.S. addict population was coupled with a marked increase in crime and violence, as addicts were compelled to steal to support their drug habits. Vietnam veterans were among these addicts, and drug-related crimes accounted for more than 75 percent of America's urban crime.[28] As recently as 2004, some 40 percent of men in federal prisons in the United States were Vietnam veterans.[29] The common factors running through their cases were PTSD and substance abuse.

Vietnam Sparks the War on Drugs

In response to the demand for drugs and the influx of marijuana and heroin on the streets of America following the Vietnam War, the government developed new approaches to drug interdiction and supply reduction. In May 1971, Congressmen Robert Steele (CT) and Morgan Murphy (IL) released a report on the growing heroin epidemic among U.S. servicemen in Vietnam. Facing the news that a generation of soldiers was about to return home from Vietnam with heroin and marijuana habits, President Nixon urged Congress to pass a $370 million emergency appropriation to fight the epidemic. The first task of John R. Bottles, the "Drug Czar," was to go to Saigon to address the growing drug use among troops in Vietnam.

Meanwhile, the U.S. military announced it would begin performing urinalyses on all returning servicemen, in what was known as "Operation Golden Flow." Beginning in September 1971, military personnel who tested positive for drugs were unable to return home until they completed a seven-day drug-detoxification program in Vietnam and then transferred to a Veterans Administration (VA) or Department of Defense (DoD) treatment center. Drug screening among servicemen was viewed as an effective deterrent because only 4.5 percent of the soldiers tested positive for heroin.[30] Despite the declaration of the War on Drugs and concerted efforts to reduce the drug supply, heroin has continued to flow into the United States, and rates of addiction have grown since 1971.

Some military personnel brought back heroin for their own use and minor dealing, while others facilitated the trafficking of raw opium and heroin. Servicemen returning to the States found the heroin in the U.S. to be weak compared to what they were using in Southeast Asia. In the 1960s, the heroin on the streets of New York was only about 5 percent pure; the other 95 percent consisted of powdered baby formula and other fillers added by intermediate dealers between Southeast Asia and the streets of America to extend the quantity and resale value of heroin.

Military connections with the KMT and the use of military cargo planes and soldiers' caskets to import pure, potent heroin was the basis of the film *American Gangster,* based on the true story of Harlem's infamous heroin kingpin, Frank Lucas. Lucas, the French Corsicans, and the Cosa Nostra had established connections with opium producers in Southeast Asia, and the U.S. provided a vulnerable population.[31] Lucas traveled to the Golden Triangle (Burma, Laos, Thailand) himself to purchase heroin directly from the drug lords at their opium-processing farms. This way, he was able to obtain heroin that was up to 97 percent pure and sell higher-quality heroin to his customers for greater profit by eliminating scores of middlemen.

Lucas paid military personnel to look the other way while kilos of heroin were loaded into the false bottoms of coffins constructed specifically for shipping home heroin undetected. Lucas's network even smuggled 125 kilos of heroin into the U.S. on an airplane carrying Henry Kissinger back from a mercy mission in Bangladesh by paying a U.S. general $100,000 to turn a blind eye.[32]

In the late 1970s, it was estimated that New York City was annually consuming two tons of heroin, valued at $2 billion. While New York has long been a barometer of the nation's heroin problems, similar usage rates were recorded in Philadelphia, Boston, Chicago, Baltimore, San Diego, Los Angeles, and Washington, DC. The United States heroin epidemic has affected every socioeconomic and age group—whether urban, suburban, or rural—and it has been widespread on both domestic and international American military bases. Heroin use has afflicted white-collar and blue-collar workers, high schools, middle schools, and elementary schools.[33]

In Southeast Asia, the CIA operated Air America during the 1960s as a front for CIA covert operations that included trafficking opium and weapons to develop support for clandestine war operatives, such as the Hmong army.[34] Air America's participation in the transportation of heroin and raw opium has been well documented in the front-line research conducted by Alfred McCoy and other experts in Vietnam and Laos.[35,36]

Military pilots who had learned aeronautic tactics that would keep them below the radar in Vietnam, Cambodia, and Laos—"treetop fliers"—found a new use for their skills, running marijuana and cocaine into the U.S. from Mexico and Central and South America. These enterprising vets were key factors in the increase in drug trafficking between the U.S. and Latin America following the Vietnam War.

This practice was immortalized by singer-songwriter Stephen Stills in his song "Treetop Flier," about the drug-trafficking pilots who applied their skills from Vietnam:

> ... People ask me, "Where'd you learn to fly that way?"
> Over in Vietnam, chasin' NVA
> The government taught me, and they taught me right....

The lyrics go on to illustrate how the Vietnam veteran pilots used their skills to stay under the tree line to avoid detection while smuggling drugs across the U.S. border for fast cash. One infamous U.S.-based drug-trafficking airline was Air America, established in Scranton, Pennsylvania, with the help of Vietnam veteran and former Air Force pilot Frederick John Luytjes. The name of the stateside airline was a play on the original Air America created by the CIA. Air America employed both veterans and civilians running cocaine and marijuana between Colombia, Florida, and Georgia. By the time the Pennsylvania-based Air America drug ring was busted in 1986, they had smuggled 7.5 tons of cocaine into the U.S. and sent more than $25 million in profits back to Colombia.[37]

In addition to trafficking drugs, Luytjes' Air America specialized in outfitting small private planes, such as Pembrokes and Cessnas, with storage space, fuel systems, and engines that would enable them to make long-range flights encumbered with up to 2,500 pounds of the drugs they transported back to the U.S each flight.

Interestingly, Keith Miller, one of the key DEA agents who finally brought down Air America, was himself a Vietnam veteran.[38]

The cocaine influx was most notable in Florida, the primary location of cocaine airdrops and boat delivery. The U.S. economy was in a recession in the late 1970s—with the exception of Miami, where billions of dollars in cocaine trafficking and sales fueled a boom in the sale of homes, airplanes, helicopters, racehorses, boats, cars, jewelry, and Rolex watches, all paid for in cash and checks written from Panamanian banks. In addition to the acquisition of individual wealth through drug deals, legitimate commercial business, such as nightclubs and restaurants, flourished.

Conclusion

The 1960s represented a cultural turning point in how the world viewed military conflict and drugs. To an extent much greater than generally appreciated, this sea change resulted from the actions of the CIA, whose alliances with drug warlords were critical contributing factors in the plentiful availability of heroin in Vietnam and eventually within the U.S. Although it is difficult to fathom, there is well-documented evidence that United States diplomats and CIA agents were involved in the international narcotics trade. Their involvement is documented on three levels: 1) *complicity* through their alliances with groups that actively engaged in drug trafficking; 2) *condoning* and covering up for known heroin traffickers; 3) *active participation* in the transport of raw opium and heroin. As Alfred McCoy puts it in *The Politics of Heroin in Southeast Asia*, "America's heroin plague is of its own making."[39]

Increased acceptance of drug use among Americans in response to the political unrest in the 1960s and the influx of pure and inexpensive hash, marijuana, and heroin from Southeast Asia created demand that grew throughout the 1960s and 1970s and has remained strong, with cyclical highs and lows for cocaine use. Changes in cultivation and trafficking dictate which drugs dominate the U.S. market at any given time. The desire and demand following the Vietnam War were met by the productivity and large-scale transport of narcotics in the Caribbean, Mexico, and South and Central America.

CHAPTER 10

Mexico's Drug War

Violence is now woven into the very fabric of the community [Juárez, Mexico], and has no single cause and no single motive and no on-off button.[1]

Charles Bowden, author of *Murder City:*
Ciudad Juárez and the Global Economy's New Killing Fields (2010)

THE CHINESE OPIUM WARS of the mid 1800s are linked to the current illicit drug market in the U.S. and the drug-fueled violence in Mexico. The Opium Wars transformed the Chinese economy by destabilizing agriculture, textile, and trade, resulting in the loss of traditional jobs for a substantial number of Chinese. This economic crisis led to the Chinese Diaspora. Many Chinese emigrated to Mexico and the United States in search of employment in the growing railroad and infrastructure industries. Some Chinese migrants brought with them the tradition of opium smoking and opium (poppy) cultivation, at which time poppy cultivation first became visible in Sinaloa, Mexico's mountainous region.[2,3]

Since the late 1800s, opium cultivation in the region has been handed down from generation to generation. Opium cultivated in Sinaloa was shipped from Badiraguato, Sinaloa, to border cities of Mexicali, Nogales, and Tijuana, Mexico and then on to the U.S. along the Pacific Railroad. Over time, the opium trade grew into a lucrative and criminal enterprise. In the 1950s and 1960s, the Herrera Organization ruled the opium and heroin trade from Sinaloa.[4] In the 1970s and 1980s, the Guadalajara Cartel assumed rule over the opium trade until its leader was arrested and the organization split into what is now the Sinaloa, Juárez, and Tijuana cartels. The Beltrán Leyva Cartel eventually grew out of the Sinaloa Cartel. Sinaloa's emergence as the crucible of Mexico's drug trade and current national narco-crisis thus began in part with the Chinese cultivation of opium-producing poppy plants as Sinaloa became a significant source of opium in the West.[5,6] In recognition of the wealth potential from opium cultivation, the region encompassing Sinaloa, Durango, and Chihuahua became known as the "Golden Triangle."[7,8]

The Pacific coast state of Sinaloa, Mexico, is located some 650 miles south of the U.S. border; its proximity to the U.S. provided a large market for the opium, which was legal in the late 1800s. It wasn't until 1914 that opium and its derivatives, morphine and heroin, became controlled substances in the U.S. under the Harrison Narcotics Tax Act.

An unintended consequence of the U.S. prohibition policies was that the decreased availability of opium drove up its price, resulting in opium production and trafficking becoming more lucrative in Mexico. Around this time, entrepreneurial small-scale trafficking was curtailed, and larger, more organized gangs and cartels gained control of narcotics trafficking in Mexico.[9] Concurrent with the implementation of the Harrison Narcotics Tax Act, the Mexican Civil Revolutionary War (Revolución de 1910) was taking place. During the Revolución, curtailing opium trafficking was not a priority of the Mexican government, which was in a fight for control over the country.[10]

Mexico-Based Opium Cultivation for Pain Management During World War II

World War II created an increased need for morphine, which is extracted from opium, to be used for the pain management of wounded soldiers. At that time, Japan controlled most of the world's opium supply, and Germany controlled morphine synthesis. Recognizing the vulnerability of their position, the United States turned to Mexico, specifically the state of Sinaloa, for assistance in cultivating opium to meet the medical demand for morphine among U.S. military and the civilian population. In response, poppy cultivation and opium production in Sinaloa, Mexico, was increased to meet the American demand for morphine. The expansion of the licit market for opium in Sinaloa opened the door for more widespread cultivation and the eventual diversion of opiates, including heroin, to illegal distribution trade.[11] Following World War II, the illicit drug trade in this region grew. Today, the Sinaloa Cartel is based in Sinaloa but operates throughout Mexico and is among the most powerful, violent, and notorious forces in the Mexican drug war.

In the 1940s, the Mexican state of Sinaloa was reportedly the only opium-producing region in Latin America.[12] Cultivation and trafficking of drugs appeared to be tolerated during this time because the opium production was marketed for export primarily to the U.S.; there was little evidence of a drug problem within Mexico, and the export of heroin to the U.S. proved extremely profitable. Mexico's black tar No. 3 heroin is lower grade and generally less favored than powdery No. 4 Asian heroin in the U.S. market. When President Richard M. Nixon's War on Drugs disrupted the flow of drugs from Asia and reduced the supply of No. 4 heroin, Mexico stepped in to fill the void created by an escalation in U.S. demand for heroin from the start of the Vietnam War. Mexico quickly captured nearly 90 percent of the U.S. market with their black tar No. 3 heroin.

In addition to opium, Mexico has long been recognized as a major source of marijuana. Sinaloa has had a venerable history of local cultivation and use of marijuana. During the Vietnam era of the 1960s and 1970s, there was an enormous increase in marijuana cultivation in the Sinaloa region, fuelled by growth in United States demand. In the late 1970s, with the encouragement of the U.S. Drug Enforcement Administration (DEA), Mexico's army and federal police carried out violent assaults and raids targeting those cultivating illicit drug crops in Sinaloa, which resulted in a subsequent decline in illegal crop harvests.

The U.S. War on Drugs encompasses both domestic and foreign policy, particularly along the border. In September 1969, the U.S. Customs Department Commissioner Myles Ambrose implemented Operación Intercepción (Operation Intercept) along the Mexican border in an effort to reduce marijuana smuggling from Mexico into the U.S. Operation Intercept subjected every vehicle crossing the Mexican border to a thorough, three-minute inspection. The operation lasted only two weeks due to its negative economic impact on border regions north and south and its apparent ineffectiveness in reducing the flow of marijuana north.

Following Operation Intercept, the Mexican government agreed to more aggressively attack the drug trade within its borders by cooperating with America's demands to extradite cocaine and heroin traffickers to the U.S. In 1978, the United States began using Agent Orange in Mexico to eradicate their poppy fields. Agent Orange was first utilized in Vietnam as a highly toxic defoliant to destroy the jungle's covering, which protected the North Vietnamese.

Ironically, following this crackdown, Mexico's drug trade really began to expand as the survivors emigrated throughout Mexico, expanding their narcotics network. The exiles who left Sinaloa for Tijuana, Guadalajara, and Ciudad Juárez in the 1970s included members of the Arellano Félix family, Joaquín Guzmán (a.k.a. El Chapo), and Amado Carrillo. They and their elders spent the next two decades collaborating with the Ochoa family, Pablo Escobar, and other Colombian drug kingpins, establishing new clandestine routes for delivering cocaine and marijuana to the United States.[13] The Ochoa and Escobar families were the two most significant forces in the Medellín, Colombia surge in the illicit cocaine industry and international criminal activity. After Pablo Escobar was killed in 1993, and his Columbian associates and rivals were arrested, the Mexican associates assumed the "lead" position in the global drug economy.

Changes in narcotics routes of transit have also contributed to the decades of increasing violence in Mexico. During the 1980s and 1990s, most of drugs bound for the U.S. were being flown and shipped from Colombia and channeled through the Caribbean. Many of these trade routes were shut down through U.S. policy and cooperation with Colombian and Caribbean governments. The demand for drugs in the U.S. has remained among the highest in the world; as a result, drug trafficking and the associated violence are now concentrated in Mexico.

The drug war in South America, Central America, and the Caribbean is inextricably linked to North America and Mexico. Latin America's war on drugs has several layers, which fuse government complicity, political unrest, and economic opportunity. Although the current level of violence in Mexico and the degree of media coverage might lead one to believe that this is a new threat, historical evidence demonstrates that this is not the case. General Paul C. Gorman, former head of U.S. Command in Panama, warned Congress and the American people during testimony provided in the 1988 Iran-Contra hearings that the Latin drug trade was more of a risk to America's safety and security than Moscow or any other communist threat.[14] A quarter century ago, our military commanders recognized drugs—more specifically, the international drug trade—as an unprecedented threat, in a non-traditional sense, to the national security of the U.S. The thousands of murders and drug-war casualties occurring in the U.S., Colombia, and Mexico by the mid 1980s demonstrated the prescience of General Gorman's prediction.[15]

The global demand for cocaine alone altered the social and political climate in Latin America. Although formal governmental efforts to reduce drug trafficking had been underway for decades, it was not until the late 20th century that the War on Drugs actually became weapons-based warfare under the administration of George H.W. Bush (president 1988–92) and his "Drug Czar" Bill Bennett. Together, Bush and Bennett doubled annual spending on the drug war to $12 billion. They involved the U.S. military, which used F-16 fighter jets on bombing raids against suspected Colombian drug-trafficking cartel locations and Navy submarines with radar and torpedoes against cocaine-smuggling boats in the Caribbean.[16] The War on Drugs continues to be militaristic and law-enforcement based, although critics point to the lack of evidence for its effectiveness.

Operación Intercepción was followed by Operación Cooperación, Operación Cóndor/Trigo, and other drug-war initiatives. Now, at the start of the second decade of the twenty-first century, nearly 30 percent of Mexico's farmable land is under cultivation for clandestine crops. Drug violence in Sinaloa has escalated, and the Sinaloa traffickers have generated entire dynasties of criminals who are at war in nearly every one of Mexico's 31 states and the nation's capital, Mexico City.[17] Sinaloa is currently an active site of poppy and marijuana cultivation and trafficking, with an increasingly violent *narcotraficante* culture. By 2000, Mexico was exporting heroin and marijuana, transporting the majority of Colombian cocaine, and collaborating with Chinese narco-traders in the production and export of methamphetamines. Since 2004, more than 90 percent of the cocaine that enters the United States has been trafficked through Mexico, up from 77 percent prior to 2003.[18]

In response to escalating drug-related violence and trafficking, in 2006 Mexico's President Felipe Calderón put forth a significant military effort to combat drug cartels.[19] President Calderón has made combating Mexico's drug cartels his highest law-enforcement priority, dispatching more than 45,000 military personnel and 5,000 federal police in 18 Mexican states.[20] In reaction to the pressure of the militaristic crackdown on drug cartels, there has been an escalation in drug-related violence in Mexico. The brutality inflicted by the cartels has intensified since 2006, although the violence had been escalating years before Calderón's crackdown. The drug cartels had increased their recruitment of Mexico's military; between 2000 and 2006, more than 100,000 military personnel deserted Mexico's army and joined the cartels.[21] Their military training not only results in paramilitary killing tactics, but also has minimized any upper hand that the military may have had. The result has been an unprecedented level of brutality targeting police, reporters, U.S. and Mexican government officials, and innocent civilians, as well as traffickers and members of drug cartels.

In Mexico, the War on Drugs has become a true war. Between 2006 and 2010, there were 977 gunfights between cartels/gangs and Mexican security forces, compared to just 309 between rival cartels/gangs. In the border city of Ciudad Juárez, there are about 10 drug-related murders each day, earning Juárez the nickname "Baghdad of the Border." Juárez is a gateway for billions of dollars in drugs flowing into the United States, and in recent years it has been called the most dangerous place in the world.[22] The city has been overrun by warring drug cartels and is currently dominated by the Sinaloa Cartel, who are equipped with grenades, assault weapons, and rocket launchers.

Drug trafficking and violence in Mexico and the U.S. border region have been in place for decades; however, previously violence was kept at bay by paying off corrupt government officials. Gun-control laws in Mexico are among the strictest worldwide, yet they border Arizona and Texas, two American states with significant pro-gun laws, making it relatively easy to obtain weapons. Military-style camps for cartel Sicarii (hit men) train them to become soldiers of the cartel and terrorists to the rest of us.

The presence of the Mexican military in Juárez is a stop-gap measure while civilian institutions and police forces are rebuilt. Civilian infrastructures, such as police, customs agents, and judicial and correctional systems, became increasingly infiltrated and influenced by the drug cartels. To truly effect change, President Calderón has struggled to systemically root out the corruption. Although the level of violence has escalated in recent years, the torture, beheadings, and murders have existed for decades. The vast amounts of money in the illicit drug market buy immeasurable power, enhance corruption, and sway assassins. The amount of cannabis trafficked through the Arizona region from Mexico is estimated at more than 10 million pounds (with a street value of approximately $56 billion), of which less than 10 percent is seized.

Today, there are four growing businesses in Mexico: the funeral industry (particularly near the U.S. border), the drug trade, weaponry sales, and the demand for personal armored vehicles.[23] There are approximately nine major drug cartels in Mexico, seven of which had begun to align themselves into two opposing sides in 2010. One side is comprised of Los Zetas, the Tijuana Cartel, the Juárez Cartel, and the Beltrán Leyva Cartel; the opposing forces include the Sinaloa Cartel, the Gulf Cartel, and La Familia Cartel.[24] Individually and collectively, these groups dominate the narcotics trade and are waging an increasingly violent turf war over key trafficking routes and border-crossing areas.

Traditionally, tourism has been among the most important industries in Mexico; however, the drug-related violence is changing that. In March 2009 and again in

March 2010, the U.S. government issued travel alerts warning U.S. citizens of the risks of travel in Mexico. Tourism has declined precipitously as violence, kidnappings, and gunfights have become increasingly prevalent and unpredictable.

Together, these factors underscore the volatility of the situation in Mexico and the security threat the cartels pose to the United States as well as Mexico. Mexico's drug gangs may become a greater threat to the United States than global terrorism, according to John P. Sullivan, lieutenant with the Los Angeles Sheriff's Department and co-founder of the Los Angeles Terrorism Early Warning group, which focuses on identifying emerging threats.[25] Sullivan's threat assessment was echoed in 2008 by former U.S. Attorney General Michael Mukasey, who warned that, "International drug cartels pose an extraordinary threat both here and abroad."[26]

How did the open border and peaceable relationship with our southern neighbor evolve into a national security threat? A confluence of factors led to the concentration of drug trafficking through Mexico. Mexico's significance to the United States and the symbiotic relationship between these neighboring countries was overshadowed by more pressing concerns with terrorism and wars overseas. After September 11, 2001, U.S. air and water security measures increased substantially, limiting access to the U.S. by traditional external routes. Historically, the U.S. provided economic support to Mexico to foster economic development and trade and to combat narcotics supply chains, particularly drug trafficking. However, following the U.S. invasion of Afghanistan in 2002 and in preparation for the 2003 invasion of Iraq, the U.S. decreased border security personnel and financial aid to Mexico by nearly 60 percent in 2003.

U.S. counter-narcotics aid to Mexico declined from $47,898,000 in 2002 to $18,369,000 in 2003, as fiscal and personnel resources were focused on the wars in Afghanistan and Iraq.[27,28] To put these figures into perspective, the U.S. spends approximately $2.4 billion a month in Afghanistan and was spending $12 billion a month during the height of Operation Iraqi Freedom. Referring to this financial imbalance, former U.S. Drug Czar General Barry McCaffrey rhetorically asked attendees at a meeting of the President's Foreign Policy Inbox: U.S.-Mexico Relations, "Where are our priorities?" He then challenged the U.S. to "Wake up. Pay attention. Get engaged ... and understand it's a 25-year problem."[29]

The need for the U.S. to focus on preventing terrorist attacks, the Afghan War, and the Iraq War understandably repositioned the War on Drugs lower on the list of U.S. priorities. The reduction in financial support to Mexico for counter-narcotics was due to financial commitments to the Iraq and Afghanistan wars and a pervasive War on Terror. Beginning in 2002, the Bush Administration turned its attention to the immediacy of Iraq and Afghanistan, and their focus was naturally redirected from counter-narcotics enforcement and the larger War on Drugs to counterterrorism and the wars in the Middle East. The decreased focus on Mexico coupled with increased efforts within Mexico to combat drug cartels created the perfect storm.

The drug-related violence in Mexico quickly became a national security issue, and the Bush Administration promised to put 8,500 National Guardsmen on the U.S.-Mexican border by the end of July 2006. As of July 2006, there were fewer than 1,000 U.S. National Guardsmen in place. The human resources simply were not available due to the increased demands in every area of the country trying to fill the void of U.S. military deployed for combat in Iraq and Afghanistan. The Bush Administration asked all 50 states to send troops to the U.S.-Mexican border, but by the summer of 2006, only 10 agreed to do so. Kristine Munn, a spokeswoman at the National Guard Bureau in Washington, was quoted as saying, "It's not a combat priority," reflecting the ripple effects of the U.S. engagement in wars in Afghanistan and Iraq on our homeland security.[31]

The U.S. preoccupation with its two wars led to a dangerous situation of escalating drug trafficking on the U.S.-Mexico border, in which the cartels took the lowered focus of U.S. border protection as an opportunity. The situation truly exemplifies the oft-quoted Chinese translation of crisis as a "dangerous opportunity."[32] The illicit drug trade on the Mexico border and within the country took advantage of the power vacuum first during the Mexican Revolution and more recently during the U.S. engagement in wars in Iraq and Afghanistan. Today, as a neighbor to the United States, Mexico is front and center with U.S. policymakers because of the violence, human trafficking, money laundering, and drug trade.

Increasing drug-fueled violence and crime in Mexico resulted in the reinstatement of pre-OEF and pre-OIF levels of U.S. financial support to Mexico under the Merida Initiative (a.k.a. Operation Mexico). In October 2007, the Bush Administration initiated a $500 million aid package for Mexico known as the Merida Initiative, aimed at helping Mexico address its violence and security crisis. In February 2008, an additional $450 million was added in counter-narcotics assistance. In 2010, President Obama again increased financial and personnel resources along the U.S.-Mexico border, including the approved use of predator drone airplanes. However, even resuming significant funding to Mexico under the Merida Initiative has failed to reduce the violence. The Merida Initiative provides $1.4 billion over three years for the U.S. to assist the Mexican government with training, equipment, and intelligence for the War on Drugs.

The Beltrán Leyva Cartel reportedly infiltrated the U.S. Embassy in Mexico, and Mexican cartel activity on U.S. soil has brought the drug war to the doorstep of America's communities. The cartels have penetrated cities across the U.S., leaving a trail of slayings and kidnappings in more than 195 cities as geographically dispersed as Anchorage, Atlanta, Boston, Buffalo, Honolulu, Las Vegas, Phoenix, and Seattle.[30]

The Role of Mexico's Political History and the Drug Trade

Coinciding with the shift in U.S. resources away from Mexico and the border region were significant changes in Mexico's political structures. In 2000, the National Action Party (PAN) won the presidency, ending 70 years of single-party rule by the Institutional Revolutionary Party (PRI) and ending the PRI's complicity and oversight of Mexico's drug trade. When Mexican president Felipe Calderón took office in December 2006, he called the armed forces in to the fight against the cartels. During his first two years in office, President Calderón sent more than 25,000 troops to known hotbeds of drug trafficking. The new party rule and the allocation of troops to fight the illicit drug trade created dangerous opportunities for Mexico's drug cartels.

According to an exposé aired on National Public Radio (NPR), drug trafficking and organized crime had infiltrated the ruling Institutional Revolutionary Party (PRI) in Mexico for decades, through bribery and corruption. The PRI had a monopoly on power and controlled the media, oil fields, politics, and the drug trade. Terrence Poppa, author of *Drug Lord* and reporter for the *El Paso Herald Post*, argues, "It was an organized type of protection that ran all the way to Mexico City, and involved the top layers of government, including the president of Mexico."[33]

In 2000, PRI lost the presidency to Vicente Fox and his National Action Party (PAN), shifting Mexico's policies towards the drug cartels. Despite this shift in policy, the strength of the drug cartels proved to be a monster the PAN party could not control. Subsequent President Felipe Calderón, also of the PAN party, continued Fox's opposition to the cartels.

During the period when the cartels were paying off local, state, and federal PRI officials, who turned a blind eye to their dealings, the cartels in turn abided by strict rules of operation, such as not killing or kidnapping civilians and limiting their overt armed conflict over turf battles with other cartels. According to George Grayson, professor at the College of William and Mary, "If in fact the cartels broke the rules of the game, the PRI had the capacity to come down on them like a ton of bricks."[34]

Cartels responded to President Calderón's crackdown on drug trafficking by beheading and killing Mexican police and soldiers. In May 2008, Edgar Millan Gomez, Mexico's acting federal police chief, and four senior Mexican officers were assassinated by agents with ties to powerful drug cartels and other gangs. To date, Mexican drug-related violence has resulted in the deaths of more than 40,000 people, of which 30,913 were execution-style killings.[35,36] Each year, the death tolls have nearly doubled. In 2007 there were more than 2,500 related deaths; there were more than 4,000 in 2008, nearly 8,000 in 2009, and 15,273 in 2010.[37,38,39,40] The increasing militarization of the drug war and the arrest of several high-profile drug traffickers have so far failed to stem the flow of drugs or violence.

The drug-war statistics reflect complex social, political, and economic factors, which have depressed economic opportunity while escalating violence and increasing economic stability. Corporations are reluctant to do business in Mexico because of the rampant violence and corruption, which has resulted in a 30 percent decline in tourism in recent years. Inadequate social and economic opportunities foster a breeding ground for the drug trade and proliferation of substance abuse, factors that are just as true for the U.S. as for other countries.

Drug trafficking is a threat to U.S. and Mexican national security, not only because of the crime that accompanies it, but also because of the significant wealth generated that enables traffickers to corrupt police and government institutions.[41] With the end of the PRI's one-party rule in Mexico has come the need to run expensive election campaigns, which the drug cartels are reported to be funding.[42] With funding comes influence, demands, immunity, and protection. Murders and street gun battles are only part of a more entrenched problem that includes corrupt police forces and inefficient judiciary. Little progress will be made until Mexico's local and state-level police and judiciary are reformed.[43]

Killing and Corruption

The four strata of "enforcement" in Mexico's War on Drugs include: 1) international agencies, such as Interpol and the DEA; 2) Mexico's national military and, to a lesser extent, U.S. military; 3) Mexico federal police and U.S. federal agents; and 4) Mexico's state/regional and local law enforcement. The stratum most vulnerable to corruption has been the state/regional and local level. The narco-criminals offer better pay, are better equipped, and are more energized than the local and state police in Mexico. As such, the cartels focus their greatest efforts on corrupting the local and state police.

The corruption among Mexico's police and border patrol is not new. In the mid 1960s, the Brotherhood of Eternal Love paid off police and border-patrol agents to ignore the Brotherhood's smuggling of hundred-pound loads of marijuana across the border.[44] In 1984, Mexican journalist Manuel Buendía exposed the ties between Mexico's drug lords and the Mexican secret police and CIA. Buendía alleged that both the Mexican secret police and the CIA funded security that protected drug trafficking from South and Central America through Mexico and into the U.S. In the midst of his investigative journalism, Manuel Buendía was gunned down.[45] U.S. General Barry McCaffrey reported that such drug-related organized criminals have dismantled squad-sized police and army units through abduction, torture, murder, and decapitation; to further terrify the population, the corpses of executed police and military are displayed in public places.[46]

Although the exact numbers are not known, some of the police and military personnel moonlight as henchmen for traffickers.[47] In some cases, the cartels have focused on bribing lower-level police to gain their cooperation, while at other times they have bribed senior officials to gain cooperation and forced them to fire honest police at the lower levels. Drug cartels' infiltration of the police, judiciary, and political parties has compromised the government's ability to fight the drug cartels and the drug problem. In 1997, General Jesús Gutiérrez Rebollo, the former Mexican drug czar, was arrested for working to protect the Juárez cartel's drug trade.[48] In 2008, Noé Ramírez Mandujano, the Calderón administration's "drug czar," was charged with providing protection and receiving payments of $450,000 a month from Mexico's Sinaloa drug cartel. Noé Ramírez Mandujano began his alliance with the Sinaloa cartel early in the Calderón administration and ran the attorney general's organized crime unit until August 2008.[49] In recognition of this extensive corruption, President Calderón implemented routine polygraph tests and background checks on all law-enforcement personnel.

The Key Cartels

As if it weren't already difficult to identify who is actually working to uphold the law in Mexico, Los Zetas further complicate the state of affairs. Their name, "Zeta," comes from the Mexican Federal Preventive Police radio code for high-ranking officers, "Z1."[50] The original founders of Los Zetas were former members of the Mexican Army's elite special forces, who had been trained to combat Mexico's drug cartels at the School of the Americas in the United States.[51] Los Zetas are primarily former members of Mexico's elite army known as Grupo Aeromóvil de Fuerzas Especiales (GAFE). In 1997, a core group of Los Zetas began working for the Gulf Cartel because of their ability to pay vastly higher wages.

Lieutenant Arturo Guzmán Decena was the first to defect from the GAFE, bringing with him approximately 30 fellow deserters who were enticed by significant salaries. It is estimated that 200 trained members of the GAFE have defected and joined Los Zetas since the late 1990s. Los Zetas have since expanded, recruiting former federal, state, and local police officers and rogue members of the Guatemalan Army special forces, known as Kaibiles.[52,53] Acting as hired guns, Los Zetas would track down and kill rival cartel members, collect debts, secure drug supply and trafficking routes or *plazas,* carry out executions, and engage in gun battles against the Mexican Police.

The DEA considers Los Zetas to be the most technologically advanced, sophisticated, and violent of the paramilitary enforcement groups connected with drug and human trafficking.[54] They make this statement based both on their experience with Los Zetas and on the fact that, as members of the GAFE, they were trained at the School of the Americas, alongside French and Israeli special forces. The GAFE were trained in rapid deployment, aerial assaults and ambushes, marksmanship, small-group tactics, intelligence collection, communications, counter-surveillance techniques, and prisoner rescues.[55] Los Zetas are known to wear military and federal police uniforms, drive similarly labeled vehicles, and use grenade launchers while conducting cartel drug-trafficking activities in Mexico City, Nuevo Laredo, along the U.S.-Mexico border, in the Gulf Coast region, and in the Mexican states of Tabasco, Yucatan, Quintana Roo, Chiapas, Guerrero, Oaxaca, and Michoacán.

Los Zetas are now considered lethal paramilitaries analogous to Al-Qaeda. Their criminal activities extend beyond drug trafficking and include kidnapping, murder for hire, assassinations, extortion, money laundering, and human trafficking. Similar to Al-Qaeda, Los Zetas have adopted a cell-like structure to limit the information that any one member of the organization knows about his associates. Zeta cells have been located in the U.S., and the Department of Homeland Security is fully engaged with the FBI and the DEA in the increasingly terrorist-like characteristics of the drug war.[56]

Since the 2002 murder of Guzmán Decena and the 2003 arrest of their original recruiter, Gulf Cartel boss Cárdenas Guillén, Los Zetas have become increasingly independent from the Gulf Cartel and have established their own drug-trafficking routes and stockpiled weapons in safe houses in the U.S.[57] They are now reportedly working with 'Ndrangheta, an Italian organized-crime syndicate significantly involved in cocaine trafficking in Europe.[58,59]

The paramilitary groups and the cartels have overtaken social order, and narco-traffickers control the streets of Nuevo Laredo. The U.S.-Mexican border city of Nuevo Laredo (population ~350,000) was left without a police chief because of the drug violence. No one was willing to step up and assume the police-chief role until a 56-year-old local shop owner, Alejandro Domínguez Coello, accepted the post on the morning of June 8, 2005. Six hours after assuming the post, he lay dead, riddled with more than 30 gunshot wounds, reportedly at the hands of Los Zetas.[60]

As organized and sophisticated as Los Zetas are, they are also an "everyman" organization with street-level groups and "gangs," such as Las Ventanas, Los Mañosos, Las Leopardos, and Dirección. Las Ventanas (the Windows) are bike-riding teens who serve as lookouts for police and other suspicious individuals. Los Mañosos (the Discerning "Cunning" Ones) acquire weapons, whereas Las Leopardos (the Leopards) are prostitutes who extract information from their clients. The Dirección (Command) are communications experts who intercept phone calls, follow and identify suspicious automobiles, and conduct kidnappings and executions.[61]

Drug kingpin Beltrán Leyva, the former leader of the cartel that bears his name, was killed by Mexican marines in December 2009. The Beltrán Leyva Cartel had successfully infiltrated the U.S. Embassy at one time. After Leyva's death, his brother, Hector, battled for business control of the cartel with Texas-born Edgar Valdez Villarreal, "The Barbie." Valdez allegedly served as the top enforcer for Arturo Beltrán Leyva and was responsible for the spate of brutal slayings in and around Mexico City. Valdez has been linked to heinous crimes, including the execution and mutilation of his enemies, the display of beheaded corpses, and the slaughter of the family of a Mexican marine who was slain in the operation that killed Beltrán Leyva.[62]

The U.S. government indicted Valdez for allegedly smuggling tons of cocaine into the States, and they offered a $2 million reward for Valdez's capture, whereas Mexico also offered a $1 million reward for Valdez. The bounties appear to have been effective in ferreting out Valdez, who was captured on August 30, 2010. Concerns over the ineffective and corrupt judicial and penitentiary system in Mexico have raised the likelihood that Valdez will be extradited to the U.S. to avoid escape from jail, as orchestrated for cartel leaders such as Joaquín Guzmán, "El Chapo."[63,64]

The cartels and their narco-trafficking paramilitary gangs are currently aligned and dominated by three groups. The Gulf Cartel is headquartered along the Texas border in Tamaulipas state, and their progeny, Los Zetas, now control virtually all of the Gulf of Mexico from the northern to southern borders, except smaller areas controlled by the Gulf Cartel. The Sinaloa Cartel covers the region from the Northern Mexico border region of Ciudad Juárez through the central corridor of Mexico, just past the Sinaloa state between the Sierra Madre Mountains and the Pacific Ocean.

The Sinaloa Cartel also established its own paramilitary gang, Los Negros. Los Negros, attempting to wrest control from Los Zetas in Nuevo Laredo, are believed to be responsible for the recent rise in violence there. In July 2010, the Mexican army shot and killed a senior member of the Sinaloa Cartel, "El Nacho" (Ignacio

Coronel Villarreal), near Guadalajara, Mexico. El Nacho was a top associate of El Chapo (Joaquín Guzmán) and El Mayo (Ismael Zambada García), leaders of the Sinaloa cartel.

The drug lords draw support of citizens through charitable acts and community service. One such drug lord is the Sinaloa Cartel's El Chapo, who gives handouts to those who want to help cultivate drugs. As one citizen said of Chapo, "He supports the people, and the people support him."[65] Just as the drug lords offer the people of Mexico economic benefit for partaking in their business, the Mexican government has taken to offering subsidies to their citizens who do not grow drugs. The effect of the economic recession on Mexico's developing economy has been identified as a significant factor in fostering corruptible citizens and law enforcement, a situation exacerbated by the global economic recession of 2009.

Who Can be Trusted?

Cartel assassins receive orders to carry out executions and are often paid without even knowing which cartel they are working for. Within this cell-like structure, murderous criminals may know who their boss is, yet never know who their boss's boss is or which organization they worked for. The assassins kill for phantoms and work for a death machine with no apparent commander. Even the identities of the police and the military are hidden, as most federal police wear balaclava masks to hide their identity from the cartels. Charles Bowden, noted journalist, author, and expert on drug-war violence along the U.S.-Mexico border, notes that violence has become woven into the very fabric of Mexico. The nation is a web of hidden complicities where the cartels are the military, the police, and the government and nobody actually knows who anyone truly is or where their allegiance lies.[66,67]

Charles Bowden observes that Mexican authorities are unable to suppress the violence in part because they are committing much of it. The murders and violence in Ciudad Juárez have established a systemic pattern that "functionally has no top or bottom, no center or edge, no boss or obedient servant. Think of something like the ocean, a fluid thing without king and court, boss and cartel. Violence courses through Juárez like a ceaseless wind, and we insist it is a battle between cartels, or between the state and the drug world, or between the army and the forces of darkness. But consider this possibility: Violence is now woven into the very fabric of the community, and has no single cause and no single motive and no on-off button."[68]

This systemic pattern supports the accusations made by hundreds of federal police regarding the corruption within their ranks. On August 7, 2010, fed up with internal corruption in the federal police force, nearly 200 armed federal police officers staged a raid on a hotel in Ciudad Juárez where their commander, Salomón Alarcón, a.k.a. "El Chaman," was staying. The group of federal police blocked off the streets to prevent Alarcón's escape and detained him at gunpoint. The catalyst for the raid stemmed from charges that Alarcón was allied with the Sinaloa Cartel, had participated in kidnappings and killings, and had allegedly planted drugs on his own officers to force them to become involved in extortion plots. When the officers gained entry into Alarcón's hotel room, they found him with weapons and drugs. Police held Alarcón captive under media attention until the Federal Police Commissioner General agreed to suspend him, pending a full investigation into the allegations.[69] Shortly thereafter, three more federal commanders were also taken in and accused of being on the payroll of the Sinaloa Cartel.[70]

Dead bodies with notes attached declaring their criminal affiliation began to appear in Ciudad Juárez in 2010, reminiscent of the vigilante-like tactics of Los Pepes (Los Perseguidos por Pablo Escobar), who stepped in to reclaim Colombia from Pablo Escobar.[71] In July 2010, two headless bodies appeared propped up against a wall, and their respective heads sat atop ice chests in front of the bodies. On the ice chests were written messages declaring that the men were carjackers, kidnappers, extortionists, and members of the Aztecas, a drug-dealing street gang working for the Juárez Cartel. Two weeks later, headless bodies were found in a charred car with a note declaring that the victims were extortionists.[72,73] Are these the acts of vigilantes, members of another cartel, or perhaps police fed up with the low rate of conviction and internal corruption within their ranks?

Narco-Terrorism and Mexico

The violence is no longer just between the cartels; police, journalists, and politicians have become frequent targets of drug killings. One effective narco-terrorism tactic has been the notorious kidnappings and killings of victims known as "levantados" (pickups). Levantados are police and narco-traffickers who are kidnapped and mutilated; their bloodied corpses appear later, displayed in public.[74] The murder and symbolic mutilation of police is prevalent in the Sinaloa capital city of Culiacán and in Ciudad Juárez. The brutality of the levantados killings can be seen in pictures of dead policeman dressed like caricatures of Mexican cowboys, wearing sombreros with threatening signs warning anyone who dares to oppose the powerful drug lords that they will be executed.[75]

Musicians developed a new brand of music, called "narcocorrido," which embraces the drug lords as heroes and sings about their exploits.[76] Cartels terrorize their communities, blaring narcocorrido songs heralding drug dealers and broadcasting their songs over police scanners as they investigate the most recent bloodbath.[77]

Mexican cartels post videos documenting their notorious decapitation of anyone who opposes them; they are disseminated as "narco messages" to threaten rival cartels and government officials. The cartels have been influenced by terrorists, mimicking the heinous acts of Al-Qaeda, the mujahideen, and Hezbollah. In 2009, Admiral James Stavridis, then commander of U.S. Southern Command, testified before the House Armed Services Committee that the nexus between illicit drug-trafficking funds, routes, corruptive influences, and "Islamic radical terrorism" is a growing threat to the U.S., particularly along the southern border with Mexico. Stavridis directly linked the drug war with the new face of war (guerilla and terrorist organizations rather than nation states). In Stavridis' statement to the Armed Services Committee, he said that "[i]dentifying, monitoring and dismantling the financial, logistical, and communication linkages between illicit trafficking groups and terrorist sponsors are critical to not only ensuring early indications and warnings of potential terrorist attacks directed at the United States and our partners, but also in generating a global appreciation and acceptance of this tremendous threat to security."[78]

For years, Hezbollah, an Iranian-backed, Lebanon-based group designated by the U.S. as a terrorist organization, has been operating drug-trafficking rings in South America along the Brazil, Argentina, and Paraguay borders through Tijuana, Mexico, with links to the Detroit area.[79,80] Hezbollah operatives in the Western Hemisphere also work with Latin American drug cartels to traffic cocaine into the lucrative growing markets of Europe.[81]

Hezbollah has become increasingly active in Central America and Mexico in recent years. Strategic Forecasting Inc. (Stratfor) stated in a recent global intelligence report that Mexico is "an ideal place for the Iranians and Hezbollah to operate because Mexico has long been a favorite haunt for foreign intelligence officers from countries hostile to the United States, ranging from Nazi Germany to the Soviet Union, due to its close proximity to the United States and its very poor counterintelligence capability."[82]

According to Sue Myrick, North Carolina Congresswoman and member of the House Intelligence Committee, Hezbollah's drug agents undergo intensive Spanish-language training, and then disguise themselves as Mexican civilians and enter the U.S. under false identities.

Known for their tunnel-digging skills, Hezbollah is alleged to be working with Mexico's cartels to dig tunnels under the U.S. border for trafficking drugs, humans, and weapons.[83] Mexican officials also report that Hezbollah has been training Mexican drug-cartel members in bomb-making techniques in preparation for car bombings of Mexican and U.S. border personnel. In August 2010, a series of car-bomb explosions were set off near police stations and in front of Mexico's leading news-broadcasting headquarters.[84]

The U.S. and Mexican governments have raised concerns about the Iranian and Hezbollah network in Latin America and the potential for terrorist-group infiltration in the region and potential threats along the U.S.–Mexico border. In response to the escalating violence, the nexus between terrorist organizations and drug cartels, and the identification of Mexican drug cartels operating in America, the U.S. announced plans to deploy predator drone aircraft along the Mexican border as part of a new effort to stem the drug cartels and their organized crime. In August 2010, U.S. Congress passed a six-million-dollar bill to fund enhanced security efforts along the border. The U.S. military also began to train Mexico's armed forces to go after their country's increasingly violent drug cartels using the skills and experience they had gained from fighting insurgencies in Afghanistan and Iraq.[85]

Supply and Demand

Sandwiched between the biggest marijuana- and cocaine-producing continent in the world (South America) and the greatest consumer of illicit drugs (North America) is Mexico. Mexico is also affected by the illegal arms trade that extends from North America through Mexico to South and Central America, fueling street crime, youth gangs, organized crime, and drug production and trafficking. This cycle of arms and drug trade across the U.S. Mexican border goes both ways. The drug demand in the U.S. drives the narcotics trade through Mexico, and the easy availability of guns in the U.S. has turbo-charged drug violence in Mexico, where officials calculate that 90 percent of confiscated firearms originate north of the border.[86]

Following an official visit to Mexico in March 2009, Secretary of State Hillary Clinton publicly stated the importance of addressing the U.S. demand for drugs with respect to the narcotraficante-related violence in Mexico. She also indicated complicity of the U.S. with regard to the violence stemming from the illegal sale and trade of weapons to Mexico through the United States.

Some politicians have criticized the acknowledgement by the Obama Administration that U.S. demand is a culpability factor in Mexico's narco-terrorism.[87] Even the CIA lists the United States as the world's largest consumer of Mexican heroin and Colombian cocaine that is shipped through Mexico and the Caribbean. Mexico is the primary transshipment country for U.S.-bound cocaine from South America, with an estimated 90 percent of annual cocaine movements toward the U.S. stopping in Mexico. In addition to being a key transshipment point, Mexico also produces and distributes ecstasy, heroin, marijuana, and methamphetamine to the U.S. markets.

Mexico is also a major drug-producing nation; cultivation of opium poppies in 2005 amounted to 3,300 hectares, yielding a potential production of 8 metric tons of pure heroin, or 17 metric tons of black tar heroin, the dominant form of heroin in the western United States. In 2005, marijuana cultivation was 5,600 hectares, yielding potential production of 10,100 metric tons, a modest decrease from the decade-high cultivation peak of 2003. In 2005, Colombia produced slightly more than two-thirds of the worldwide crop of coca leaf (208,500 hectares), followed by the next highest producers, Peru and Bolivia. This represented a 40 percent increase in potential pure cocaine production from the previous year.[88]

In 2005, the U.S. consumption of export-quality cocaine was estimated to have been in excess of 42 percent (more than 380 metric tons) of Latin American cocaine production. In 2005, Latin America produced only 1 percent of global opium, most of which was refined into heroin destined for the U.S. market. Outside of North and South America, the world is supplied primarily by opium from Afghanistan and Southeast Asia. The economic situation in Mexico makes drug trafficking a viable, attractive business option, which challenges the stability of Mexico's economy and government.

Thus, Mexico's violent-crime wave is an outgrowth of the illicit drug trade, which is a problem for the United States as much as for Mexico. A study on drug policies conducted by the RAND Corporation revealed that militaristic efforts in Latin America and overseas were the least effective way to decrease drug use (cocaine specifically), and imprisoning addicts is prohibitively expensive. The RAND study used mathematical modeling to evaluate what worked in the War on Drugs against the cocaine/crack epidemic. This study concluded that the only cost-effective way to put a dent in the market was drug treatment, which is a demand-reduction approach. Demand reduction is complicated—encompassing everything from primary prevention with children to drug treatment for adolescents and adults—to reduce the market for drugs. The $400 million funding of the Merida Initiative was directed primarily toward equipment and communications systems, rather than training and institution building. However, the aid package did not address how to reduce U.S. drug demand.

What has been the reluctance to rein in the demand in the U.S.? Consider the fact that the highest profits are realized in the countries of narcotics destinations, and not in the countries of origin where the drugs are produced. As such, it may appear as if the objective of the drug interdiction campaign is to alter market share and not to eradicate the cultivation, production, and trafficking.[89] Drug profits contribute significantly to the foreign-exchange earnings of Mexico, and Mexico is a significant money-laundering center. Furthermore, the U.S. has a vested interest in the solvency of Mexico's banks; twice since 1982, Mexico almost defaulted on their loans to the U.S. banks. To prevent the potential collapse of the U.S. banks carrying Mexico's debt, their loan defaults were averted by emergency U.S. government loans. Before issuing the first rescue loan in 1982, the U.S. government established, through the CIA and the DEA, that profits from Mexico's drug exports represent an estimated 75 percent of the country's export earnings.[90]

There is no simple, clear answer to the drug cultivation, trafficking, and demand that plague South America, Central America, Mexico, and North America. The War on Drugs is visibly a militaristic defense against narco-traffickers, cartels, and the government officials trying to contain them. There are many cities in America that experience urban warfare conditions, imposed not so much by law enforcement, but between rival gang members fighting for their financial piece of the narcotics pie.

Charles Bowden has studied the War on Drugs and the economic quality of life in Mexico for decades. His thorough assessment of the 40-year-old War on Drugs is that it "has produced cheaper drugs of higher quality at lower prices in thousands of U.S. cities and towns. It has helped create one of the largest prison populations in the world."[91] Bowden's assessment of the War on Drugs is true, yet we have no way of knowing how much worse the levels of violence and drug abuse may have been in the absence of efforts in Mexico and the U.S. Many voices criticize the war on drugs, but few offer tangible alternatives, and there are no simple solutions. Although it is easy to criticize the use of force, we must consider the increasingly well-armed drug dealers and cartels.

Amidst the growing violence is increasingly vocal discourse about legalization of drugs. Even the United Nations Office on Drugs and Crime (UNODC) states that drug-control policies have generated a criminal market of macro-economic dimensions that employs violence and corruption. Blanket statements calling for legalization of all drugs is too simplistic of a response. However, thorough and careful analysis of data comparing the health and safety risks of drugs and the quality of life and level of crime in countries that have decriminalized some drugs provides insight into potential viable solutions. There may be some merit to legalization of a soft drug, such as marijuana, as it has been modeled in the Netherlands under the Dutch Drug Policy, which views alcohol and other drug use as public health and safety issues and eventually led to the decriminalization of marijuana under its categorization as a soft drug. The Dutch highly regulate their marijuana market, and as a result, people are able to purchase it in regulated shops at a price so low that there simply aren't financial incentives to traffic marijuana illicitly. If marijuana were legalized in the U.S., it is estimated that the cartels in Mexico would take an enormous hit to their power structure through the loss of billions of dollars.

The solution to the War on Drugs must be comprehensive and address demand reduction as much as it seeks to control supply. A simplistic, single-sided approach that focuses only on the criminal element is no more the answer than suggestions to legalize all drugs. Drugs are not harmful simply because they are illegal; they are illegal because they can be very harmful.

Conclusion

Images of dead bodies, decapitated police officers, and civilian bystanders flood the papers, television, and environment of Mexico, desensitizing the populace and disassembling society's ability to determine right from wrong. The violence is likely to rage on, as the citizens and youth of Mexico are desensitized to the violence and deviance that surrounds them. The possibility of drug abuse rises, and the moral objectives of the communities become irrelevant and skewed.

Drug violence alters daily life in Mexico. Elected officials and candidates for office who are perceived as threats to the cartels are killed on a regular basis, and journalists and reporters who cover news of cartel violence are gunned down on the job. The governor of Nayarit, Mexico, closed the state's schools early due to escalating violence and threats of attacks on the schools by drug cartels. The U.S. State Department ordered a pull-out of all children of its diplomatic personnel in Mexico's business capital of Monterrey because of the escalating drug-war violence, including a shootout in front of the elite American School Foundation.[92] Drug cartels have killed not only lone vulnerable police: in June 2010 they flagrantly attacked a caravan of federal police officers, killing 10 officers en route to Mexico City.[93]

The July 2010 temporary closure of the U.S. Consulate in Ciudad Juárez, Chihuahua, Mexico, is evidence of the warlike atmosphere and level of violence. The consulate was closed abruptly and indefinitely until its security could be reviewed and enhanced.[94]

Whereas drugs are the central focus of the violence, corruption, crime, and security threat in Mexico, the political history of Mexico's corrupt and unstable government and law enforcement appear to be the fulcrum of these problems, and the drugs are the commodity around which they are currently organized. If or when drug trafficking is curtailed in Mexico, the billions of dollars funding the cartels and the corruption from the drug trade will be diminished and should weaken criminal networks. However, if the weak government systems and pervasive corruption are not rectified, another commodity will assume the place of drugs, as we are already seeing with the diversification in revenue streams from cartels dealing not only in drugs, but also in human trafficking, kidnapping, extortion, and arms trade.

The gruesome August 2010 discovery of 72 migrant workers from Honduras, El Salvador, Ecuador, and Brazil who had been executed by a drug gang provided evidence of the cartels' diversification beyond drugs and into extortion and human trafficking. Within days of the discovery of the massacre in Tamaulipas, near the Texas border, the state prosecutors charged with investigating the case had disappeared and are feared dead.[95]

As of the writing of this book, Ciudad Juárez, the Mexican sister city to El Paso, Texas, is the most dangerous city on earth. Monterrey, Mexico, is among the limited locations where the U.S. State Department will allow only adult children to accompany diplomats; the others include Lebanon, the Republic of Chad, the Sudan, and Yemen.[96] The drug war has shaped a more violent atmosphere in some Mexican cities than exists in cities in Afghanistan and Iraq, where there are two wars underway. The drug war in Mexico has raised concern over the voracious appetite for drugs in North America and the role of U.S.-led drug prohibition in fueling the violence.

The PRI party has begun to regain popularity in light of the violence that has erupted as the PAN party struggles to clean up the corruption and crime that were endemic of the PRI rule. Terrence Poppa told NPR that in his view, "the best reason for ending drug prohibition is to save Mexico, to save the democracy of Mexico that the Mexican people have struggled so hard to gain."[97]

No issue has a greater impact on stability and development in Mexico and Central America than drug-related crime. Security and economic-development challenges are rooted in the culture of illegality embodied most graphically by the triple threat of small-arms proliferation, drug trafficking, and criminal and youth gangs.[98] The region is one of the most violent in the world, with a homicide rate three times the global average.[99] In January 2011, the U.S. military's Joint Forces Command issued a report warning that Mexico (along with Pakistan) is at risk of "rapid and sudden collapse."[100] The War on Drugs, like the War on Poverty, implies that you can win it once and for all. In reality, these social ills have been with us throughout recorded history, and they require constant tending. Although the escalating drug war in Mexico is not directly related to the war in Afghanistan (OEF), their corresponding economic, corruption, and narcotics problems have eroded the legitimacy of banking, business, government, and military sectors in both countries.

CHAPTER 11

Drugs and the Afghan Wars

The catalogue of casualties caused by Afghan narcotics is gruesome. We need to go back to the dramatic opium addiction in China a century ago to find comparable statistics.

Antonio Maria Costa, executive director,
United Nations Office on Drugs and Crime[1]

PRIOR TO THE MID 1970s, opium cultivation in the Afghan-Pakistan border region was primarily limited to cultural use, traditional medicine, and limited regional recreational use. By the late 1970s, opium cultivation from this region began to be co-opted for heroin production and international trafficking to fill the void created by interruptions in Southeast Asia's Golden Triangle (Laos, Vietnam, Thailand) that followed the end of the Vietnam War. As presented in Chapter 7, the CIA, in connection with the Vietnam War, became entwined with warlords who were also drug lords, and through their support the drug trade flourished in Southeast Asia and led to the development of the Golden Triangle, the epicenter of the global heroin trade until the late 1970s.

Following the Vietnam War, the U.S. turned its attention to Afghanistan and the increasing presence of the Soviets. By 1980, Afghanistan was the new frontline of the Cold War, and it was there that the U.S. government implemented its largest post-Vietnam covert operation to date. The U.S. could not directly engage in support of Afghanistan's fight against the Soviets without risking escalation to nuclear war. Replicating the strategies the U.S. had used in Laos in the 1960s and 1970s to support and fund insurgent groups in regions where the U.S. could not be acknowledged as fighting, the U.S. covertly supported Afghanistan's battle against the Soviets and Pakistan's backing of the Afghans. The CIA worked closely with their Pakistan counterpart, the Inter-Services Intelligence (ISI), which served as the intermediary liaison between the CIA, Afghan exiles, and the mujahideen.

During the Soviet-Afghan war (1979–1989), the U.S. covert operations again became entwined with Afghan and Pakistan drug traffickers, and the region covering Afghanistan, Iran, and Pakistan became opium's new empire, the Golden Crescent. Poppy cultivation in the region was escalating just as a confluence of regional wars erupted—the Soviet invasion of Afghanistan (1979), the Islamic revolution in Iran (1979), and the Iran-Iraq war (1980–1990). The escalation in the drug trade served several purposes: money for weapons to support the freedom fighters battling the Soviets, funds for Pakistan to support the Afghan refugee settlements, and the use of drugs as a destabilizing force against the Soviets. These cultural, economic, political, social, and geographic factors cultivated a fertile environment for an opium and heroin boom in the region during the 1980s.

Soviet-Afghan War

During the Soviet invasion of Afghanistan, Pakistan provided military and humanitarian aid to Afghan refugees and enabled the mujahideen to establish and operate some 300 refugee camps in their North-West Frontier Province (NWFP). Afghanistan and Pakistan developed a mutually beneficial relationship: Pakistan provided humanitarian support to the Afghans, and the refugee resettlement region provided a means of defense along Pakistan's western border. Pakistan was under military and financial stress with the Soviet-Afghan war on their western border, as they were simultaneously at war on their eastern border with India over the disputed Kashmir territory.

Within the Afghan refugee resettlement, some wealthier Afghans invested in opium-poppy cultivation in Pakistan as a means of generating currency to support their opposition to the Soviet invasion. In the absence of central law, Afghan refugees and Pashtun immigrants, with the collaboration of Pakistani locals, established robust poppy cultivation along the 1,400-kilometer (870-mile) Afghanistan-Pakistan border and throughout the NWFP. The intensification of opium production in the geographically isolated and rugged region of the Afghanistan-Pakistan border along Pakistan's NWFP was largely attributed to the Soviet-Afghan War and the Iranian Revolution.[2] Lieutenant General Fazle Haq, governor of the NWFP, overlord of the mujahideen guerrillas, and close confidant and advisor to Pakistan's President General Muhammad Zia-ul-Haq, suggested that Zia use the money from the drug trade to finance the military and challenges they were facing on both the western and eastern borders. Thus began the interdependence between the drug trade, Pakistan, and the Afghan mujahideen. The drug trade was tolerated and even enabled because it generated significant amounts of money on demand as the need arose.[3] General Haq and President Zia allowed hundreds of heroin refineries to be established in the NWFP, even though Pakistan had "officially" banned poppy cultivation in 1979.[4]

As early as 1982, Pakistani army trucks were carrying CIA weapons from Karachi, Pakistan, to General Haq's province, where they offloaded arms and picked up large shipments of heroin.[5] During this time, Pakistan also played an important role in the

Iran-Contra Affair, providing transshipment, storage, and arms-trafficking services with Iran and the multibillion-dollar arms supply of Afghanistan.[6] General Haq moved Pakistan's heroin money through the notorious Bank of Credit and Commerce International (BCCI).[7] BCCI was involved in money laundering in connection with the Iran-Contra Affair and Panamanian President Manuel Noriega.

Norman Bailey, a member of the National Security Council (NSC) who monitored terrorist activities through finance tracking, reported that in the early 1980s, the CIA and the NSC were aware that BCCI was involved in drug-money transactions and neither agency took any action, presumably because Pakistan was a critically important U.S. ally in the region.[8] BCCI had a 1,500-employee clandestine division of the bank they named the "black network" that engaged in global intelligence operations, along with a mafia-style enforcement squad. The base of operations for the "black network" was in Karachi, Pakistan, and they engaged in bribery, extortion, kidnapping, and murder. On the business side, BCCI had offices throughout the world and conducted money laundering for the drug trade, the lucrative arms-trade business, and precious metals.[9]

During this same time, General Haq was listed with Interpol as an international drug trafficker while he was simultaneously considered by the CIA to be an asset. As a CIA asset, Haq's drug-trafficking activities were exempt from U.S. action because of the agreement between the CIA and the Department of Justice that exempted the CIA from having to report drug trafficking by its assets to the Justice Department during the years of 1982 to 1995.[10] Despite his being listed by Interpol as an international drug trafficker, U.S. government officials including William Casey, CIA director (1981–1987), and George H.W. Bush, former CIA director and then–vice president, met with Haq. In 1984, Casey and Bush met with Haq in Pakistan to discuss the details of the Afghan arms pipeline and the role of Pakistan in supporting the Afghans in their Soviet resistance. As vice president, George H.W. Bush worked closely with President Zia, the ISI, and his government because their country was the frontline against the Soviets.

On August 17, 1988, the day before President Bush gave his acceptance speech as the Republican Party candidate for the 1988 presidential race, President Zia was killed in a suspicious plane accident. He was returning from a demonstration of U.S. weaponry when his plane crashed, killing Zia, Arnold Ralph, the American ambassador to Pakistan, and 30 others. Bush paid tribute to Zia in his acceptance speech, acknowledging the special relationship the U.S. had developed with President Zia and Pakistan. That same day, *The New York Times* report of the plane crash that resulted in Zia's death included reference to the open secret about the ties between drug traffickers and senior figures in the Zia government.[11] U.S. officials would later state that everybody knew that Haq was running the drug trade, and shortly thereafter the involvement of Zia's government in the heroin trade became an accepted historical fact.[12,13,14]

By 1990, U.S. newspapers were publishing major stories on the links between specific mujahideen groups, the ISI, and the illegal narcotics trade. Moreover, papers reported that U.S. officials were failing to act on reports of drug trafficking by

Afghan rebels and Pakistanis. Afghans had given U.S. officials firsthand accounts of heroin smuggling under the direction of Gulbuddin Hekmatyar, an Afghan warlord and guerilla leader with close ties to the Pakistani military and the ISI.[15] Gulbuddin Hekmatyar became closely tied to Osama Bin Laden in the 1980s, and Bin Laden greatly strengthened Hekmatyar's opium-smuggling operations.[16]

Operation Mosquito

It has also been alleged that French and American intelligence operatives were deeply enmeshed in this drug trade during the Soviet-Afghan War. In early 1981, during the initial days of the Reagan Administration, Count Alexandre de Marenches, former head of France's secret foreign intelligence service (the DGSE), proposed "Operation Mosquito," a Franco-American alliance venture to counter the Soviet Communist threat in Afghanistan.[17] Inspired by the wartime tactics of the Vietcong, who used drugs as a tool of war against enemy soldiers, de Marenches proposed to senior advisors in the Reagan Administration that they strategically use drugs as tools of war against the Soviets. Operation Mosquito involved supplying drugs (primarily raw opium, heroin, and hashish) to the Soviet military in addition to littering the country with anti-communist propaganda.[18] This proposition came about in part through the association between U.S. Deputy Director of Central Intelligence (DDCI) General Vernon Walters and de Marenches. Prior to becoming the DDCI, Walters had been the U.S. defense attaché in Paris, where the two had become close friends and allies.[19]

France reportedly backed out of formal involvement in Operation Mosquito, but many of the ideas proposed by de Marenches stuck and were implemented with aid from the U.S. In 1981, President Reagan approved this covert program to weaken Soviet soldiers fighting in Afghanistan by addicting them to illegal drugs. Members of the Reagan Administration in turn proposed the use of this drug warfare tactic to Afghanistan's mujahideen.[20] They encouraged Afghanistan's opium-growing mujahideen guerilla to weaken their Russian opponents with an influx of drugs during the Soviet-Afghan War.[21] Drug development in the Afghan-Pakistan region grew as drugs began to be used as weapons of war against Afghanistan's enemies, while narcotics trafficking provided the mujahideen funding for the Soviet opposition.[22]

Growth in Trafficking and Addiction
Related to the Soviet-Afghan War

The proliferation of heroin and hash in Afghanistan impacted the Soviet troops; a RAND study reported that the majority of Russian troops were using drugs regularly in the Democratic Republic of Afghanistan.[23] For many Soviet soldiers, the drug problems they developed in Afghanistan continued long after their return to the Soviet Union. Among the citizens of many former Soviet countries, addiction has continued to escalate since the collapse of the Soviet Union. Their exposure to the drugs and the abundance of drugs, combined with the collapse of the USSR, created a population that was highly susceptible to substance abuse.

Central Asia and the Balkans are now key transit routes for Afghan heroin. The geographic proximity coupled with limited economic opportunities has led many people in the region to become involved in the drug trade. Twenty years after the end of the Soviet-Afghan War and the collapse of the USSR, more Russians per year died from drugs than the total number of Red Army soldiers killed during the Soviet-Afghan war. In 2009, Russia estimated that between 30,000 and 40,000 people per year died directly related to substance abuse. Today, Russians consume 75 to 80 tons of Afghan heroin per year, and by 2009 the number of heroin addicts in the Russian Federation had increased tenfold since the start of Operation Enduring Freedom (OEF) in 2001.[24]

The Afghan and Pakistan heroin trade required connections beyond the Middle East. When the wars in the Golden Crescent disrupted the traditional drug-trafficking routes between the region and Europe, Pakistan-based drug cartels were forced to develop alternative narcotics-trafficking routes and forge new alliances with syndicates who could move the heroin to Europe. Evidence of the Pakistan-sanctioned European drug-trafficking ring is provided by the Oslo, Norway, arrest of Hamid Hasnain, General Zia's personal banker, who was implicated in the world heroin trade and brought to trial in Islamabad, Pakistan.[25] Pakistan cartels needed new routes and associates, which they found through connections with Corsican syndicates. As discussed in previous chapters, U.S. intelligence agencies worked with Corsican syndicates at the end of World War II and early in the Cold War.

The Golden Crescent heroin trade grew significantly with the aid of the French Marseille Corsican syndicates and the Sicilian mafia. The growth in heroin production in the NWFP impacted the source countries, Afghanistan and Pakistan, as well as the citizens in their target markets of Europe and the United States. As early as 1979, Europe and the U.S. began to be flooded with potent, cheap heroin from the Golden Crescent, with Afghanistan and Pakistan furnishing 70 percent of the world's supply of high-grade heroin. With this influx of Afghan heroin, the number of overdoses and drug-related deaths in New York City increased 77 percent.[26]

Concomitantly, plentiful and cheap opium from Afghanistan began fueling addiction in Pakistan, Afghanistan, and Iran in the 1980s. Officially, the first documented case of heroin addiction in Pakistan was identified in the city of Baluchistan, in 1979; by 1988 Pakistan had an estimated 650,000 heroin addicts.[27] Between 1979 and 1999, the rate of opium and heroin addiction in Pakistan had grown by nearly seven percent annually, with current estimates at four million opium/heroin addicts and an additional 100,000 new addicts annually.[28,29]

The Afghan Narconomy and How Drugs Are Bankrolling Terrorist Organizations

Similar to the dynamics of poverty, corruption, and despair that have enabled Mexico's drug problems, Pakistani police in the 1980s and 1990s were often culpable in the growth of drug trafficking in the region. Heroin was sold in Pakistani cities under the watchful eyes of police, who had a stake in the local drug trade. Karachi's drug peddling thrived in the presence of the police, who rarely intervened in gunfights between rival drug gangs.[30]

According to Ahmar Mustikhan, it is an undisputed fact among Pakistanis that the military junta that ruled Pakistan in the 1980s is responsible for their country's heroin crises. Mustikhan stated, "During the bloody communists-versus-Mujahideen war in Afghanistan—the former helped by the erstwhile Red Army and the latter aided by the American CIA—the West looked the other way while heroin addiction made inroads in Pakistani society. It is an open secret that the Afghan Mujahideen transported the first consignments of the deadly powder to Pakistan in the early 1980s when Afghanistan was under Russian occupation."[31]

Pakistan is pivotal to the global drug trade that is funding terrorist groups. However, gaining control of the narcotics trade to interrupt funding for insurgents and terrorists is a global security issue that affects nearly every corner of the world. The Liberation Tigers of Tamil Eelam (LTTE) has funded its terrorist organization through the drug trade operating out of Pakistan and northern Sri Lanka for decades. The LTTE and their affiliated gangs capitalized on their established transit routes and contraband smuggling operations in South Asia and have engaged in transcontinental drug trafficking since 1983.[32] They are also reported to be linked to the billion-dollar drug markets in Canada and Europe.[33]

LTTE identified and infiltrated weak security-access points, such as the western coast of India nearest to Pakistan, thus enabling Pakistan-based drug cartels to access transit points along the coast and recruit drug couriers from India. The LTTE was responsible for the December 2008 terrorist attacks in Mumbai, India, that resulted in the slaughter of hundreds of innocent citizens over the course of a day of terror.

The opium-based economy in Afghanistan existed long before the U.S.-led invasion in 2001. For decades, the Taliban, warlords, insurgents, and government officials have used opium as a source of taxable revenue and a tool of political influence and control. When the country's infrastructure was destroyed during the Soviet-Afghan War, many Afghan farmers turned to growing opium poppies because there were limited alternative sources of stable guaranteed income. Afghan refugees who fled to the NWFP in neighboring Pakistan began cultivating opium to fund their fight against the Soviets. A decade after the withdrawal of Soviet troops, the provinces in Taliban-led Afghanistan were producing nearly 75 percent of the world's illicit opium, and in 2000 the Taliban led a brutal enforced ban on opium cultivation, which resulted in a 98 percent drop in poppy production within a single year.[34]

Opium cultivation and production are labor intensive, requiring roughly 45 hours of human labor to produce one kilogram of raw opium.[35] Drug lords rely on desperate poverty to sustain a workforce willing to do this type of intensive manual labor. The farmers' debt keeps them linked to the next poppy harvest, and their crop is dictated by whomever they owe money to, likely the Taliban or Al-Qaeda. Poppy farmers unable to pay their debt are often forced to give up their daughters to the drug lords in partial exchange for reduction of their debt.[36] Poverty, illiteracy, deprivation, and disempowerment are the underpinning of the problems that perpetuate drug cultivation and addiction in the region. Warlords and drug lords benefit from the manipulation of impoverished and uneducated masses. The citizens are certainly not encouraged to develop critical thinking; they are told what to do by the warlords and drug lords. Education and political participation are privileges, not rights, in Afghanistan and Pakistan. These factors interact to perpetuate the vulnerability of farmers, some willing and others forced to grow opium poppies.

Opium, heroin, and hash are processed in narcotics "labs" throughout Afghanistan and the NWFP; the narcotics provide profitable economic funding to individuals and families as well as some antigovernment groups. In addition to the financial profits from the drug trade, there is addiction and significant domestic use of opiates among Afghanis. Afghan citizens are plagued by problems caused by opium cultivation and the drug trade. As is the case in any community that produces and trades unregulated, underground, or illicit goods, Afghanistan is vulnerable to corruption and money laundering through informal financial networks and inter-group violence. Drug lords have replaced warlords in the struggle for power, and insurgents including Al-Qaeda and the Taliban are receiving much of their money from the Afghan opium drug trade.

The amount of opium cultivated and trafficked in the Afghan region has escalated and receded in tandem with the wars in the region. Today, Afghanistan and the NWFP are the epicenter of the world heroin trade, where poppy cultivation has been invigorated by the Taliban, Al Qaeda, and their Pakistan-based supporters, all unified by drug money and their opposition to the presence of the U.S., NATO, and their western allies. Just as narcotics trafficking funded the Afghan freedom fighters during the Soviet-Afghan war, the drug trade continues to be a primary source of funding for Al-Qaeda and a substantial source of economic revenue for the Taliban in 2010. The practice is the same; only the enemy has changed.

In 2001, the Taliban had virtually eliminated opium production in Afghanistan; this astonishing feat was confirmed in a report from the United Nations Office on Drugs and Crime. What makes this so significant is that in the years prior to this, Afghan heroin accounted for 90 percent of the European drug market. A Taliban-led brutally enforced ban on opium in 2000 resulted in a 98 percent drop in poppy production within one year.[37] The Helmand Province, which was under Taliban control at the time, reported no poppy cultivation, whereas the provinces under control of the Northern Alliance produced 185 tons of opium. The 2000 opium ban imposed by the Taliban resulted in a limited supply and dramatic price increases. The Taliban supreme leader Mullah Mohammed Omar imposed the ban. Skeptics of the Taliban's success in reducing Afghan's opium production have speculated that the intent of the ban was to drive up the price of opium. The drastic reduction does demonstrate that opium cultivation can be eradicated or greatly curtailed of the Afghans' own accord if the ruling forces choose to do so.

When the U.S. began fighting in Afghanistan in response to the September 11, 2001, attacks against the U.S., the Taliban was ousted from provincial power. With the Taliban removed from power, many of the farmers reinstated their cultivation of opium poppies.[38] This spontaneous resumption of poppy cultivation was in response to the desire for economic means by farmers and the cultivation of revenue streams to fund the oppositional forces of Al Qaeda and the Taliban. The Taliban and Al Qaeda have embraced drug cultivation, and today the insurgency is funded in large part through the drug trade. Drug traffickers provide financing to the Taliban in exchange for protection of their drug routes, production labs, and opium-poppy fields.

One of the key drug lords providing financial support in the form of drug proceeds to the Taliban is Haji Juma Khan. Khan was arrested and charged with conspiracy to distribute narcotics with intent to support a terrorist organization in October 2008, through a joint operation involving the U.S. DEA, Interpol, and Turkish and British officials.[39]

By 2003, the United States began to view the increasing opium-poppy cultivation and drug trafficking as a threat to the stability and security of Afghanistan. By 2004, the U.S. government made counternarcotics a top priority and provided $380 million for Afghan- and United Kingdom–led counter-narcotics efforts. These funds have been used to train Afghan narcotics interdiction units, construct border and highway checkpoint facilities, and supply operational support and nonlethal equipment to Afghan eradication teams. However, according to the Report to Congress from the Government Accountability Office, these efforts failed to have any significant effect on the illicit narcotics industry because of limited security and stability across Afghanistan.

Early in Operation Enduring Freedom, the World Bank and the United Nations began raising concerns about Afghanistan becoming a "narco-state." Today, that concern has been realized. In 2009, the drug trade accounted for 30 percent of Afghanistan's gross domestic product.[40] It is estimated that 1 in 17 people in the Afghan-Pakistan border region are directly involved in the drug trade, and 12 percent of the Afghan population lives off of the opium trade.[41] This has created a narco-culture throughout Afghanistan and resulted in what I call a "narconomy."

In her book *Seeds of Terror: How Heroin Is Bankrolling the Taliban and Al Qaeda*, journalist and author Gretchen Peters observes that the Taliban's poppy/opium ban turned out to be the ultimate insider-trading con. Taliban leaders, such as Haji Bashir Noorzai, had purchased mass quantities of opium prior to the 2001 ban, when the price was low, and then sold it after the ban, when the price rose.[42] Peters contends that the poppy ban was staged in an attempt to gain recognition of the Taliban as a legitimate government, and their hopes of receiving millions in international aid for their drug-reduction efforts. Regardless of the receptivity from the international community, the Taliban were guaranteed substantive income in the coming years, when the price of opium and heroin would rise dramatically in response to the perceived shortage of opium caused by the reduction in poppy cultivation in 2001.

In 2005, Pakistan's opium-poppy cultivation was estimated to be 800 hectares, yielding potential production of four metric tons of pure heroin. The Pakistani federal and provincial authorities are actively conducting anti-poppy cultivation campaigns and impose fines and arrests when the ban on poppy cultivation is not observed. However, the financial crimes that stem from drug trafficking—namely, funding insurgents and terrorism, fostering corruption, and smuggling—remain key problems in Pakistan, Afghanistan, and the region. Pakistan remains a significant transit point for drugs (heroin, opium, and hashish) from Afghanistan bound for Western markets, the Gulf States, and Africa.

According to the CIA, Afghanistan is currently the world's largest producer of opium, accounting for 90 percent of the global supply. It is estimated that 80 to 90 percent of the heroin consumed in Europe comes from Afghanistan's opium. However, very little Afghan heroin reaches the U.S., whose primary source of heroin comes from Latin America, which produces only about 1 percent of the global heroin supply.[43] Figure 11-1 illustrates the growth in opium production in Afghanistan coinciding with Operation Enduring Freedom.

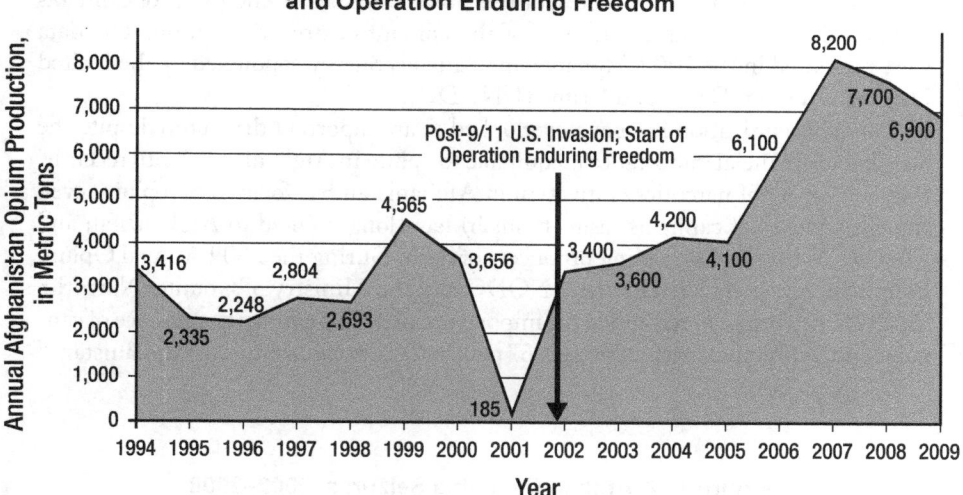

Figure 11-1 Afghanistan Opium Production and Operation Enduring Freedom

In 2006, there was an increase in poppy cultivation and trafficking of opium and heroin in the majority of the country, 21 out of 34 provinces. Helmand Province and Southern Afghanistan along the NWFP border experienced the greatest increase in poppy cultivation. Of the 34 provinces in Afghanistan, three reported increases of more than 50 percent, and another 12 provinces increased opium production 10 to 50 percent. Only six provinces, all located in the eastern region, were declared as non-cultivating provinces in 2006. [44]

Through international leadership, counternarcotics efforts have made some progress in recent years, and opium cultivation decreased to negligible levels in several provinces in 2009. However, the decrease in opium farming in these provinces does not make them opium-free. Many of these provinces now serve as opium refineries and transshipment networks at times aided by Afghan government officials. Whereas the total quantity of hectares of opium-poppy cultivation has declined in Afghanistan, the actual yield of raw opium has dropped by negligible amounts. This is due to the fact that Afghan farmers are now extracting more opium sap per poppy bulb and therefore per hectare. Afghan poppies yield more opium per hectare than Southeast Asia's Golden Triangle poppies, which have a yield of about 10 kg of opium per hectare. This is because Afghan poppies from fertile regions have increased their yield per hectare by 20 percent; whereas they previously produced 49 kg of opium per hectare, they now yield 56 kg of opium per hectare. Although total poppy cultivation decreased by 22 percent between 2008 and 2009 in terms of hectares planted, actual opium production decreased only by 10 percent.[45]

Cannabis

The data reflected in Figure 11-2 are from the Afghan Annual Reports Questionnaires 2002–2008, and they represent the annual number of kilograms of cannabis seized; seizures are a valid indicator of the amount of drug cultivation. The data were presented in the 2009 Afghanistan Cannabis Survey conducted by the United Nations Office on Drugs and Crime (UNODC).[46]

Cannabis cultivation has been overlooked as an important drug crop despite the fact that its financial importance is equitable to opium in Afghanistan. Until recently, the monitoring of narcotics cultivation in Afghanistan has focused on opium, even though seizures of cannabis resin (hashish) have long pointed to Afghanistan and Morocco as the world's leading producers of hash. During the 2009 Annual Opium Poppy Surveys conducted by the UNODC and the Ministry of Counter Narcotics (MCN), they began to recognize the importance of documenting the presence of cannabis cultivation that exists alongside 67 percent of the opium crops in Afghanistan.[47]

Figure 11-2 Afghan Cannabis Seizures, 2002–2008

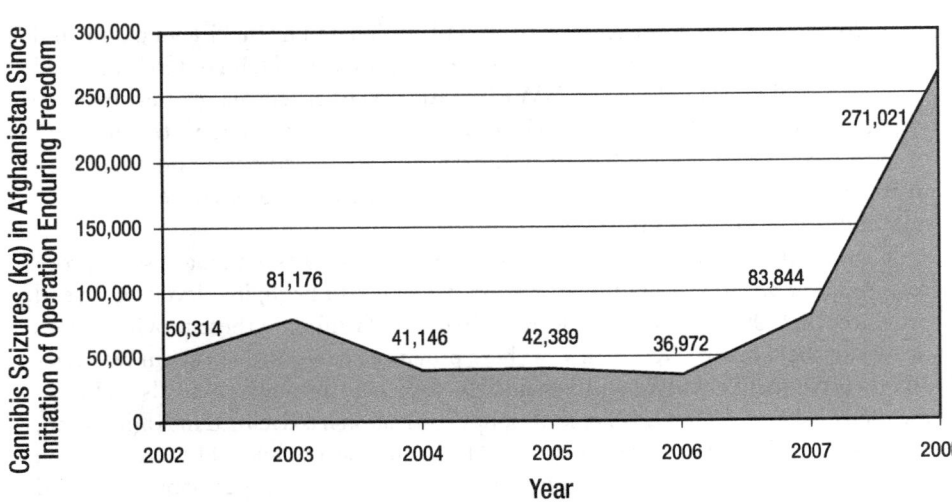

Prior to 2009, systematic surveys to document cannabis cultivation and production had not been conducted. The cannabis survey was implemented under the technical framework of the UNODC Illicit Crop Monitoring Programme (ICMP), which helps the international community monitor the extent and evolution of illicit crops within the context of the Political Declaration and Plan of Action on International Cooperation Towards a Balanced Strategy to Counter the World Drug Problem. Opium and heroin are used by a very small percentage of the world population (~0.05 percent of the world population), whereas cannabis is much more widely used (~4.3 percent of the world population) and has a larger world market.[48]

Afghanistan's role as the top opium producer in the world has been well known in recent years; less well publicized is the fact that it is also the world's largest producer of hashish. Although there are other countries that cultivate larger cannabis acreage or hectares, the Afghan cannabis crops yield more resin used to produce hashish than those in any other country. Afghan cannabis yields more than three times as much resin (145 kg of resin per hectare) compared to Moroccan cannabis (40 kg of resin per hectare). Annually, Afghanistan cultivates 10,000 to 24,000 hectares of cannabis, which results in production of 1,500 tons (1,360,777 kg) to 3,500 tons (3,175,147 kg) of hashish for the world market. Net income per hectare of cannabis ($3,341 U.S.) is higher than from opium ($2,005). Cannabis cultivation and harvesting also requires significantly less manual labor than cultivating and harvesting opium poppies; it is three times less expensive to cultivate each cannabis hectare compared to each opium hectare.

As with opium cultivation, cannabis cultivation is concentrated in regions of instability. Poverty and fear keep the farmers tied into the agricultures of opium and cannabis, and their cultivation, production, and trafficking are taxed by those who control the territory and provide key sources of revenue for insurgents. Two-thirds of the farmers who grow opium poppies also grow cannabis. In 2010, southern Afghanistan was the primary region for cannabis cultivation, whereas it had previously been concentrated in the northern provinces.[49]

Growth in Addiction Related to Operation Enduring Freedom

The human impact of the drug production originating in Afghanistan has resulted in catastrophic consequences around the globe, from such regionally diverse cities as Oslo, London, Moscow, Paris, Tehran, and Kabul. Among the most vulnerable are the Afghans, where drug use and addiction is a growing problem, particularly among residents and refugees. Drug addiction and HIV (transmitted through shared needles) are spreading illness, misery, and death, particularly along opiate-trafficking routes in Afghanistan, the Islamic Republic of Iran, the Russian Federation, Central Asia, and Europe.[50]

After decades of war, Afghans, including young children, are increasingly escaping the pain of war and poverty by using opium, heroin, and synthetic opiates (Propoxyphene, Fentanyl, Pentazocine, Methadone). The abundance of cheap opium and heroin make it an inexpensive means of forgetting their troubles and misery. Until now, Afghans have rationalized the cultivation and trafficking of drugs to fund their defense of an Islamic state while poisoning the "infidels" of Europe, Russia, and the U.S. However, the demand for heroin and opium within Afghanistan has doubled between 2004 and 2009, with 1 in 12 Afghans abusing drugs and more than one million opiate addicts.[51] Each day, some 1,500 men gather to use heroin in Kabul at the former Russian Cultural Center to get their heroin fix, while they are protected by policemen in riot gear.[52] The social unrest and violence has resulted in millions of Afghan refugees flooding the neighboring countries of Iran and Pakistan. Many of the Afghan refugees living in and returning from Iran bring with them a serious heroin addiction.

The primary drugs of abuse are opium and heroin, and the rates of use and addiction have nearly doubled between 2005 and 2010. A study published by the former UNODC executive director in 2010 reported that nearly eight percent of Afghans between the ages of 15 and 64 suffer from drug addiction, a rate double the world average. UNODC Executive Director Antonio Maria Costa attributes the recent escalation as such: "Three decades of war-related trauma, unlimited availability of cheap narcotics and limited access to treatment have created a major, and growing, addiction problem in Afghanistan."[53]

Most troubling of the emerging trends in Afghan drug use is the fact that 50 percent of drug-using parents in the northern and southern regions of the country give opium to their children, including young toddlers. Afghan children are affected by intergenerational trauma from the decades of war coupled with a life of addiction. Future generations may have more to overcome with limited economic, educational, and social opportunities and inadequate addiction treatment.

The impact of drug abuse, overdose, and addiction stemming from Afghanistan is profound. Heroin and hashish are trafficked through neighboring countries, where they are used and sold along the way to their final destinations in Europe and Russia. Today, Russia's demand for heroin is in part an outgrowth from the prolific use and availability of heroin to Soviet soldiers during the Soviet-Afghan War. Following the Soviet-Afghan War, heroin supplies flooded Russia and Europe.

In the early 1990s, Tajikistan and Turkmenistan emerged as major transit countries for Afghan narcotics bound for Russian and Western European markets. This influx of heroin in Europe and Russia has created a new generation of addicts. In 2010, one of the most active transit cities was Almaty, Kazakhstan, which has become a hub for hash and heroin bound for Europe. The UNODC estimates that less than five percent of illicit drug trafficking is intercepted; based on recent seizures, they calculate that 80 tons of heroin are trafficked annually from Afghanistan to Russia via Central Asia. This region of Central Asia is a significant overland trafficking route for Afghan narcotics and is now referred to as the New Silk Road.

Similar to the trafficking ploys between Mexico and the U.S., the drugs trafficked through Kazakhstan are hidden inside tankers, vehicles, and railway cars and carried on and inside human mules traveling on buses or in cars and walking across the border. In addition to the escalating rates of addiction in the region, the annual growth in intravenous drug use is estimated at 3 percent and is connected to rising rates of HIV infection and HIV/AIDS-related death.[54] A 2009 report from UNODC reported the following statistics in direct relation to the impact of the rising Afghan opium trade.

> Presently more people die from Afghan opium (~100,000/year) than any other drug in the world. The number of people who die from heroin overdoses in NATO countries (more than 10,000/year) is five times higher than the total number of NATO troops killed in Afghanistan since the start of the war in 2001. Iran has an estimated 1,000,000 opiate users and has one of the world's most serious opiate-addiction problems. Central Asia primarily has been a conduit for the transshipment of drugs; however, the region is now a major consumer of Afghan heroin. Consequently, rates of HIV infection have skyrocketed in Central Asia due to increased intravenous heroin use in the region.[55]

Creating a Monster

Part of the difficulty of reversing the drug trade that has emerged in the Golden Crescent is the fact that it was allowed, enabled, and even supported at the highest levels of government in Pakistan, Afghanistan, and to some extent the United States.[56] During the Cold War, the U.S. role was complicity in enabling warlords to become drug lords in the region. The overriding objective of the U.S. in the region was to prevent Soviet expansion into Pakistan. The drug trade between Afghanistan and Pakistan's NWFP are entwined and created a monster narco-culture that is now difficult to control.

The 1982 secret legal memorandum that exempted CIA officers from having to report on known narcotics activities among CIA assets enabled escalation of drug cultivation and trafficking in the Golden Crescent as well as South America. U.S. Attorney General William French Smith granted CIA Director William Casey a legal exemption for CIA officers, agents, and assets (such as Pakistan President General Muhammad Zia-ul-Haq) from being required to report on drug smuggling in order to help protect CIA assets, intelligence sources, and methods.[57] Eventually, the CIA exemption for acting on known narcotics trafficking was rescinded by President Bill Clinton in 1995, which has helped the U.S. amend their complicity in the drug trade during the Cold War, particularly during active wartime.[58]

This type of corruption is not unheard of, but it is surprising considering the fact that among the corrupt politicians involved in the drug trade have been Afghan President Hamid Karzai's brother, Ahmad Wali Khan Karzai, and General Mohammed Daud Daud, Afghanistan's most powerful anti-drug czar.[59,60] The duplicitous role of General Daud, Afghanistan's deputy minister of the interior responsible for counternarcotics, is just one example. Despite being widely implicated in opium smuggling, Duad was appointed deputy interior minister responsible for counter-narcotics.[61] In 2005 in Jalalabad, a specially trained unit of Counternarcotics Police conducted a precision ambush of drug dealer Sayyed Jan. When the officers caught Jan moving 183 kilograms of pure heroin, they also discovered that Jan had a signed letter of protection from their own boss, General Mohammed Daud, the Afghan drug czar. [62]

General Daud had safeguarded shipments of illegal opiates while simultaneously commanding thousands of Counternarcotics Police sworn to fight the drug trade. The extent of the corruption goes beyond a few bureaucrats skimming cream off the top to supplement their salaries. There were reports that Daud has reaped significant profits in Afghanistan's multibillion-dollar narcotics industry. A 2009 published report from Kabul gave details about Afghan officials involved in the drug trade and their protection of drug traffickers, who in turn support the Taliban. [63]

As noted in the well-sourced *Globe and Mail* investigation of General Daud, his involvement "highlights the wider implications of drug cartels operating inside the Kabul administration. It's a toxic triangle of alliances, as corrupt officials work with drug traffickers who, in turn, help the Taliban ... in effect, running branches of the state for illegal gain." [64] In May 2011, General Daud was assassinated by a suicide bomber linked to the Taliban.

Within weeks of Daud's assassination, Ahmad Wali Khan Karzai (a.k.a. AWK), half-brother of President Karzai, was assassinated in his Kandahar home, by his police commander, Sardar Mohammad, who was immediately killed by Karzai's bodyguards in a hail of gunfire. Mohammad was an unlikely assassin; he had cooperated and shared intelligence with U.S. officials, and at the time his brothers-in-law were security guards for the CIA's Kandahar base. [65] However, Mohammad had reportedly met with the Taliban in Pakistan in the weeks prior to the assassination, and the Taliban has claimed responsibility for AWK's assassination.

AWK was a powerful and controversial figure widely reported to have been a drug baron on the CIA payroll as well as a warlord defender of the Afghan people. [66,67] Documents posted by WikiLeaks include communications from American diplomats who portrayed AWK as a Mafia-like figure, involved in the opium drug trade and other illegal activities. [68,69] One document included a statement from Frank Ruggiero, a U.S. diplomat, which read, "While we must deal with AWK as the head of the Provincial Council, he is widely understood to be corrupt and a narcotics trafficker." [70]

NATO's Anti-Corruption Task Force wanted to reign in AWK; however, they recognized the potential blowback for taking down President Karzai's brother for his involvement in corruption and the narcotics trade. [71] AWK had extensive ties to the U.S. and was seen as the go-to person by the CIA and U.S. government and military officials. [72] His ties to the U.S. stem from his years living in Chicago, after fleeing Afghanistan during the communist takeover in 1979. He remained in Chicago until 1992, when he moved to Pakistan. [73]

Reversing the Tide

To systematically address concerns over Afghanistan becoming a narco-state, the U.S. has developed a five-pillar strategy to reduce poppy cultivation, drug production, and trafficking. The plan is intended to offer incentives to stop the growing of opium poppies through: 1) alternative livelihoods projects, combined with strong disincentives in the form of; 2) forced eradication; 3) interdiction; 4) law enforcement; and 5) spreading the Afghan government's antinarcotics message. These U.S. efforts are also expected to build the Afghan government's capacity to conduct counter-narcotics efforts on their own.[74]

Gretchen Peters has evaluated the five-pillar strategy and the reality of the conditions in Afghanistan and proposed four additional points, creating a nine-point strategy including the following: 6) diplomatic initiatives to support regional peace and free trade; 7) launch properly equipped counterinsurgency strategies; 8) blend counterinsurgency and counternarcotics efforts; and 9) target criminals and isolate and obstruct their drug money.[75]

Shortly after taking office, President Barack Obama presented a new international and U.S. strategy for Afghanistan and Pakistan in March 2009. The 2009 strategy focused on addressing the root causes of the regions' narcotics cultivation and trade. For decades, the drug trade has funded opposition forces and "terrorist" organizations and fostered corruption, which destabilizes the Afghan government and economy.[76] In presenting the strategy, President Obama openly addressed the fact that although Afghanistan has an elected government, it is undermined by corruption, and the economy is undercut by a thriving narcotics trade that encourages criminality while funding the insurgency. Obama also articulated the need to measure the growth of Afghanistan's economy and its illicit narcotics production as a means of assessing progress toward stabilizing the country, which has been at war for decades.

To make lasting progress and to develop an Afghan economy that isn't dominated by the illicit narcotics trade, President Obama laid out a plan to provide training and funding for agricultural specialists, educators, engineers, police, and lawyers. The new approach also addressed the issues of narco-funded corruption that have undermined trust and stability in the Afghan government in ways similar to those that are simultaneously plaguing Mexico. However, the Afghan plan differs in many ways from the traditional defense-based approach to the drug wars in North, Central, and South America. The emphasis in Afghanistan seems to be a shift away from primarily a militaristic intervention and toward economic development and prevention; however, treatment for addiction remains extremely limited.

It is noteworthy that the U.S. is not engaged in an intergovernmental war with Mexico or countries in Central or South America; however, the U.S. approach to combating drug use and narcotics trafficking in the western hemisphere has remained primarily militaristic, with financial support for military aid, training, and equipment. However, during the U.S. engagement in the war in Afghanistan (OEF), the articulated approach to prevent the narcotics trade was focused on education, economic development, and diplomacy. These are laudable yet long-term solutions that will take years to yield measurable change.

Meanwhile, the U.S. and NATO have stepped up the militaristic approach to drug interdiction. In June 2009, some 7,000 new U.S. troops sent to Afghanistan were deployed in the volatile southern province of Helmand, the world's largest opium poppy–growing region and Afghanistan's most violent province. The violence in this region stems from the Taliban militants, the drug lords they protect, the insurgents, and the U.S. and NATO fight to reduce opium production. In 2009, the U.S. and NATO increased attacks on Afghan drug labs after concluding that the opium trade and the insurgency are intertwined and are believed to be making hundreds of millions of dollars from the drug trade each year.[77] Since then the situation has become further complicated because the Taliban is no longer a single group with a leader.[78] It has evolved into multiple fragmented and decentralized components unevenly engaged in the narcotics trade with the potential for devolving into competing cartel-like structures.

Conclusion

Opium-poppy cultivation represents 34 percent of the combined legal and illegal economies in Afghanistan, and more than two million people depend on the crop for income. Total eradication does not seem possible, and there are well-founded concerns that social protests could further destabilize the country and region. Some policy analysts have recommended legitimate poppy licensing combined with bilateral U.S.-Afghan agreements. A similar Turkish-U.S. agreement was successfully co-developed and implemented in Turkey in the 1970s. This transformed opium cultivation in Turkey from an unregulated, uncontrolled, and primarily illicit enterprise to a government-supervised, licensed, medicinal-producing system. If total eradication is not feasible in Afghanistan, a controlled licensing process similar to Turkey's may be a pragmatic solution to the current crisis.[79]

The ensuing decades of war-related trauma coupled with unlimited availability of cheap narcotics and limited access to treatment have created a significant addiction problem in Afghanistan and the Golden Crescent.[80] According to the U.S. Department of State's Counternarcotics Strategy for Afghanistan, the drug trade in Afghanistan has undermined virtually every aspect of the Afghan government's efforts to build political stability, economic growth, internal security, and rule of law. Insurgents and drug traffickers are increasingly entwined, and vast networks of drug traffickers operate virtually untouched, sheltered by the rugged Afghan terrain. These isolated and ungoverned areas are known as global "black spots": they are outside of effective, recognized, governmental control; they are dominated by illicit social structures (e.g., criminal organizations, terrorist groups, warlords); and they cultivate and export global insecurity.[81] This reality has led to a strategic shift in drug interdiction and eradication, focusing dually on counter-insurgency and counter-narcotics.

The billions of dollars generated by the narcotics trade buy protection from law enforcement and create corrupt government officials, which in turn erodes trust in the government at every level and has destabilized an already fragile rule of law. The money generated from the sale of opium and heroin has also impacted the international banking system and weakened the reputation of banks in the Persian Gulf, where much of the heroin money-laundering occurs. Drugs have the capacity to corrupt the political atmosphere of the producing country, which is Afghanistan in this case.

Without the political patronage and the narco-favorable political atmosphere, drug production would not be possible.[82] Until Afghan officials take a leadership role in confronting internal smuggling routes, processing havens, and criminal rackets, the country will continue to operate as a narconomy and a narco-state. As former UNODC Executive Director Antonio Maria Costa noted, "A marriage of convenience between insurgents and criminal groups is spawning narco-cartels in Afghanistan linked to the Taliban. Drug money is addictive and is starting to trump ideology."[83] Similar to the patterns of drug cultivation that began as a means to fund political interests in Colombia and Myanmar, the drug trade in Afghanistan has gone from being a funding source for insurgency to supporting ideology and has become an end in itself. [84]

The Afghan drug trade generates billions of dollars annually, and concern has been raised about the potential for the battle to control drug money in Afghanistan leading to the type of inter-group warring we see with the Mexican cartels.[85,86,87] Pakistan—more specifically Taliban influences in Pakistan—triangulate the conflict and the flow of narcotics. Originally, the U.S. needed the strategic alliance of Pakistan to gain control of Afghanistan and the Taliban. Now the U.S. needs Afghanistan to help keep an eye on Pakistan, which, along with Mexico, the U.S. lists as being at risk of "rapid and sudden collapse."[88] Informed observers, including U.S. Secretary of State Hillary Clinton, have described Afghanistan as a narco-state.[89] The problems in Afghanistan are systemic and complex. Controlling drugs in Afghanistan will not solve all of their problems; however, Afghanistan's problems cannot be solved without controlling drug use, cultivation, production, and trafficking.[90]

CHAPTER 12

PTSD and Substance Abuse Among Veterans of the Afghan and Iraq Wars

There is no other feeling in the world that comes close to hunting another human being.... It is as addictive as any drug.

James Massey, Iraq veteran, *The Good Soldier*, 2009

The rush of battle is often a potent and lethal addiction, for war is a drug.

Chris Hedges, *The Hurt Locker*, 2009

OPERATION ENDURING FREEDOM (OEF, 2001–present) and Operation Iraqi Freedom (OIF, 2003–present; combat troops pulled in 2010) have been protracted, non-traditional wars; the enemies are not clearly defined governments following agreed-upon rules of engagement. Deployment to Iraq and Afghanistan is associated with serious psychological health problems in more than 30 percent of returning soldiers.[1] The most prevalent psychological health problem among soldiers returning from OEF and OIF is post-traumatic stress disorder (PTSD). Among those with PTSD, 80 percent also have comorbid conditions of substance abuse, major depression, and anxiety. PTSD and substance abuse are integrated, complex problems resulting in impairment in functioning, military performance, and family/marital relationships; a failure to "reset"; risk-taking; and suicidal behavior.

Lessons from Vietnam

Similar to fighting in Vietnam, the wars in Iraq and Afghanistan have presented unique psychological stressors among veterans of these wars. U.S. soldiers in the wars in Vietnam, Iraq, and Afghanistan faced continuous threats of ambush, inability to distinguish friend from foe, high casualty rates among civilians and soldiers, unidentifiable front lines, and a deteriorating sense of mission.[2] Unlike during and after Vietnam, however, society and the mental-health field now have greater understanding and insight into the residual trauma that affects veterans for decades. There is unprecedented awareness of the level of PTSD among those who have served in Afghanistan and Iraq.

In January 2009, the United States National Institute on Drug Abuse (NIDA) sponsored a conference in Bethesda, Maryland, entitled "Addressing Substance Abuse and Comorbidities Among Military Personnel, Veterans, and Their Families: A Research Agenda." During this important national meeting, leading military and medical personnel associated with the Veterans Health Administration discussed the historical trend of increased substance-abuse problems that affect veterans and society following every war. Experts noted that there have been documented increases in alcohol and other drug use following every war for which data have been collected.[3] Based on my extensive research, this goes back to at least the Civil War. One only has to reflect on Vietnam for a clear example of the devastation and escalation of substance abuse among veterans and their families following the war.

Despite this well-known fact, the U.S. was seven years into OEF and six years into OIF before the military and federal agencies were pulled together to discuss and strategize ways to address war-related substance-abuse and mental-health problems among active-duty military and reservists, and OEF and OIF veterans.

The Links Between PTSD and Substance Abuse

As a hallmark of these wars, PTSD has been linked directly to atrocities veterans have witnessed and, in some cases, perpetrated. Improvised incendiary explosive devices (IED's) and bombings have been hallmarks of both OEF and OIF. As a result, many soldiers who have seen combat have witnessed the instantaneous decimation of the human body from an explosion and have come in contact with fragments of human beings. Understandably, veterans who have handled human remains have higher levels of PTSD symptoms than their fellow soldiers who have not. Furthermore, substance abuse is likely to be triggered in an effort to self-medicate and manage their PTSD symptomology.[4] The combat events that many soldiers have witnessed have increased their risk for PTSD, suicidal ideation, and substance abuse.

Combat-related PTSD symptoms generally are grouped into three symptomatic categories: hyper-arousal and increased startle responses, re-experiencing of the traumatic event, and withdrawal or avoidance behavior and emotional numbing.[5] These symptomatic categories often trigger one another. Memories and re-experiencing are triggers that incite the need to numb and avoid the intense feeling this brings about. Thus, alcohol and other drugs are often used and adapted as coping mechanisms for emotional numbing and avoidance.[6] When PTSD is coupled with alcoholism, the likelihood of suicidal ideation increases nearly tenfold.[7]

The Effects of Close Combat in OEF and OIF

Killing is one of the objectives of war, and the closer the killer is to his human targets, the greater the emotional toll. Similar to Vietnam, there has been closeness between killer and target in the current wars in Iraq and Afghanistan. This relationship inevitably affects today's soldiers as it did during the Civil War, the Vietnam War, and other close-combat incursions. "Physical distance between enemies facilitates emotional distance from destructive acts."[8] Whereas high-tech precision warfare puts distance between soldiers and killing, OEF and OIF soldiers are engaged in close-contact combat, often in populated areas where enemy combatants and innocent civilians are indistinguishable.

For some soldiers there is an addictive thrill to the adrenaline of combat and the rush of hunting another human being. In the 2009 documentary *The Good Soldier*, Iraq War Veteran Staff Sergeant James Massey confesses he was caught up in the adrenaline-fueled bloodlust. Reflecting on the mental state that made him a formidable soldier during the Iraq War, he states "there is no other feeling in the world that comes close to hunting another human being.... It is as addictive as any drug." In response to what he observed to be the killing of innocent and unarmed civilians in Iraq, his view of killing changed, and the hook of the adrenaline dissipated. Haunted by the memories, Massey now protests the war in Iraq and atones for his actions, carrying a placard proclaiming, "I killed innocent civilians for our government."

OEF- and OIF-Related Suicide and Substance Abuse

With a suicide rate double the U.S. national average, substance abuse and suicide among servicemen and women has become front and center for the U.S. military.[9,10] Much to their credit, the Army has undertaken unprecedented efforts during wartime to study and address these problems. Each day, five U.S. soldiers try to kill themselves, representing a five-fold increase from before the start of OEF and OIF. The rate of suicide among OEF and OIF veterans has been escalating, with present rates double the already-high rate of 115 suicides among the Army branch in 2007, with another 2,100 soldiers attempting suicide.[11] In 2009, among just the Army branch of the military, there were 74 drug-overdose deaths and 239 suicides (160 in active duty, 79 reservists) and another 1,713 known suicide attempts.[12] Upon examination of the circumstances behind these deaths, the Army found a direct link between increased military-life stressors and the service members' high-risk behavior (self-harm, illicit drug use, binge drinking, criminal activity, etc.).

In previous wars, soldiers have been provided regular periods of rest and recuperation, with troops rotating between periods of prolonged combat. This has not been the practice in OEF and OIF deployment, where troops are often engaged in daily combat operations lasting 10 to 12 hours each.[13] This level of sustained combat and repeated deployment exceeds the historical practices of U.S. military. At no other time in our history have troops been required to serve on the front lines in heavy combat zones for up to a year or more without significant time breaks to allow them to recover from the physical, psychological, or emotional strains experienced in combat. With two simultaneous wars underway, OEF and OIF service members are at the breaking point because they have faced deployment after deployment without the rest, recovery, and treatment they need.

Armed-forces personnel are subject to an array of stressors as part of their military work assignments and duties, well beyond the stress civilians face. The stressors include the rigors of service, long and repeated deployments, increased demands due to personnel shortages, combat trauma, life-altering injuries, and separations from family that result in a sense of isolation, hopelessness, and life fatigue. Alcohol consumption, stress, and emotional problems are interrelated, with a particularly robust connection between stressful life events and depression for women in the military, and stress and alcohol abuse for servicemen.[14] Because the military operates as a cohesive unit, the actions and moods of each individual affects his or her unit as a whole. In relation to this, the Army has noted a troubling subset population who increasingly place themselves and their fellow service members at risk by using and distributing illicit drugs and prescription drugs.

The illicit trade of licit prescribed drugs is a growing problem because of the proliferation of prescriptions for stimulants (amphetamines) and pain-management drugs (synthetic opiates). In 2009, approximately 106,000 Army soldiers were prescribed medications for pain, depression, or anxiety that carry with them a high potential for addiction and abuse.[15] Although the Army is increasingly prescribing addictive pain medications, they will not provide coverage for veterans who become addicted to pain medication—even when the addiction is the result of using the drug as prescribed for pain resulting from a combat injury.[16]

The Army has become increasingly vigilant about the use of opiates, particularly in light of the increased prescribing of synthetic opiates (e.g., Oxycodone, Oxycontin). To assess the extent of possible abuse and addiction, they measure the level of authorized (legal as prescribed) and unauthorized (illegal abuse) use. Due to the increasing prevalence of drug prescriptions to members of the military, the Army has a substantial problem with drug diversion and dealing of prescription drugs.[17]

Prescription-drug abuse is not the only problem for OEF and OIF service members. Heroin use is becoming ever more prevalent and is now included in the Army's routine drug screening. Between 2008 and 2009, the rate of unauthorized opiate use rose as a result of the increasing use of heroin by soldiers who were tested.[18] The U.S. Army public documents do not make reference to the source of heroin; however, news reports from Afghanistan have reported on the ease with which anyone can buy heroin in the local markets, such as the Bagram Bazaar.[19] Given the fact that OEF is being fought in the region where 90 percent of the world's heroin is produced, one would assume that the heroin is coming from Afghanistan.

As was the case in Vietnam, military medics are often known to be the "dealers." As a soldier, they are your best bet if you are looking to get drugs of any kind.[20] Soldiers describe it as a "don't ask, don't tell" policy in the military, with vastly differing opinions concerning drug use from one level of authority to the next. The collection and reporting of illicit drug use and abuse of prescription narcotics carries with it great risk for active military personnel. The statistics provided by the U.S. military regarding the rates of alcohol and other drug abuse by soldiers are considered by most to be an underrepresentation of the actual problem, because they are primarily based on random urine screens. The military does periodically conduct surveys of self-reported alcohol and other drug use, such as the 2005 Department of Defense Health Behavior Survey.

Conducting routine urine drug screens is not the primary concern for a military that has been overextended, facing two close-combat wars in hostile territories with troops on extended deployment. Alcohol and other drug abuse is steadily rising, and soldiers are returning home with life-altering drug addictions and health-related problems, including those soldiers who have taken adulterated drugs obtained in Iraq and Afghanistan.

Stimulants for Performance Enhancement

The concern about substance abuse and addiction is not only related to illicit drug use. U.S. soldiers in Iraq use amphetamines in "prescribed and legitimate doses" to stay alert during 36-hour missions conducted in scorching 110-degree heat. The use of stimulant drugs in these scenarios is similar to the dispensing of amphetamines to soldiers during World War II, and it illustrates how drugs are used to achieve the necessary or desired mindset to undertake physically and emotionally stressful missions; however, their secondhand impact cannot be underestimated.

The need for licit (legal and medically prescribed) stimulants increases when combat fatigue hits, which is particularly evident with repeated deployments and the long missions characteristic of OEF and OIF. Additionally, stimulants are used to enhance performance during military maneuvers; however, they also increase anxiety, stress, and tension. During emotionally stressful events, such as combat, there is an increase in the neurotransmitter dopamine that is released in the brain, which makes the events more salient by laying deeper tracks in the person's long-term memory. The presence of stimulants in the bloodstream, coupled with the increase in dopamine during exposure to trauma and stress, is believed to more deeply embed the memory of the event.[21] Therefore, the use of stimulants during military operations may stimulate energy and alertness while negatively affecting emotional states by carving traumatic experiences into a person's memory.

The amphetamine Dexedrine (a.k.a. speed) is referred to in the Air Force as "go-pills," and the pills are to be taken by fighter pilots to help them stay awake and alert on their missions.[22] This has been a pilot practice dating back to World War II; it continues to this day with the exception of a brief ban on the use of stimulants following Desert Storm.[23] In 2002, two American fighter pilots, Major Harry Schmidt and Major William Umbach, killed four Canadian soldiers near Kandahar, Afghanistan, because the pilots mistakenly thought the Canadian soldiers were shooting at them. Their court defense attributed the pilots' actions to the Air Force–issued stimulant drugs they were taking at the time. The pilots had been taking the stimulant Dexedrine during the flight, under the standard-order guidelines of their commander.

In a statement to the press during the trial, Colonel Peter Demitry, chief of the U.S. Air Force surgeon-general's science and technology division, said of the practice of dispensing "go-pills": "It is the gold standard for anti-fatigue. We know that fatigue in aviation kills.... This is a life-and-death insurance policy that saves lives.... This is a common, legal, ethical, moral and correct application."[24]

Today, when pilots are finished with their missions, they are provided with Ambien or Restoril, the "no-pills," to bring them down and help them sleep and adjust after defying the body's circadian rhythms and altering neurotransmitter levels with amphetamines. The lawyer for Major Schmidt noted that the depressant sleep aid Ambien, which was given to Schmidt to help him sleep before the mission, also affected his mental state when he bombed the Canadians.

Stimulants such as the Dexadrine dispensed by the Air Force are addictive, as are the depressant sleep aids dispensed, such as Ambien. These drugs are highly regulated prescription medications for the general population because of the rapid rates of dependency, their high potential for abuse, and their health and safety risks. Dexadrine is produced by United Kingdom–based GlaxoSmithKline (GSK). GSK's own literature includes a warning that the drug has "high potential for abuse" and "may impair the ability of the patient to engage in potentially hazardous activities, such as operating machinery or vehicles." Flying an F-16 most certainly qualifies under the category of "operating machinery or vehicles." Cycling on and off stimulants, particularly through the use of depressant drugs to counteract the stimulants, causes instability in brain chemistry and disrupts the natural levels of neurotransmitters. Together, these factors can make the individual taking the drugs more susceptible to depression, anxiety, and addiction. As was the case in World War II, the use of heavy doses of stimulants—particularly chronic use—causes distorted thinking, paranoia, hyper-vigilance, aggression, and "trigger-happy" behavior.

The percentage of all people in chemical-dependency treatment who are military veterans rises and falls in direct relation to the U.S. engagement in war. As one would expect, the trauma of war impacts those who served and increases their risk of substance abuse. Figure 12-1 illustrates the steady decline in veterans in treatment for substance abuse following the 1991 Gulf War and the dramatic increase following the U.S. engagements in OEF and OIF. This graph was created by the author from the U.S. data set for all U.S. residents, covering the time period from 1992 to 2006.

Illicit drugs are not the most prevalent problem for OEF and OIF veterans and active military. Alcohol and recreational use of prescription drugs are the two most common substances of abuse today.[25] Figure 12-2 demonstrates the precipitous increase in military personnel and veterans being admitted to treatment for opiates (codeine, heroin, morphine, opium) and synthetic opiates (pharmaceuticals such as Vicodin, Oxycontin, Dilaudid). According to data from the 2005 Survey of Health Related Behaviors among Military Personnel and the National Survey on Drug Use and Health, military personnel are more likely than civilians to binge drink. Overall, 43 percent of active-duty military personnel report binge drinking, compared to 27 percent of national household residents.

While active-duty military personnel had higher rates of alcohol abuse and binge drinking across all age groups, the largest differences were found between underage youth ages 17 to 20 (44 percent military vs. 33 percent civilian) and young adults ages 21 to 25 (60 percent military vs. 46 percent civilian). Researchers have also found that the more recently a service member was deployed, the more likely he was to report moderately heavy to heavy levels of alcohol use.

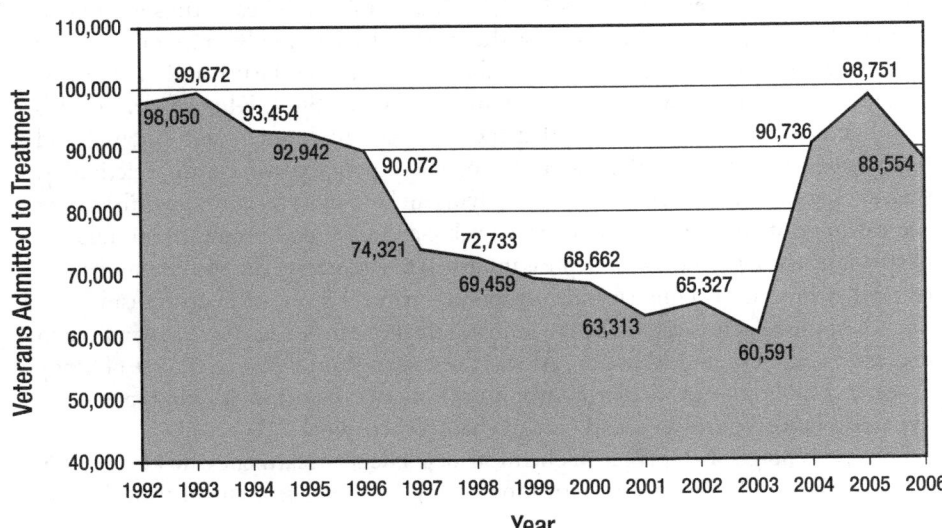

**Figure 12-1 Veterans Admitted to Treatment
for Chemical Dependency, 1992–2006**

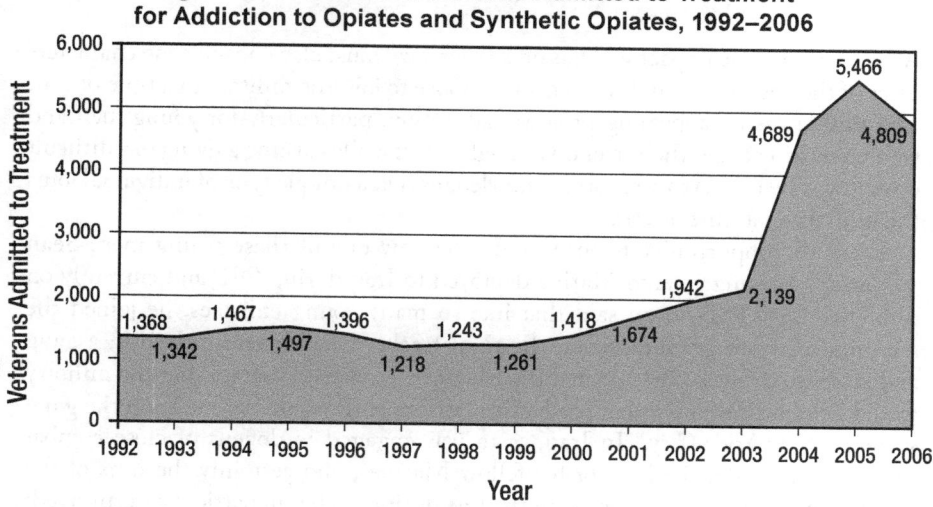

Figure 12-2 Number of Veterans Admitted to Treatment for Addiction to Opiates and Synthetic Opiates, 1992–2006

Figure 12-3 illustrates how alcohol use escalates in conjunction with recent deployment, although oddly enough, the rate of heavier alcohol use is higher among those who have never been deployed than among those who were deployed more than three years ago.[26] Noting that "most alcohol programs in the military have tended to focus exclusively on screening and treating alcoholism," researchers recommend that more preventive public health and policy efforts be implemented, such as increasing the price of alcoholic beverages on military bases, establishing and enforcing rules to restrict alcohol use in dormitories, singles housing on base, and onboard ships.[27]

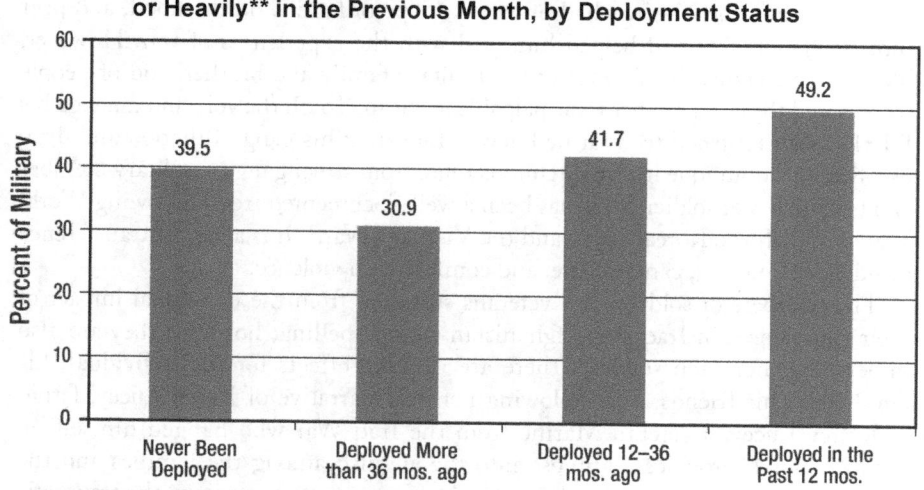

Figure 12-3 Percent of U.S. Military Who Drank Moderately to Heavily* or Heavily** in the Previous Month, by Deployment Status

* Moderately heavy = 5+ drinks in a row two to three times per month
** Heavy = 5+ drinks in a row one or more times per week

OEF and OIF Soldiers

As we consider the impact war has on soldiers, we must also consider the character- istics of the young men and women who choose to join the military in a time of war. The military is an appealing professional option, particularly for young men and women seeking to get their lives on the right track while earning a living in a difficult economy. The U.S. Army report acknowledges that a unique type of individual joins the military in a time of war.

I had the opportunity to meet and interview one of these young men: Sean Thomas,[28] a young veteran Marine deployed to Iraq during OIF and currently on disability for PTSD. Sean said that like so many young enlistees, he joined the Marines to try to get himself on the right track. "I had been involved in a gang and was into drugs before I joined the Marines. I believed that joining the military would help me develop into a productive citizen while removing me from the gang scene in New York City." In Iraq, Sean was engaged in dozens of close-combat situations. His life, the lives of his fellow Marines, and certainly the lives of the combatants he was fighting were on the line during each gun battle. Sean survived; many of his close friends did not. As reflected by the tattoo on his arm bearing the number "13," at least 13 of the combatants he fought were killed. I interviewed Sean as part of my research for this book, and despite all that I had read about the impact of war on soldiers, I was surprised by the acute awareness soldiers like Sean have with regard to the individuals they may kill in combat. Sean is a bright, physically intimidating young man who commands control of his environment. Yet the emotion and empathy conveyed in his soulful eyes as he talked about killing in combat provided a window into the confused and distant place he returns to when he recalls his combat experiences.

When Sean returned to the U.S., he found himself "unprepared to deal with life after the war." The Marines had provided a type of family, brotherhood, and peer support system that had helped him deal with the experiences of war. However, like many veterans, the absence of the military family and brotherhood of people who shared these experiences was palpable for Sean. To fill the void and manage his PTSD, Sean returned to what he knew before Iraq: his gang affiliation and drug use. Sean is not unique in this circuitous route from street gang to military member and back to street soldier. This has been a well-documented trend following World Wars I and II, the Korean War, and the Vietnam War.[29] It is a logical transference of skills: risk-taking, camaraderie, and comfort with violence.

The numbers of soldiers and veterans suffering from the emotional impact of their experiences in Iraq and Afghanistan are compelling; however, they are also impersonal. For each statistic, there are rippling effects for the individual, his family, and his friends. The following personal narrative of Kevin Lucey, father of Jeffrey Lucey, a veteran Marine from the Iraq War who hanged himself on June 22, 2004, provides a glimpse into the anguish among the families and the individuals who take their own lives in a desperate attempt to escape the traumatic memories of war.

The night before Jeffrey Lucey hanged himself, he asked his father if he could sit in his lap and rock.

> It was about 11:30 at night. And I rocked him for about 45 minutes. Now here you have a 23-year-old, 150-pound Marine that I'm just rocking, and his therapist said it was his last gasp. It was his last place for refuge, and then the next time I held him in my lap was when I was taking him down from the rafters. He had put the hose around his neck double-looped, and he was dead.[30]

Jeffrey Lucey was receiving mental-health treatment and had a very supportive family environment; however, for some emotionally tortured veterans, it is simply not enough. For them, suicide seems like a resolution to their desperation to escape their own internal thoughts. Although this illustrates a suicide and is not necessarily substance abuse–related, it provides aching insight into the residual emotional toll war has on veterans and their families, leaving them vulnerable to substance abuse.

Desperate Measures: The Sanctioned Use of MDMA to Prevent Suicide and Alleviate PTSD Among Veterans of the Wars in Afghanistan and Iraq

Due to the severity of the mental and physical burden OEF and OIF veterans are experiencing, therapists and researchers are desperately pursuing daring and bold treatments. The federal government has funded research for clinical trials to treat veterans suffering from PTSD with MDMA, which is scientifically known as 3,4-methylenedioxy-N-methylamphetamine; on the streets, it is known as "E," "X," or Ecstasy. MDMA is both a stimulant and a hallucinogen that fosters feelings of empathy, closeness, and emotional warmth. Researchers hope to help veterans discuss traumatic situations without triggering anxiety, thereby enabling them to work through flashbacks and recurring nightmares.[31]

Prior to this, it had been decades since the Department of Defense had conducted studies on animals using MDMA. In the 1950s, the U.S. Army conducted lethal-dose studies on animals of MDMA mixed with other compounds.[32] MDMA resurfaced as a therapeutic drug in the late 1970s before becoming a notoriously popular recreational club drug in the 1980s and 1990s. In the 1970s, MDMA was used to treat PTSD among Vietnam veterans, prior to becoming a controlled drug in 1985, categorized as a Schedule I illicit substance by the DEA. Schedule I drugs are deemed highly addictive with no therapeutic value.[33] There was considerable debate on the inappropriate Schedule I status the DEA placed on MDMA. When used in a controlled therapeutic setting, MDMA has been found to be effective in treating trauma. However, due to the widespread abuse of the drug in the 1980s and 1990s, concerns remain regarding the potential for a resurgence of abuse and recreational use.

Scientist Dr. Michael Mithoefer is among a growing group of researchers who believe that the feelings of emotional closeness experienced by people on Ecstasy may help soldiers talk about their experiences to therapists and work through their combat- or deployment-related trauma. Dr. Mithoefer is the psychiatrist leading a significant clinical research study with MDMA. He reported in 2009 that it was early to draw conclusions, but for people with severe PTSD, such as veterans, who were not responding to other PTSD treatments, the preliminary research findings on MDMA were very encouraging.[34]

In contrast to the empathy of MDMA, chemists have also been developing drugs that could enable soldiers to kill without guilt and remorse, which raises significant ethical and moral questions about the extent to which society needs to preserve the psychological and physical cost of war as a check against man's inhumanity toward man.[35] Dr. Roger Pitman of Harvard University has been leading research on the use of the drug Propranolol to reduce PTSD among automobile-accident victims. Pitman asserts that as a society we need to preserve the psychological and physical cost of war as a deterrent. He does not support the use of drugs for the alleviation of guilt, remorse, and trauma in the context of war. As he describes it, these feelings need to exist as a check against inhumanity.[36] Reflecting on the decades of CIA and Department of Defense drug development and testing on civilians that I discussed in Chapter 8, the scientific community has reason for concern over the ways in which such drugs may be co-opted and used once they are developed.

Conclusion

The high rates of mental health and behavioral adjustment problems among recent U.S. military combat veterans are marked by the increasing rates of substance abuse, PTSD, depression, and suicide among military personnel. It is critical that a country develop early identification, referral, and treatment for combat-related PTSD and substance abuse to reduce suffering, severity of impairment, and homelessness.[37]

As Washington State Senator Patty Murray noted in 2006: although hundreds of millions of dollars have been put forth to improve the military's ability to provide mental-health treatment to those in need, it will take more than money to resolve the problem. Murray noted that, "It takes leadership and it takes a change in the culture of war."[38] There is hope in the fact that soldiers and veterans are increasingly seeking help in the form of counseling and behavioral healthcare. In 2009, the Army recorded more than 225,000 behavioral health contacts, indicating that the Army and its soldiers recognize the importance of seeking support. The stigma associated with accessing counseling is decreasing, and military leaders realize the importance of intervention and support for soldiers in crisis.[39]

The Department of Defense and branches of the military note that there is still a resistant subset population who increasingly place themselves and their fellow service members at risk by refusing help, taking unnecessary risks, and using and distributing drugs. In addition to traditional psychiatric treatment and medication, evidence-based practices to prevent PTSD include teaching skills to enhance cognitive fitness and psychological resilience (e.g., Battlemind Training, mindfulness meditation) that can reduce the detrimental impact of trauma.[40]

Although there has been unprecedented wartime focus on addressing substance abuse and PTSD among U.S. troops, it is important to note that these can be lifelong progressive problems that require cultivated ongoing care. Left untreated, these conditions increase the risk of addiction, suicide, and homelessness.[41] Fortunately, as a society, the U.S. today seems to better recognize the importance of accepting and supporting our veterans, regardless of our personal support for the war they fought in.

CHAPTER 13

Conclusion

The Seven-Generations Cost of War

Make sure every decision we make relates to the welfare and well-being of the seventh generation to come.... We consider: Will this be to the benefit of the seventh generation?

Iroquois chief as quoted by Jeremy Rifkin
in *Time Wars: The Primary Conflict in Human History*[1]

THE IROQUOIS (HAUDENOSAUNEE), an association of Native American Indian tribes in North America, have a seven-generations philosophy that governs their actions. They believe that we not only must consider the impact of our decisions and actions on the present generation, but also contemplate, calculate, and project the potential impact each action may have on the next seven generations. When applied to ripple effects of war and drug trafficking, the seven-generations view illustrates the potential for each person to be profoundly affected by current and historical incidents.

The human web of connections links each of us. Policy decisions going back many generations can have a far-reaching impact on each and every person. But possibly nowhere is the seven-generations principle captured so demonstrably as through the ripple effect that each war has had on the global evolution of addiction. For centuries the political, physical, and psychological impacts of wars have contributed to the proliferation and use of drugs, including alcohol. The intergenerational impact of trauma among groups of people affected by war, including the social upheaval, is an emerging field of study, and we are just beginning to understand the echo effects on generations.

Understanding the effects of intergenerational trauma among Native Americans provides insight into the ways in which unsettled trauma results in collective emotional and psychological injury over an individual's lifespan and across generations.[2] Native Americans' history of subjection to genocide, racism, and refugee resettlement on reservations has resulted in disproportionate rates of alcoholism (five times the national average) and suicide rates more than double the national average.[3] In addition to the effect intergenerational trauma has on alcoholism and drug abuse, for those living on reservations and in sovereign nations, poverty and lack of law enforcement contribute to the conditions that perpetuate intergenerational trauma.

Narco-Funding for War, Paramilitary Groups, and Terrorist Organizations

This book began with an examination of the duality of war and drugs, examining the Opium Wars, and then followed the subsequent seven-plus generations of evolving drug cultivation, trafficking, addiction, and trauma in relation to military incursions, the Cold War, the War on Drugs, and the War on Terror. We also have examined how the trajectory was further complicated by the Cold War and the CIA's quid-pro-quo alliances and clandestine operations, which inadvertently supported rogue groups and their drug cultivation and trafficking in support of government and political interests. During armed conflict, history has witnessed cycles of increased illicit drug production and trafficking. Resumption of international peacetime conditions enables governments to refocus on drug diplomacy; however, during wartime, the drug trade takes a backseat to more pressing wartime matters.

The history of the Cold War has much to teach us about the dangerous environment that can be created by a fear-based singular view of global affairs, as occurred during the Cold War. America's insecurities have resurfaced through the vulnerabilities exposed by the terrorist attacks of September 11, 2001. To conceal these insecurities, a visible portion of the American culture has embraced a gun-slinging cowboy swagger.[4] A post-9/11 rhetoric has been fueled by extremist politicians and fear-based media to evoke the masculine image of the Cold Warrior in need of unchecked power to take whatever actions necessary to protect our country against the enemy.

We cannot repeat the behaviors of the past by replacing the threat of communism with terrorism to generate public fear, simply to enable the abuse of authority by people who capitalize on fear to amass influence, power, and control. Public disclosure and civilian accountability requirements in the U.S., Canada, and much of Europe should safeguard against the type of government-related Cold War civilian narcotics experiments that took place (e.g., MK-ULTRA, Project Bluebird, and Project Artichoke) and CIA complicity in drug trafficking (e.g., the Vietnam War and the Iran-Contra Affair). However, rogue nation states and terrorist organizations have no such safeguards and are not bound by any national or international policy. As noted by the U.S. Senate Select Committee on Intelligence, the same forces of globalization that can improve our lives also empower the rogue forces of disintegration (e.g., terrorist organizations) and drug traffickers, which are destroying lives.[5]

The Terrorist Nature of Drug Cartels and Criminal Syndicates

Over the past century, it is estimated that nearly 200 million human beings, mostly civilians, have died in wars. In the book *The Most Dangerous Animal: Human Nature and the Origins of War*, author David Smith notes that there is no end in sight to the slaughter. He poses two key questions that are at the root of war's suffering. Smith asks the reader to examine "What is it about human nature that makes it possible for human beings to regularly slaughter their own kind?" and "Why are we our own worst enemy?"[6] These inquiries are strikingly similar to the key statements and questions posed to people battling alcohol and other drug addictions: "Would you let another person treat you as badly as you treat yourself?" and "You are your own worst enemy." Both war and addiction are human afflictions.

Today's wars are not being fought on staged battlefields; for the most part, they are not even being fought between nation-states. They are more likely to be dispersed insurgency attacks against a government or coordinated terrorist acts against citizens. The insurgents and terrorists are motivated by religious, cultural, and jingoistic ideologies. Central Asia and the Middle East have become fertile grounds for cultivating vicious ideologues. Their power and funding have increasingly depended on international drug trafficking. Sixty percent of terrorist organizations have some ties with the narcotics trade. The connection between terrorist groups and drugs has been evident for decades.

In 1998, the United Nations Secretariat considered terrorism to be the most visible and openly aggressive form of transnational organized crime—specifically, the illicit trafficking of drugs, arms, and people.[7] The exponential growth in opium and cannabis cultivation in Afghanistan following the start of Operation Enduring Freedom has resulted in devastating rates of addiction in Afghanistan and neighboring Iran and Pakistan, in addition to its target markets in Europe and Australia. Addiction and violence hava also escalated along Afghanistan's trafficking routes and primary transit points in Africa and Central Asia.

War Fosters Alcohol and Other Drug Abuse as a Refuge from War and PTSD

In World War I, it was known as shell shock; during World War II, it was called combat fatigue. Traumatized Vietnam veterans were said to experience flashbacks; today, we understand the post-war emotional and psychosomatic trauma as post-traumatic stress disorder (PTSD). Civilians from war-torn regions are also affected by PTSD. Many lose their family members, homes, and community. PTSD is characterized by hyper-vigilance, hyper-arousal, intrusive memories, panic attacks, and the avoidance of situations that trigger memories and result in anxiety attacks and reliving wartime experiences.

The aftermath of Vietnam has shown us how the living casualties of war (civilians, refugees, and veterans) manifest as depression, suicide, alcohol and other drug abuse, homelessness, withdrawal, and displacement. Although sometimes the symptoms are immediately apparent, they often emerge in association with life stressors, bereavement, social isolation, and chronic medical illness. It often takes a decade or more before veterans enter the system seeking treatment for PTSD, and for some the diagnosis has been delayed for more than 30 years following their service.[8]

Regardless of formal diagnosis, veterans and survivors of war-torn regions have long suffered from the psychological trauma of what they've witnessed, and many spend a lifetime suppressing these memories with alcohol and other drugs. For decades following the Vietnam War, society witnessed growing numbers of homeless and addicted veterans who struggled socially, psychologically, politically, and economically because of unaddressed and underlying PTSD. Failure to address post-combat challenges often leads to problematic relationships, chemical dependency, depression, and anxiety and is associated with rising rates of suicide among military personnel and veterans.

The world has yet to realize the impact of the wars in Iraq and Afghanistan by these measures. The rate of substance abuse among OEF and OIF veterans is believed to be much higher than it was among Vietnam veterans. The fact that the degree of substance abuse and mental-health problems is being measured during wartime has raised the warning flags early, but it is also a hopeful sign that OEF and OIF veterans won't be abandoned.

Based on documented numbers of homeless veterans, it is estimated that 300,000 veterans are homeless at some point during any given year, and 70 percent (210,000) of them suffer from alcohol or drug abuse. There has also been a rise in the number of homeless female veterans, concomitant with their increasingly active role in the military and combat exposure. The societal impact of homeless veterans from OEF and OIF is yet unknown. However, among all of today's homeless veterans, 47 percent served in Vietnam more than 40 years ago.[9] Identifying effective strategies for prevention and effective intervention of PTSD among those affected by war benefits the individuals, their families, and society at large.

Geopolitical and Economic Linkages Between War and Drugs

Among those who traffic and cultivate drugs, the narcotics primarily are linked to economics, at least initially. Despite the economic links to the drug trade, the war on poverty has not followed the same type of escalating pattern. Perhaps this is in part because we have not used force and criminalization against poverty; it does not make sense to do so.

The use of the term "war" against a condition (addiction) or a commodity (drugs) undermines our ability to effectively confront the core of this problem. As Carl Trocki observed, present-day anti-drug policies are directed primarily by the world's leading economic nations. Moreover, for most of the current leading nations, drug-based economics have played a significant role in the construction of their modern state, and they have been stepping stones of a capitalist political economy. Yet there is a clear understanding that drugs and narco-based economies destroy and undermine political and social order. The question then becomes whether the drugs are the problem or the economic order is the problem.[10]

The nexus between war, the drug trade, and economic instability is evident in the 2010 United Nations Security Council Resolution 1540 conference on non-proliferation of weapons of mass destruction (WMD) and the accompanying conference report titled "WMD, Drugs, and Criminal Gangs in Central America: Leveraging Nonproliferation Assistance to Address Security/Development Needs with UN Security Council Resolution 1540." The report and the summit clearly map the triangulation between the risk of WMD proliferation in a region, drug trafficking, and economic and political instability. The report concludes that in order to take and enforce effective measures against the proliferation of WMD, counterdrug efforts and drug-related gangs must simultaneously be addressed, along with economic development.

The Addicted as Entities Separate from the Criminal Enterprise

I began writing this book just prior to the 2008 U.S. presidential election of Barack Obama and the transition from the Bush Administration to the Obama Administration. As President Obama and his administration were taking office in early 2009, the drug war was escalating in Mexico, particularly along the U.S.-Mexico border. Among the first public actions taken by the Obama Administration's new head of the Office of National Drug Control Policy (ONDCP), Gil Kerlikowske, was repudiating the "war" on drugs stance that has dominated U.S. policy and practice for nearly 40 years. Concomitant with Kerlikowske's denouncement of warfare rhetoric, U.S. Secretary of State Hillary Rodham Clinton publicly stated that the U.S. demand for drugs must be addressed if there is any hope of stemming the supply side of narcotics trafficking—a nod toward the need for prevention, harm reduction, and a public-health approach to addiction.

In light of the escalation of drug-related violence in Mexico, the national tone has again shifted away from drug use as a public-health issue with mankind as the referent object and back to drugs as an existential international threat, and organized crime and drug trafficking as the referent objects. Often missing in the discussion is the fact that the drugs provide such enormous profit to criminal organizations because they are illegal. Making drugs legal and centrally controlled would not reduce substance abuse or addiction, but it would break the criminal enterprises at the center of current drug policy. Governments may be unwilling to consider drug legalization, regulation, and control not because they would not work, but because they would work to weaken and disengage criminal elements involved in drug cultivation and trafficking.

From a public-health and safety perspective, this statement is illogical. From a security standpoint, it may not be, considering the perspective that it is better to deal with the devil you know than the devil you don't know. This means that there are global systems for dealing with drug-related crime, and criminal enterprises will never be eliminated.[11] If narcotics were legalized tomorrow, criminal organizations would move on to other illicit means of making massive money, and whatever that may be could be worse. We have already seen the expansion of mafia, cartels, and transnational organized crime expanding to weapons trafficking, human trafficking, trafficking of human organs, and dangerous dealings with radioactive materials. Therefore, from the government or political perspective of managing security threats, drugs are the known entity.

A kinder, gentler approach to addiction may seem paradoxical in the context of the drug-related violence in neighboring Mexico. However, since Mexico increased the nation's militaristic force against narco-traffickers, the violence perpetrated by the cartels and their profits have grown exponentially. In response to the escalating violence in Mexico and along the Southwest border of the U.S., the Obama Administration has responded with increased financial and technological support, such as predator drone planes, to support Mexico's drug war. Although Obama has reframed our drug problem by acknowledging that with "far too many suffering from addiction here at home, never has it been more important to have a national drug control strategy guided by sound principles of public safety and public health," there have not been improvements in access to, payment for, or availability of drug treatment, despite the passage of the Mental Health Parity and Addiction Equity Act (MHPAEA) in 2008 under President Bush. As of 2011, funding for drug treatment and prevention has not increased; however, the funding for interdiction at the border and financial support of Mexico's military has risen significantly.

ONDCP Director Kerlikowske also characterizes America's drug problem as "one of human suffering." This contrasts the language that George H.W. Bush used to describe the War on Drugs, which evoked more martial methods. In 1989, during one of his first national speeches, President Bush characterized his approach toward the War on Drugs as "Malice toward many. Charity toward none." His stance toward the drug war was an inversion of a statement from Abraham Lincoln's second inaugural address, in which he said, "Malice towards none and charity for all."[12] The difference in the language and rhetoric is noteworthy. Time will tell whether the change in tone is accompanied by a public-health approach and a shift toward treatment, demand reduction, prevention, and reconciliation.

Concluding Thoughts and Provocations

The face of war has changed dramatically in recent decades. It seems that it is also time to change our relationship with drugs and reexamine national and global policies with consideration given to the role drugs have played in military incursions, colonization, funding for oppositional forces, and the cresting wave of addiction. A simplistic single-sided approach that focuses only on the criminal element is no more the answer than suggestions to legalize all drugs. Europe, the U.S., and increasingly the international community are refocusing on the public-health aspect of drug use, separating drug-related medical, etiological, and social issues from that of drug trafficking and control problems.[13] It bears repeating that drugs are not harmful simply because they are illegal; drugs have been made illegal and controlled because they are dangerous.

Through the historical review of nearly two centuries of wars, this book has examined the linkages between drugs as a funding source for colonization, war, paramilitary groups, and terrorist organizations. This account of modern history has illustrated the underlying geopolitical, economic, and structural elements that link war and drugs to one another. The latter chapters have examined the increasingly terrorist nature of drug cartels/criminal syndicates and their parallels with the cartel-financed terrorist organizations. Although each chapter has addressed a specified period of conflict, each has illustrated how war has fostered alcohol and other drug use as a refuge from brutality and posttraumatic stress.

It is my hope that through the background presented here, the reader has been encouraged to develop a humanistic approach to the prevention and treatment of substance abuse, rather than simply to continue to view drugs as legalistic, militaristic, or prohibitionist issues. This is particularly salient when we consider the disproportionately high rates of substance abuse in people affected by the trauma of war. Through the reframing of the user as a human being independent from the violence and the criminal enterprise of the drug trade, innovative and effective approaches to the prevention of addiction may emerge.

This book has taken an international analytical view of the connections between drug use, the regions impacted by military incursion, the experiences of military personnel, and the civilian communities to which they return. As much as this book has illustrated the linkages of drug use and trafficking from one war to the next, it also calls upon the reader to ask: How will we know if and when we have won the War on Drugs—or the War on Terror, for that matter? And what will the impact be in seven generations from these wars? When drugs and addiction are examined in the absence of a threat-based view of drugs as a security threat, a policy vista opens up that currently remains firmly closed, one that offers significantly improved outcomes.[14]

Notes

Chapter 1

1. Carter, Jimmy. "Call Off the Global Drug War." *The New York Times.* June 16, 2011. http://www.nytimes.com/2011/06/17/opinion/17carter.html. Accessed on June 20, 2011.

2. Massing, Michael. *The Fix.* New York: Simon & Schuster, 1998. Print. 109.

3. Woolley, John T. and Gerhard Peters. "Richard Nixon: Statement on Establishing the Office for Drug Abuse Law Enforcement." *The American Presidency Project.* http://www .presidency.ucsb.edu/ws/?pid=3552. Accessed on July 14, 2011

4. Massing, Michael. *The Fix.* New York: Simon & Schuster, 1998. Print. 126.

5. Carlsen, Laura. "Militarizing Mexico: The New War on Drugs." *Foreign Policy in Focus: International Affairs, Peace, Justice, and Environment.* Ed. John Feffer. July 11, 2007. http://www.fpif.org/articles/militarizing_mexico_the_new_war_on_drugs. Accessed on July 16, 2011.

6. McCoy, Alfred W. *The Politics of Heroin: CIA Complicity in the Global Drug Trade, Afghanistan, Southeast Asia, Central America, Colombia.* Chicago: Lawrence Hill, 2003. Print. 113.

7. Cockburn, Alexander and Jeffrey St. Clair. *Whiteout: The CIA, Drugs, and the Press.* London: Verso, 1999. Print.

8. Scott, D. L. "Honduras, the Contra Support Networks, and Cocaine: How the U.S. Government Has Augmented America's Drug Crisis." In Block, Alan A. and Alfred W. McCoy. *War on Drugs: Studies in the Failure of US Narcotics Policy.* Boulder, CO: Westview, 1992. Print. 126–127.

9. Gintis, Herbert. *Game Theory Evolving: A Problem-Centered Introduction to Modeling Strategic Behavior.* Princeton, NJ: Princeton UP, 2000. Print.

10. Archibold, C. A. "U.S. Moves Against Top Mexican Drug Cartel." *The New York Times.* http://www.nytimes.com/2009/02/26/us/26raids.html.

11. DiNardo J. and T. Lemieux. "Alcohol, Marijuana, and American Youth: The Unintended Effects of Government Regulation." *Journal of Health Economics* 20.6: (2001) 991–1010.

12. Guse, S. L. *The Military and the Drug War: Operational Art at an Impasse?* Naval War College Report No. A512523. 1997. Print.

13. Hathaway, A. D. and P.G. Erickson. "Drug Reform Principles and Policy Debates: Harm Reduction Prospects for Cannabis in Canada." *Journal of Drug Issues.* 33.2: (2003) Print. 465–496.

14. Marshall, I. H. and H. Van de Bunt. "Exporting the Drug War to the Netherlands and Dutch Alternatives." In Gerber, Jurg and Eric L. Jensen. *Drug War, American Style: The Internationalization of Failed Policy and Its Alternatives.* New York: Garland Pub, 2001. Print. 197–217.

15. Room, Robin. "The Rhetoric of International Drug Control." *Substance Use & Misuse* 34.12 (1999): 1689–1707. Print.

16. "Global Commission on Drug Policy." *Report of the Global Commission on Drug Policy.* June 2011. Print.

17. Carter, Jimmy. "Call Off the Global Drug War." *The New York Times.* June 16, 2011. http://www.nytimes.com/2011/06/17/opinion/17carter.html. Accessed on June 20, 2011.

18. "The Anti-Vietnam Agitation and the Teach-In Movement: The Problem of Communist Infiltration and Exploitation." Staff study prepared for the Internal Security Subcommittee, Senate Judiciary Committee. Senate Document No. 72, 89th Congress, 1st Session. October 25, 1965. Print. 256.

19. MacAllister, William B. *Drug Diplomacy in the Twentieth Century: An International History.* London: Routledge, 2000. Print.

20. "A Short History of the Collection of UN Crime and Justice Statistics at the International Level." http://www.unodc.org/unodc/en/data-and-analysis/A-short-history-of-the -collection-of-UN-crime-and-justice-statistics-at-the-international-level.htm. Accessed on August 20, 2010.

21. World Health Organization (WHO) Collaborating Centre for Drug Statistics Methodology. *http://www.whocc.no/atcddd/.* Accessed on August 20, 2010.

22. U.S. Government Accountability Office. "Drug Control: Agencies Need to Plan for Likely Declines in Drug Interdiction Assets, and Develop Better Performance Measures for Transit Zone Operations." GAO Report No. GAO-06-200. November 30, 2005. http:// www.gao.gov/htext/d06200.html. Accessed on August 20, 2010.

23. Teslik, Lee Hudson. "The Forgotten Drug War." The Council on Foreign Relations. April 6, 2006. http://www.cfr.org/publication/10373/#3. Accessed on August 20, 2010.

24. Hanes, William Travis and Frank Sanello. *Opium Wars: The Addiction of One Empire and the Corruption of Another.* Naperville, IL: Source, 2002. Print.

25. Wong, J.Y. *Deadly Dreams: Opium, Imperialism, and the Arrow War 1856–1860.* Cambridge, England: Cambridge University Press, 1998. Print. 331–334.

26. MacKenzie, Deborah. "Trauma of War Hits Troops Years Later." *New Scientist* (2005). http://www.newscientist.com/article/mg18725143.800-trauma-of-war-hits-troops-years -later.html. Accessed on August 20, 2010.

27. MacKenzie, Deborah "Mental Effects of War Delayed for Months." *New Scientist.* http://www.newscientist.com/article/dn12917-mental-effects-of-war-delayed-for-months .html. Accessed on August 20, 2010.

Chapter 2

1. Hagel, J. M., B. MacLeod, and P. J. Facchini. "Opium Poppy." In *Biotechnology in Agriculture and Forestry: Volume 61 Transgenic Crops VI.* Berlin: Springer, 2007. Print.

2. Asad, Amir Zada, and Robert Harris. *The Politics and Economics of Drug Production on the Pakistan-Afghanistan Border: Implications for a Globalized World.* Hampshire, England: Ashgate, 2003. Print. 26.

3. Lewis, Bernard. *The Assassins: a Radical Sect in Islam.* New York: Basic, 2003. Print.

4. Grossman, Dave. *On Killing: The Psychological Cost of Learning to Kill in War and Society.* New York: Little, Brown, and Company, 1996. Print.

5. Holmes, Richard. *Acts of War: The Behavior of Men in Battle.* New York: Free, 1989. Print.

6. Smith, David Livingston. *The Most Dangerous Animal: Human Nature and the Origins of War.* New York: St. Martin's Press, 2007. Print. 153–154.

7. Lehmann, A. C. and L. J. Mihalyi. "Aggression, Bravery, Endurance, and Drugs: A Radical Re-evaluation and Analysis of the Masai Warrior Complex." *Ethnology* 21.4: (1983) Print. 335–347.

8. Smith, David Livingston. *The Most Dangerous Animal: Human Nature and the Origins of War.* New York: St. Martin's Press, 2007. Print. 153.

9. Ibid.

10. Waller, James. *Becoming Evil: How Ordinary People Commit Genocide and Mass Killing.* Oxford: Oxford UP, 2002. Print.

11. Ferguson, Niall. *The Pity of War.* New York: Basic, 1999. Print. 351.

12. Ibid., 352.

13. Ibid., 352.

14. Smith, David Livingston. *The Most Dangerous Animal: Human Nature and the Origins of War.* New York: St. Martin's Press. 2007. Print. 153.

15. Poem by Australian Soldier printed in *Aussie* 1918 in Niall Ferguson. *The Pity of War.* New York: Basic, 1999. Print. 351.

16. Burns, Marcelline, Thomas E. Page, and Sevil Atasoy. *Medical-Legal Aspects of Abused Substances: Old and New, Licit and Illicit.* Tucson: Lawyers & Judges Pub, 2005. Print.

17. Ulrich, A. "Hitler's Drugged Soldiers." *Spiegel Online.* Trans. Christopher Sultan. 2005. http://amphetamines.com/nazi.html. Accessed on August 20, 2010.

18. Waller, James. *Becoming Evil: How Ordinary People Commit Genocide and Mass Killing.* Oxford: Oxford UP, 2002. Print.

19. Ibid., 118–210.

20. United States Army. "Army Health Promotion Risk Reduction Suicide Prevention Report." 2010. Print. 55.

21. Goldsmith, Kristofer Shawn. Testimony Before the United States Congressional Progressive Caucus and Iraq Veterans Against the War. May 15, 2008. Washington D.C. United States. C-SPAN Public Affairs Forum. Program ID 205390-1 Transcript.

22. United States Army. "Army Health Promotion Risk Reduction Suicide Prevention Report." 2010. Print. 55.

23. Beah, Ishmael. *A Long Way Gone: Memoirs of a Boy Soldier.* New York: Farrar, Straus & Giroux, 2008. Print.

24. Singer, P. W. *Children at War.* Berkeley: University of California Press, 2006. Print.

25. Saviano, Roberto and Virginia Jewiss. *Gomorrah: A Personal Journey into the Violent International Empire of Naples' Organized Crime System.* New York: Picador, 2008. Print.

26. McAllister, Andrew and Christof Putzel. "Cocaine Mafia." *Current TV.* Vanguard: Global News Now & Video Journalism. http://current.com/shows/vanguard/91650781_cocaine-mafia.htm. Accessed on May 1, 2010.

27. Scott, Peter Dale. *Drugs, Oil, and War: The United States in Afghanistan, Colombia, and Indochina.* Lanham, MD: Rowman & Littlefield, 2003. Print. 40.

28. United Nations Office on Drugs and Crime. 2009 Afghanistan Opium Survey Summary Findings. 2010. Print.

29. U.S. Government Accountability Office. "Afghanistan Drug Control." GAO Report No. GAO-07-78. 2006. Print.

30. McCoy, Alfred W. *The Politics of Heroin: CIA Complicity in the Global Drug Trade, Afghanistan, Southeast Asia, Central America, Colombia.* Chicago: Lawrence Hill, 2003. Print. 461.

31. Zepezauer, Mark. *The CIA's Greatest Hits.* Tucson, AZ: Odonian, 1994. Print.

32. McCoy, Alfred W. *The Politics of Heroin: CIA Complicity in the Global Drug Trade, Afghanistan, Southeast Asia, Central America, Colombia.* Chicago: Lawrence Hill, 2003. Print.

33. Scott, Peter Dale. *Drugs, Oil, and War: The United States in Afghanistan, Colombia, and Indochina.* Lanham, MD: Rowman & Littlefield, 2003. Print. 40.

34. Collier, Paul, V. L. Elliott, and Havard Hegre. *Breaking the Conflict Trap: Civil War and Development Policy.* Washington, DC: World Bank, 2003. Print. ix–x.

35. Associated Press. "7,000 Marines Patrolling Southern Afghan Desert." National Public Radio. (June 8, 2009). http://www.npr.org. Accessed on August 20, 2010.

36. Cole, A. "U.S. Relies More on Contractors to Fight Drug Trade." *Wall Street Journal.* July 5, 2008. A5.

37. Northrop Grumman. "Northrop Grumman Corporation Wins U.S. Department of Defense Counter-Narcoterrorism Technology Program Support Contract." (October 3, 2007). http://www.irconnect.com/noc/pages/news_printer.html?d=127965&print=1. Accessed on September 1, 2009.

38. United States Sentencing Commission. *2002 Sourcebook of Federal Sentencing Statistics.* 2003.

39. "UNICOR Online | Electronics | Guided Missile Components | Components & Support Equipment." UNICOR—Federal Prison Industries. https://www.unicor.gov/electronics/guided_missile/component.cfm. Accessed on July 16, 2011.

40. "America's Prisons: We're in the Jailhouse Now." *The Economist—World News, Politics, Economics, Business & Finance.* June 22, 2011. http://www.economist.com/blogs/democracy inamerica/2011/06/americas-prisons. Accessed on July 16, 2011.

41. United States Sentencing Commission. *2002 Sourcebook of Federal Sentencing Statistics.* 2003.

42. Faust, Drew Gilpin. *This Republic of Suffering: Death and the American Civil War.* New York: Vintage, 2008. Print. 60.

43. McFall, M. and J. Cook. "PTSD and Health Risk Behavior." *The National Center for PTSD Research Quarterly.* 17.4: (2006) 1–7.

44. Pitman, R., K. Sanders, R. Zusman, et al. "Pilot Study of Secondary Prevention of Posttraumatic Stress Disorder with Propranolol." *Biological Psychiatry* 51.2: (2002) Print. 189–92.

45. Vaiva, G., F. Ducrocq, K. Jezequel et al. "Immediate Treatment with Propranolol Decreases Posttraumatic Stress Disorder Two Months after Trauma." *Biological Psychiatry* 54.9: (2003) Print. 947–49.

46. Henry, Michael, Jennifer R. Fishman, and Stuart J. Youngner. "Propranolol and the Prevention of Post-Traumatic Stress Disorder: Is It Wrong to Erase the 'Sting' of Bad Memories?" *The American Journal of Bioethics* 7.9: (2007) Print. 12–20.

47. Baard, E. "The Guilt-Free Soldier: New Science Raises Specter of World Without Regret." *The Village Voice.* http://www.villagevoice.com/2003-01-21/news/the-guilt-free-soldier/1. Accessed on January 22, 2003.

48. Sanders, E. "The Last Drug Czar: Obama's Point Man in the War on Drugs Is Calling Off the Troops. But That Doesn't Mean Legalization Is Around the Corner." *The American Prospect.* http://www.prospect.org:80//cs/articles;jsessionid=aK9Lr1eHm-Wfp -16xn?article=the_last_drug_czar. Accessed on June 29, 2009.

Chapter 3

1. Asad, Amir Zada, and Robert Harris. *The Politics and Economics of Drug Production on the Pakistan-Afghanistan Border: Implications for a Globalized World.* Hampshire, England: Ashgate, 2003. Print. 26.

2. Sneader Walter. "The Discovery of Heroin." *Lancet* 352.9141: (1998) Print. 1697–1699.

3. Berridge, Virginia and Griffith Edwards. *Opium and the People: Opiate Use in Nineteenth-Century England.* New Haven: Yale UP, 1987. Print. xix–xx.

4. Inciardi, James A. *The War on Drugs III: The Continuing Saga of the Mysteries and Miseries of Intoxication, Addiction, Crime, and Public Policy.* Boston: Allyn and Bacon, 2002. Print. 24.

5. McCoy, Alfred W. *The Politics of Heroin: CIA Complicity in the Global Drug Trade, Afghanistan, Southeast Asia, Central America, Colombia.* Chicago: Lawrence Hill, 2003. Print. 87–88.

6. Wong, J.Y. *Deadly Dreams: Opium, Imperialism, and the Arrow War (1856–1860) in China.* Cambridge, England: Cambridge UP, 1998. Print. 331–334.

7. Tan, Chung. *China and the Brave New World: A Study of the Origins of the Opium War (1840–42).* Durham, NC: Carolina Academic, 1978. Print. 1–12.

8. Tan, Chung. "The British-China-India Trade Triangle 1771–1840." *Indian Economic and Social History Review* 21.4: (1974) Print. 411–31.

9. Bello, David Anthony. *Opium and the Limits of Empire: Drug Prohibition in the Chinese Interior, 1729–1850.* Cambridge, MA: Harvard University Asia Center, 2005. Print. 13.

10. Stevenson, R. "Hobart Paper 124." *Winning the War on Drugs: To Legalize or Not?* Proc. of London Institute of Economic Affairs. 1994. Print. 76.

11. U.S. Department of Commerce. Statistical Abstract 1915. Cited in McCoy, Alfred W. *The Politics of Heroin: CIA Complicity in the Global Drug Trade, Afghanistan, Southeast Asia, Central America, Colombia.* Chicago: Lawrence Hill, 2003. Print.

12. Asad, Amir Zada, and Robert Harris. *The Politics and Economics of Drug Production on the Pakistan-Afghanistan Border: Implications for a Globalized World.* Hampshire, England: Ashgate, 2003. Print. 27.

13. Ward, G. "A Fair, Honorable and Legitimate Trade." *American Heritage* August–September: (1986). Print.

14. Allen, Nathan. *An Essay on the Opium Trade.* Cornhill, MA: John P. Jewett and Co., 1850. Digitized version of original publication.

15. Greenberg, Michael. *Trade and the Opening of China 1800–1842.* Cambridge: Cambridge UP, 1951. Digitized version of original publication. 221.

16. MacAllister, William B. *Drug Diplomacy in the Twentieth Century: An International History.* London: Routledge, 2000. Print. 13.

17. Hanes, William Travis and Frank Sanello. *Opium Wars: The Addiction of One Empire and the Corruption of Another.* Naperville, IL: Source, 2002. Print. 25.

18. Ibid., 94.

19. Ibid., 220.

20. Wong, J. Y. *Deadly Dreams: Opium, Imperialism, and the Arrow War (1856–1860) in China.* Cambridge: Cambridge UP, 1998. Print.

21. MacAllister, William B. *Drug Diplomacy in the Twentieth Century: An International History.* London: Routledge, 2000. Print. 13.

22. Ashin, S. "Opium in Szechwan 1881–1911." *Journal of Southeast Asia History* 7.2: (1966) Print. 93–99.

23. Hanes, William Travis and Frank Sanello. *Opium Wars: The Addiction of One Empire and the Corruption of Another.* Naperville, IL: Source, 2002. Print. 83.

24. *New-York Evangelist.* March 7, 1840. Digitized version of original.

25. U.S. Bureau of the Census. "Population of the 100 Largest Urban Places." (1840) Digitized version of original publication.

26. "Remonstrance of a Chinese in Opium" *The Liberator* (April 10, 1840) Digitized version of original.

27. Trocki, Carl A. *Opium, Empire, and the Global Political Economy: A Study of the Asian Opium Trade, 1750–1950.* London: Routledge, 1999. Print

28. Hanes, William Travis and Frank Sanello. *Opium Wars: The Addiction of One Empire and the Corruption of Another.* Naperville, IL: Source, 2002. Print.

29. Ward, G. "A Fair, Honorable and Legitimate Trade." *American Heritage* August–September (1986) Print.

30. Stelle, C.S. "American Trade in Opium to China, 1821–39." *The Pacific Historical Review* 10.1: (1941) 57–74. Digitized version of original.

31. "CIA—The World Factbook." Central Intelligence Agency. https://www.cia.gov/library/publications/the-world-factbook/geos/bm.html. Accessed on August 29, 2008.

32. Ibid.

33. Asad, Amir Zada, and Robert Harris. *The Politics and Economics of Drug Production on the Pakistan-Afghanistan Border: Implications for a Globalized World.* Hampshire, England: Ashgate, 2003. Print. 18.

34. United Nations Office of Drugs and Crime. UNODC Calculations Based on International Opium Commission, Shanghai, February 1909 and World Drug Report 2008. Print.

35. Executive Office of the President of the United States, the White House. "The National Drug Control Strategy." 1996. Print.

36. Woodward, J. Arthur, Robert Retka, and Lin Ng. "Construct Validity of Heroin Abuse Estimators." *Substance Use & Misuse* 19.1 (1984): 93–117.

37. Technical Paper: United States. National Institutes of Health. National Institute on Drug Abuse. "Technical Paper: A Method for Estimating Heroin Use Prevalence." 495 DHEW Publication No. (ADM)77-439. Washington, DC.

38. Trocki, Carl A. *Opium, Empire, and the Global Political Economy: A Study of the Asian Opium Trade, 1750–1950.* London: Routledge, 1999. Print. 10.

39. Leonard, George Jay. *The Asian Pacific American Heritage: A Companion to Literature and Arts.* New York: Garland, 1999. Print. 317.

40. Bello, David Anthony. *Opium and the Limits of Empire: Drug Prohibition in the Chinese Interior 1729–1850.* Cambridge: Harvard UP, 2005. Print. 17.

Chapter 4

1. Ward, Geoffrey C., Ken Burns, and Ric Burns. *The Civil War.* New York: Vintage, 1994. Print.

2. Sutherland, Daniel E. *Seasons of War: The Ordeal of a Confederate Community, 1861–1865.* Baton Rouge: Louisiana State UP, 1998. Print. 89, 163.

3. Flannery, Michael A. *Civil War Pharmacy: A History of Drugs, Drug Supply and Provision, and Therapeutics for the Union and Confederacy.* New York: Pharmaceutical Products, 2004. Print. 183.

4. Ibid., 96.

5. Grossman, Dave. *On Killing: The Psychological Cost of Learning to Kill in War and Society.* New York: Little, Brown and Company. 1996. Print. 18–22.

6. Ibid.

7. Ibid.

8. Da Costa, J. M. "On Irritable Heart: A Clinical Study of a Form of Functional Cardiac Disorder and Its Consequences." *American Journal of Medical Science* 61: (1871) 17–52. Digitized version of original.

9. Hyams, K. C., F. S. Wignall, and R. Roswell. "War Syndromes and Their Evaluation: From the U.S. Civil War to the Persian Gulf War." *Annals of Internal Medicine.* 124.5: (1996) Print. 398–405.

10. Faust, Drew Gilpin. *This Republic of Suffering: Death and the American Civil War.* New York: Vintage, 2008. Print.

11. Stolemyer, S. "Bivouacs of the Dead." In Faust, Drew Gilpin. *This Republic of Suffering: Death and the American Civil War.* New York: Vintage, 2008. Print. 69.

12. Thompson, W. E. "Historical Surgical Instruments in the Museum of the Royal College of Surgeons of England." *Journal of Bone & Joint Surgery, British Volume* 36-B.1: (1954) Print. 135–9.

13. Miller, R. J. and B. Tran. "More Mysteries of Opium Revealed: 300 Years of Opiates." *Trends in Pharmacological Sciences* 21.8: (2000) Print. 299–304.

14. Asad, Amir Zada, and Robert Harris. *The Politics and Economics of Drug Production on the Pakistan-Afghanistan Border: Implications for a Globalized World.* Hampshire, England: Ashgate, 2003. Print. 32.

15. "Resources of Our Fields and Forests." *The Charleston Mercury.* April 29, 1863. Digitized version of original.

16. Quinones, M. A. "Drug Abuse During the Civil War 1861–1865." *International Journal of the Addictions* 10.6: (1975) Print. 1007–20.

17. Courtwright, D. "Opiate Addiction as a Consequence of the Civil War." *Civil War History* 24: (1978) Print. 106–7.

18. Starkey, G. "The Use and Abuse of Opiates and Amphetamines." In Healy, Patrick and J. Manak (Eds.). *Drug Dependence and Abuse Resource Book.* Chicago: National District Attorney's Association, 1971. Print. 481–484.

19. Flannery, Michael A. *Civil War Pharmacy: A History of Drugs, Drug Supply and Provision, and Therapeutics for the Union and Confederacy.* New York: Pharmaceutical Products, 2004. Print. 33.

20. Billings, J. "Medical Reminiscences of the Civil War." *Transactions of the College of Physicians* 27: (1905) Print. 115–21.

21. Bishop, E. S. "Legitimate Use of Narcotics in Wartime." *American Journal of Public Health* 9: (1919) Print. 321–29.

22. Bishop, Ernest Simons. *The Narcotic Drug Problem.* New York: Macmillan, 1920. Print. 24–25.

23. Courtwright, D. "Opiate Addiction as a Consequence of the Civil War." *Civil War History* 24: (1978) Print. 101–111.

24. Ashley, Richard. *Heroin.* New York: St. Martin's Press. 1972. Print. 5.

25. Jones, Hardin and Helen Jones. *Sensual Drugs—Deprivation and Rehabilitation of the Mind.* Cambridge: Cambridge UP, 1977. 189.

26. Quinones, M. A. "Drug Abuse During the Civil War 1861–1865." *International Journal of the Addictions* 10.6: (1975) Print. 1007–20.

27. Flannery, Michael A. *Civil War Pharmacy: A History of Drugs, Drug Supply and Provision, and Therapeutics for the Union and Confederacy.* New York: Pharmaceutical Products, 2004. Print. 37–38.

28. Ibid., 6.

29. Ibid., 109.

30. Quinones, M. A. "Drug Abuse During the Civil War 1861–1865." *International Journal of the Addictions* 10.6: (1975) Print. 1007–20.

31. Terry, Charles Edward and Mildred Pellens. *The Opium Problem.* Montclair, NJ: Patterson Smith, 1970. Reprint.

32. Carnwath, Tom and Ian Smith. *Heroin Century.* London: Routledge, 2002. Print.

Chapter 5

1. "Opium Degrading the French Navy." *The New York Times.* April 27, 1913.

2. McCoy, Alfred W. *The Politics of Heroin: CIA Complicity in the Global Drug Trade, Afghanistan, Southeast Asia, Central America, Colombia.* Chicago: Lawrence Hill, 2003. Print. 90–91.

3. MacAllister, William B. *Drug Diplomacy in the Twentieth Century: An International History.* London: Routledge, 2000. Print. 35–36.

4. McCoy, Alfred W. *The Politics of Heroin: CIA Complicity in the Global Drug Trade, Afghanistan, Southeast Asia, Central America, Colombia.* Brooklyn, NY: Lawrence Hill, 1991. Print. 113.

5. Ibid., 114.

6. Schulte-Bockholt, A. *The Politics of Organized Crime and the Organized Crime of Politics: A Study in Criminal Power.* Oxford: Lexington Books, 2006. 60.

7. McCoy, Alfred W. *The Politics of Heroin: CIA Complicity in the Global Drug Trade, Afghanistan, Southeast Asia, Central America, Colombia.* Brooklyn, NY: Lawrence Hill, 1991. Print. 114.

8. MacAllister, William B. *Drug Diplomacy in the Twentieth Century: An International History.* London: Routledge, 2000. Print. 160–161.

9. Ibid.

10. Ibid., 167.

11. MacAllister, William B. *Drug Diplomacy in the Twentieth Century: An International History.* London: Routledge, 2000. Print.

12. McCoy, Alfred W. *The Politics of Heroin: CIA Complicity in the Global Drug Trade, Afghanistan, Southeast Asia, Central America, Colombia.* Chicago: Lawrence Hill, 2003. Print.

13. McCoy, Alfred W., Cathleen B. Read, and Leonard P. Adams. *The Politics of Heroin in Southeast Asia.* New York: Harper & Row, 1972. Print.

14. McCoy, Alfred W. *The Politics of Heroin: CIA Complicity in the Global Drug Trade, Afghanistan, Southeast Asia, Central America, Colombia.* Chicago: Lawrence Hill, 2003. Print.

15. "Guns, Drugs, and the CIA." *Frontline.* Transcripts of V. Marchetti, Central Intelligence Agency officer. Original airdate May 17, 1988. http://www.pbs.org/wgbh/pages/frontline/shows/drugs/archive/gunsdrugscia.html. Accessed on August 30, 2010.

16. McCoy, Alfred W. *The Politics of Heroin: CIA Complicity in the Global Drug Trade, Afghanistan, Southeast Asia, Central America, Colombia.* Brooklyn, NY: Lawrence Hill, 1991. Print. 47.

17. Ibid.

18. "Guns, Drugs, and the CIA." *Frontline.* Transcripts of V. Marchetti, Central Intelligence Agency officer. Original airdate May 17, 1988. http://www.pbs.org/wgbh/pages/frontline/shows/drugs/archive/gunsdrugscia.html. Accessed on August 30, 2010.

19. Moynihan, D. "Memorandum for Honorable John N. Mitchell, Attorney General." In *Foreign Relations* E-1, Documents on Global Issues: 1969–1972. http://www.state.gov/r/pa/ho/frus/nixon/e1/45827.htm. Accessed on August 20, 2010.

20. McCoy, Alfred W. *The Politics of Heroin: CIA Complicity in the Global Drug Trade, Afghanistan, Southeast Asia, Central America, Colombia.* Chicago: Lawrence Hill, 2003. Print. 461.

21. Peters, Gretchen. *Seeds of Terror: How Heroin Is Bankrolling the Taliban and Al Qaeda.* New York: St. Martin's Press, 2009. Print. 44.

22. Ibid.

Chapter 6

1. Grinspoon, Lester and Peter Hedblom. *The Speed Culture: Amphetamine Use and Abuse in America.* Cambridge, MA: Harvard UP, 1975. Print.

2. Owen, Frank. *No Speed Limit: The Highs and Lows of Meth.* New York: St. Martin's Press, 2007. Print.

3. Graham, James. *Vessels of Rage, Engines of Power: The Secret History of Alcoholism.* Lexington, VA: Aculeus, 1994. Print. 170.

4. Grinspoon, Lester and Peter Hedblom. *The Speed Culture: Amphetamine Use and Abuse in America.* Cambridge, MA: Harvard UP, 1975. Print.

5. Owen, Frank. *No Speed Limit: The Highs and Lows of Meth.* New York: St. Martin's Press, 2007. Print.

6. Northwestern University Library. "World War II Poster Collection from Northwestern University Library." http://www.library.northwestern.edu/govinfo/collections/wwii-posters/. Accessed on August 24, 2010.

7. Grinspoon, Lester and Peter Hedblom. *The Speed Culture: Amphetamine Use and Abuse in America.* Cambridge, MA: Harvard UP, 1975. Print.

8. McCoy, Alfred W. *The Politics of Heroin: CIA Complicity in the Global Drug Trade.* Brooklyn, NY: Lawrence Hill, 1991. Print. 106.

9. Freiberg, Peter S. "Tests, Use, and Misuse in the German Wehrmachted." *Man, Medicine, and the State: The Human Body as an Object of Government Sponsored Medical Research in the 20th Century.* By Wolfgang U. Eckart. Stuttgart: Franz Steiner Verlag, 2006. 61–65. Print.

10. Bernadac, C. (1967). Les medecins maudits. Paris: Editions France-Empire. Based on records pertaining to Dr Kurt Ploetner, United States Army Intelligence and Security Command. Fort Meade, Maryland. Print. 58–62.

11. Pross, C. "Breaking Through the Postwar Cover-Up of Nazi Doctors in Germany." *Journal of Medical Ethics* 17: (1991) 13–17.

12. Marks, John. *Search for the Manchurian Candidate: CIA and Mind Control.* New York: W.W. Norton, 1992. Print.

13. Freiberg, Peter S. "Tests, Use and Misuse in the German Wehrmachted." *Man, Medicine, and the State: The Human Body as an Object of Government Sponsored Medical Research in the 20th Century.* By Wolfgang U. Eckart. Stuttgart: Franz Steiner Verlag, 2006. 61–70.

14. Vasagar, J. "Nazis Tested Cocaine on Camp Inmates." *The Guardian*. November 19, 2002. http://www.amphetamines.com/nazidrug.html. Accessed on August 20, 2010.

15. Sato, A. "Methamphetamine Use in Japan after the Second World War: Transformation of Narratives." *Contemporary Drug Problem* 35: (2008) Print. 717–745.

16. Vasagar, J. "Nazis Tested Cocaine on Camp Inmates." *The Guardian* (November 19, 2002) http://www.amphetamines.com/nazidrug.html. Accessed on August 20, 2010.

17. Ulrich, A. Translated from German by Sultan, C. "The Nazi Death Machine: Hitler's Drugged Soldiers." *Spiegel Online International* (May 6, 2005) www.spiegel.de/international /0,1518,354606,00.html. Accessed on August 20, 2010.

18. Morrell, T. G. and D. Irving. *Die geheimen Tagebücher des Dr. Morell: Leibartz Adolf Hitlers*. München Goldmann, 1983. English translation Morrell, T. G. and D. Irving. *The Secret Diaries of Hitler's Doctor*. New York: McMillan, 1983.

19. Heston, L. L. and R. Heston. *The Medical Casebook of Adolf Hitler: His Illnesses, Doctors, and Drugs*. New York: Stein and Day, 1980.

20. Burns, M., T. E. Page, and S. Atasoy, eds. *Medical-Legal Aspects of Abused Substances: Old and New—Licit and Illicit*. Tuscson, AZ: Lawyers & Judges Publishing Company, 2005.

21. Morrell, T. G. and D. Irving. *Die geheimen Tagebücher des Dr. Morell: Leibartz Adolf Hitlers*. München Goldmann, 1983. English translation Morrell, T. G. and D. Irving. *The Secret Diaries of Hitler's Doctor*. New York: McMillan, 1983.

22. Heston, L. L. and R. Heston. *The Medical Casebook of Adolf Hitler: His Illnesses, Doctors, and Drugs*. New York: Stein and Day, 1980.

23. Doyle, D. "Adolph Hitler's Medical Care." *Journal of the Royal College of Physicians in Edinburgh* 35.1: (2005) 75–82.

24. Heston, L. L. and R. Heston. *The Medical Casebook of Adolf Hitler: His Illnesses, Doctors, and Drugs*. New York: Stein and Day, 1980.

25. Kaplan, R. "Doctor to the Dictator: the Career of Theodor Morell, Personal Physician to Adolf Hitler." *Australasian Psychiatry* 10.4: (2002) 389–392.

26. Heston, L. and R. Heston. *The Medical Casebook of Adolf Hitler: His Illnesses, Doctors and Drugs*. New York: Stein and Day, 1980.

27. Redlich, F. *Hitler: Diagnosis of a Destructive Prophet*. London: Oxford UP, 1999.

28. Manvell, R. *Goering*. Greenhill Books, London, 2006.

29. Lowinson J., P. Ruiz, R. Millman, and J. Langrod. *Substance Abuse: A Comprehensive Textbook*. Fourth Ed. Philadelphia: Lippincott, Williams, & Wilkins, 2005. 557.

30. Letters from Heinrich Boell, the first German awarded the Nobel Prize for Literature (1972) in the post-war period.

31. Stephens, R. *Germans on Drugs: The Complications of Modernization in Hamburg*. Ann Arbor, MI: U of Michigan P, 2007. 12.

32. Owen, F. *No Speed Limit: The Highs and Lows of Meth*. New York: St. Martin's Press, 2007.

33. Ikuta, B. (1951). On stimulants. *The Science and Crime Detection, 4*. 28–53.

34. Owen, F. *No Speed Limit: The Highs and Lows of Meth*. New York: St. Martin's Press, 2007. 15–18.

35. Beaudreault, Amy R. "Methamphetamine in the United States: Perceptions and Educational Programming Needs in Extension Education." Ohio State University Dissertation. 2009. 14–15.

36. Herrmann, N. and G. Eryavec. "Lifetime Alcohol Abuse in Institutionalized World War II Veterans." *American Journal of Geriatric Psychiatry* 4.1: (1996) 39–45.

37. Hermann, N. and G. Eryvac. "Delayed Onset Post-Traumatic Stress Disorder in World War II Veterans." *Canadian Journal of Psychiatry* 39.7: (1996) 439–41.

38. Alongi, Paul. "Vet's Daughter Said His Suicide Was a Statement about VA Benefits: 89-Year-Old Killed Self Outside Clinic." *The Greenville News* (May 5, 2008) http://www .greenvilleonline.com/apps/pbcs.dll/article?AID=/20080505/NEWS01/805050314/1001. Accessed on July 1, 2010.

Chapter 7

1. Pross, C. "Breaking Through the Postwar Cover-Up of Nazi Doctors in Germany." *Journal of Medical Ethics* 17: (1991) Print. 13–17.

2. Blackman, Shane J. *Chilling Out: The Cultural Politics of Substance Consumption, Youth and Drug Policy.* Maidenhead: Open UP, 2004. Print.

3. Dubavitch, N. "New Research on CIA History." Audio of lecture at the Kennedy Center at Brigham Young University.

4. McCoy, Alfred W. *The Politics of Heroin: CIA Complicity in the Global Drug Trade, Afghanistan, Southeast Asia, Central America, Colombia.* Chicago: Lawrence Hill, 2003. Print. 18–19.

5. Asad, A.Z. and R. Harris. *The Politics and Economics of Drug Production on the Pakistan-Afghanistan Border.* Hampshire, England: Ashgate Publishing, 2003. 29.

6. Cockburn, Alexander and Jeffrey St. Clair. *Whiteout: The CIA, Drugs, and the Press.* London: Verso, 1999. Print. 189.

7. McCoy, Alfred W. *The Politics of Heroin: CIA Complicity in the Global Drug Trade, Afghanistan, Southeast Asia, Central America, Colombia.* Chicago: Lawrence Hill, 2003. Print. 162–178, 265, 444, 454, 475–487.

8. Peters, Gretchen. *Seeds of Terror: How Heroin Is Bankrolling the Taliban and Al Qaeda.* New York: Thomas Dunne, 2009. Print. 34–39, 54–58.

9. McCoy, Alfred W. *The Politics of Heroin: CIA Complicity in the Global Drug Trade, Afghanistan, Southeast Asia, Central America, Colombia.* Chicago: Lawrence Hill, 2003. Print.

10. Cockburn, Alexander and Jeffrey St. Clair. *Whiteout: The CIA, Drugs, and the Press.* London: Verso, 1999. Print. 219–225.

11. McCoy, Alfred W. *The Politics of Heroin: CIA Complicity in the Global Drug Trade, Afghanistan, Southeast Asia, Central America, Colombia.* Chicago: Lawrence Hill, 2003. Print. 174–177.

12. Cooker, R.A. "Forces of Change in the Thailand Opium Zone." *Geographical Review* 78.3: (1988) Print. 241–256.

13. Cockburn, Andrew and Leslie Cockburn. "Guns, Drugs and the CIA." *Frontline.* PBS. May 17, 1988. Television. Transcript.

14. McCoy, Alfred W. *The Politics of Heroin: CIA Complicity in the Global Drug Trade, Afghanistan, Southeast Asia, Central America, Colombia.* Chicago: Lawrence Hill, 2003. Print.

15. Central Intelligence Agency. "Scope of Investigation: The California Story—Central Intelligence Agency." https://www.cia.gov/library/reports/general-reports-1/cocaine/report/scope.html. Accessed on August 27, 2010.

16. McCoy, Alfred W. *The Politics of Heroin: CIA Complicity in the Global Drug Trade, Afghanistan, Southeast Asia, Central America, Colombia.* Chicago: Lawrence Hill, 2003. Print. 384–385.

17. Scott, D.L. "Honduras, the Contra Support Networks, and Cocaine: How the U.S. Government Has Augmented America's Drug Crisis." In Block, Alan A. and Alfred W. McCoy. *War on Drugs: Studies in the Failure of US Narcotics Policy.* Boulder, Colo: Westview, 1992. Print. 126–27.

18. Westermeyer, J. "Influence of Opium Availability on Addiction Rates in Laos." *American Journal of Epidemiology* 109.5: (1979) 550–562.

19. Blum, William. *Killing Hope: US Military and CIA Interventions Since World War II.* Monroe, ME: Common Courage, 1995. Print. 142.

20. McCoy, Alfred W. *The Politics of Heroin: CIA Complicity in the Global Drug Trade, Afghanistan, Southeast Asia, Central America, Colombia.* Chicago: Lawrence Hill Books, 2003. 318, 384, 385.

21. Ibid.

22. United States Senate. "Drugs, Law Enforcement and Foreign Policy: A Report Prepared by the Subcommittee on Terrorism, Narcotics and International Operations of the Committee on Foreign Relations." 1989. 100th Congress 2nd Session. December 1988. Washington, DC. Print. 121.

23. McCoy, Alfred W. *The Politics of Heroin: CIA Complicity in the Global Drug Trade, Afghanistan, Southeast Asia, Central America, Colombia.* Chicago: Lawrence Hill, 2003. Print.

24. United States Congress. "The Select Committee to Study Governmental Operations with Respect to Intelligence Activities, Foreign and Military Intelligence." Church Committee Report, no. 94-755. 94th Congress 2nd Session. 1976. Washington, D.C.

25. McCoy, Alfred W. *The Politics of Heroin: CIA Complicity in the Global Drug Trade, Afghanistan, Southeast Asia, Central America, Colombia.* Chicago: Lawrence Hill, 2003. Print.

26. Webb, Gary. "America's 'Crack' Plague Has Roots in Nicaragua War: Colombia–San Francisco Bay Area Drug Pipeline Helped Finance CIA-Backed Contra." *San Jose Mercury News.* August 18, 1996. Print.

27. Webb, Gary. "Shadowy Origins of 'Crack' Epidemic: Role of CIA-Linked Agents a Well-Protected Secret Until Now." *San Jose Mercury News* August 19, 1996. Print.

28. Webb, Gary. "War on Drugs Has Unequal Impact on Black Americans: Contra Case Illustrates the Discrepancy: Nicaraguan Goes Free; L.A. Dealer Faces Life." *San Jose Mercury News* August 20, 1996. Print.

29. *The Oliver North File: His Diaries, E–Mail, and Memos on the Kerry Report, Contras and Drugs.* National Security Archive Electronic Briefing Book No. 113. The George Washington University. http://www.gwu.edu/~nsarchiv/NSAEBB/NSAEBB113/#4. Accessed on August 30, 2010.

30. United States Senate. "Drugs, Law Enforcement and Foreign Policy: A Report Prepared by the Subcommittee on Terrorism, Narcotics and International Operations of the Committee on Foreign Relations." 1989. 100th Congress 2nd Session. December 1988. Washington, D.C. 145–146.

31. U.S. Senate Subcommittee on Terrorism, Narcotics, and International Operations. "Report: Drugs, Law Enforcement and Foreign Policy." 1994. 41.

32. Cockburn, A., and L. Cockburn. "Guns, Drugs and the CIA." *Frontline.* PBS. May 17, 1988. Television. Transcript.

33. Webb, Gary. "America's 'Crack' Plague Has Roots in Nicaragua War: Colombia–San Francisco Bay Area Drug Pipeline Helped Finance CIA-Backed Contra." *San Jose Mercury News.* August 18, 1996. Print.

34. "Town Meeting on Allegations of CIA Involvement in Drug Trafficking." CNN. November 15, 1996. Television.

35. Webb, Gary. *Dark Alliance: The CIA, the Contras, and the Crack Cocaine Explosion.* New York: Seven Stories P, 1999. Print.

36. Ibid.

37. *American Drug War: The Last White Hope.* Dir. Kevin Booth. Sacred Cow Productions, 2008. DVD.

38. Webb, Gary. *Dark Alliance: The CIA, the Contras, and the Crack Cocaine Explosion.* New York: Seven Stories P, 1999. Print.

39. United States. National Institutes of Drug Addiction. "National Household Survey on Drug Abuse Survey Data from 1979, 1982, 1985, 1988, and 1990–2001." Office of National Drug Control Policy. http://www.whitehousedrugpolicy.gov/publications/factsht/druguse/. Accessed on August 30, 2010.

40. Kraar, Louis. "The Drug Trade: Think of It as a Huge, Multinational Commodity Business with a Fast-Moving Top Management, a Widespread Distribution Network, and Price-Insensitive Customers." CNNMoney.com. June 20, 1988. http://money.cnn.com/magazines/fortune/fortune_archive/1988/06/20/70695/index.htm. Accessed on August 30, 2010.

41. Cockburn, Alexander and Jeffrey St. Clair. *Whiteout: The CIA, Drugs, and the Press.* London: Verso, 1999. Print.

42. Zimmerman, S. *A history of Smuggling in Florida: Rum Runners and Cocaine Cowboys.* Charleston, SC: The History Press, 2006. Print

43. Hitz, Frederick P. "Obscuring Propriety: The CIA and Drugs." *International Journal of Intelligence and Counterintelligence* 12.4: (1999) Print. 448–462.

44. CIA Inspector General's Office Report of Investigation. "Volume I: The California Story: Allegations of Connections Between CIA and the Contras in Cocaine Trafficking to the United States" (96-0143-IG). January 29, 1998. https://www.cia.gov/library/reports/general-reports-1/cocaine/report/index.html. Accessed on August 1, 2009.

45. Weir W. *In the Shadow of the Dope Fiend.* New Haven, CT: Archon, 1995. Print. 83.

46. Chepesiuk, Ron. *The War on Drugs: An International Encyclopedia.* Santa Barbara, CA: ABC-CLIO, 1999. Print. 43.

47. McCoy, Alfred W. *The Politics of Heroin: CIA Complicity in the Global Drug Trade, Afghanistan, Southeast Asia, Central America, Colombia.* Chicago: Lawrence Hill, 2003. Print. 461.

48. Davidson, Joe. "Recruiting, with Unintended Consequences." *The Washington Post.* August 27, 2008. http://www.washingtonpost.com/wp-dyn/content/article/2008/08/26/AR2008082603066.html. Accessed on August 5, 2011.

49. *National Security Archive Electronic Briefing Book No. 2: The Contras, Cocaine, and Covert Operations.* http://www.gwu.edu/~nsarchiv/NSAEBB/NSAEBB2/nsaebb2.htm. Accessed on July 5, 2010.

50. Valentine, Douglas. *The Strength of the Wolf: The Secret History of America's War on Drugs.* London: Verso, 2004. Print.

51. Central Intelligence Agency. *The World Factbook: Colombia.* https://www.cia.gov/library/publications/the-world-factbook/geos/co.html. Accessed on August 28, 2010.

52. United Nations Office of Drugs and Crime. *World Drug Report 2009.* 2010. Print. 65.

53. Ibid.

54. GlobalSecurity.org. Paramilitary Groups in Latin America. *Revolutionary Armed Forces of Colombia Fuerzas Armadas Revolucionarias de Colombia – FARC.* http://www.globalsecurity.org/military/world/para/farc.htm. Accessed on October 1, 2010.

55. Federal Bureau of Investigation. "Department of Justice Press Release: High-Ranking Member of Colombian FARC Narco-Terrorist Organization Extradited to U.S. on Terrorism, Drug Charges." December 31, 2004. http://www.fbi.gov/dojpressrel/pressrel04/narcoterrorist 123104.htm. Accessed on August 28, 2010.

56. Ibid.

57. Ibid.

58. BBC News. "Female Farc Commander Tried in US." http://news.bbc.co.uk/2/hi/americas/6246641.stm. Accessed on August 28, 2010.

59. Greste, Peter. "Haiti 'Weak Link' in Drug Chain." BBC World News. May 16, 2000. http://news.bbc.co.uk/2/hi/americas/750434.stm. Accessed on March 1, 2010.

60. Ibid.

61. United Nations Office of Drugs and Crime. Report for 2010. Print. 167–68. Print.

62. MacAllister, William B. *Drug Diplomacy in the Twentieth Century: An International History.* London: Routledge, 2000. Print. 161.

63. Ibid.

64. Caryl, C. "The New Silk Road." *Newsweek.* September 17, 2001. http://www.newsweek.com/2001/09/16/the-new-silk-road-of-death.html. Accessed on July 1, 2010.

65. Moore, J. "The Evolution of Islamic Terrorism: An Overview." *Frontline.* PBS. Transcript. http://www.pbs.org/wgbh/pages/frontline/shows/target/etc/modern.html. Accessed on March 1, 2010.

66. Central Intelligence Agency Office of Soviet Analysis. "Organized Crime in the USSR: Its Growth and Impact." CIA Special Collections. February 1991. Released 2000 to CIA FOIA Library.

67. BBC World News. "Drug Submarine Found in Colombia." September 7, 2000. http://news.bbc.co.uk/2/hi/americas/915059.stm. Accessed on March 1, 2010.

68. Navarro, M. "Russian Submarine Drifts into Center of a Brazen Drug Plot." *The New York Times.* March 7, 1997. http://www.nytimes.com/1997/03/07/us/russian-submarine-drifts-into-center-of-a-brazen-drug-plot.html?pagewanted=1. Accessed on March 1, 2010.

69. Miroff, Nick and William Booth. "Mexican Drug Cartels' Newest Weapon: Cold War–Era Grenades Made in U.S." *Washington Post.* July 17, 2010. http://www.washingtonpost.com/wp-dyn/content/article/2010/07/16/AR2010071606252.html. Accessed on September 3, 2010.

70. United Nations Office on Drugs and Crime. *World Drug Report.* 2005. Print.

71. Judah, Ben. "Russia: Ominous Demographics." ISN. October 14, 2009. www.isn.ethz.ch/isn/Current-Affairs/Security-Watch/Detail/?id=108474&lng=en. Accessed on September 2, 2010.

Chapter 8

1. Lee, M., and B. Shlain. *Acid Dreams: The Complete Social History of LSD: The CIA, the Sixties, and Beyond.* New York: Grove Press, 1992. 286–287.

2. Cockburn, A., and J. St. Clair. *Whiteout: The CIA, Drugs, and the Press.* London: Verso, 1998. 145–215.

3. Ibid., 196.

4. United States Senate. "Human Drug Testing by the CIA, 1977: Hearings Before the Subcommittee on Health and Scientific Research of the Committee on Human Resources." September 20 and 21, 1977. 95th Congress, 1st Session. Washington, DC: U.S. Govt. Print. Off., 1977. Print. 151.

5. Ketchum, J.S. *Chemical Warfare Secrets Almost Forgotten: A Personal Story of Medical Testing of Army Volunteers with Incapacitating Chemical Agents During the Cold War.* ChemBook, Inc., 2006.

6. Lee, M., and B. Shlain. *Acid Dreams: The Complete Social History of LSD: The CIA, the Sixties and Beyond.* New York: Grove Press, 1992. 235.

7. Willing, R. "Researchers Tested Pot, LSD on Army Volunteers." *USA Today*. April 6, 2007. http://www.usatoday.com/news/washington/2007-04-05-army-experiments_N.htm.

8. "What Lies Beneath: British Experiences in the Cold War." Original footage archived in the Imperial War Museum, London. 1964. http://www.whatliesbeneath.org.uk/server.php?show=nav.24233.

9. Ross, C.A. "Ethics of CIA and Military Contracting by Psychiatrists and Psychologists." *Ethical Human Psychology and Psychiatry* 9.1: (2007) 25–34.

10. United States Senate. "Human Drug Testing by the CIA, 1977: Hearings Before the Subcommittee on Health and Scientific Research of the Committee on Human Resources." September 20 and 21, 1977. 95th Congress 1st Session. Washington, DC: U.S. Govt. Print. Off., 1977. Print.

11. U.S. Advisory Committee Staff. "Methodological Review of Agency Data Collection Efforts: Initial Report on the Central Intelligence Agency Document Search." Memorandum to the Members of the Advisory Committee on Human Radiation Experiments. June 27, 1994. Washington, DC.

12. Ibid.

13. United States Senate. "Human Drug Testing by the CIA, 1977: Hearings Before the Select Committee on Intelligence and the Subcomittee on Health and Scientific Research of the Committee on Human Resources." August 3, 1977. 95th Congress 1st Session. Washington, DC: U.S. Govt. Print. Off., 1977. Print. Appendix C 109.

14. Ibid.

15. Cockburn, A. and J. St. Clair. *Whiteout: The CIA, Drugs, and the Press*. London: Verso, 1998. 190.

16. Lee, M. and B. Shlain. *Acid Dreams: The Complete Social History of LSD: The CIA, the Sixties and Beyond*. New York: Grove Press, 1992. Print.

17. Letter from Olson Family Attorneys David Kairys and David Rudovsky to James R. Schlesinger, Deputy Director of Defense. July 28, 1975.

18. Cockburn, A. and J. St. Clair. *Whiteout: The CIA, Drugs, and the Press*. London: Verso, 1998. 192–193.

19. Jacobs, J. and P. Avery. "The Diaries of a CIA Operative." *The Washington Post*. September 5, 1977. A1.

20. Albarelli, H. *A Terrible Mistake: The Murder of Frank Olson and the CIA's Secret Cold War Experiments*. Waterville, OR: Trine Day, 2009.

21. Haydon, H. "French Insanity Blamed on LSD." *The Sun*. March 11, 2010. http://www.thesun.co.uk/sol/homepage/news/2888558/French-insanity-blamed-on-LSD.html.

22. Albarelli, H. *A Terrible Mistake: The Murder of Frank Olson and the CIA's Secret Cold War Experiments*. Waterville, OR: Trine Day, 2009.

23. Blume, M. "France's Unsolved Mystery of the Poisoned Bread." *The New York Times*. July 23, 2008. http://www.nytimes.com/2008/07/24/arts/24iht-blume.1.14718462.html

24. Samuel, H. "French Bread Spiked with LSD." *The Telegraph U.K.* March 11, 2010. http://www.telegraph.co.uk/news/worldnews/europe/france/7415082/French-bread-spiked-with-LSD-in-CIA-experiment.html.

25. Cockburn, A., and J. St. Clair. *Whiteout: The CIA, Drugs, and the Press*. London: Verso, 1998.

26. Lee, Martin A., and B. Shlain. *Acid Dreams: The Complete Social History of LSD: The CIA, the Sixties, and Beyond*. New York: Grove Press, 1992.

27. United States Senate. "Project MKULTRA: The CIA's Program of Research in Behavior Modification." Joint Hearing Before the Select Committee on Intelligence and the Subcommittee on Health and Scientific Research of the Committee on Human

Resources 95th Congress 1st Session. August 3, 1977. Washington, DC: U.S. Govt. Print. Off., 1977.

28. U.S. Drug Enforcement Agency. "Controlled Substance Schedules." 2010. http://www.justice.gov/dea/pubs/scheduling.pdf.

29. Nutt, D., L. A. King, W. Saulsbury, and C. Blakemore. "Development of a Rational Scale to Assess the Harm of Drugs of Potential Misuse." *Lancet* 369: (2007) 1047–53.

30. Halser, Felix, U. Grimberg, M. Benz, et al. "Acute Psychological and Physiological Effects of Psilocybin in Healthy Humans: A Double Blind, Placebo-controlled Dose-effect Study." *Psychopharmacology* 172 (2004): 145–56.

31. Robson, Phillip. "Therapeutic Aspects of Cannabis and Cannabinoids." *British Journal of Psychiatry* 178 (2001): 107–115.

32. Richards, B. "The Gang That Couldn't Spray Straight: How the CIA's LSD Spray Bombed in San Francisco." *The Washington Post.* September 21, 1977. A1.

33. United States Senate. "Project MKULTRA: The CIA's Program of Research in Behavior Modification." Joint Hearing Before the Select Committee on Intelligence and the Subcommittee on Health and Scientific Research of the Committee on Human Resources 95th Congress 1st Session. August 3, 1977. Washington, DC: U.S. Govt. Print. Off., 1977.

34. Buckman, J. "Social and Medical Aspects of Illicit Use of LSD." *International Journal of Social Psychiatry* 17.3: (1971) 163.

35. Ibid., 163–176.

36. Ibid., 163–176.

37. Wolfe, T. *The Electric Acid Kool-Aid Test.* New York: Farrar, Straus and Giroux, 1968.

38. Lee, M. A. and B. Shlain. *Acid Dreams: The Complete Social History of LSD: the CIA, the Sixties, and Beyond.* New York: Grove Press, 1992. 239.

39. Schou, N. "How the Brotherhood of Eternal Love Is Connected to the Weather Underground Via the Black Panthers." *OC Weekly.* September 17, 2009.

40. Lee, M. A. and B. Shalin. *Acid Dreams: The Complete History of LSD: The CIA, the Sixties, and Beyond.* New York: Grove Press, 1992. 268–271.

41. Schou, N. "Distant Karma Catches Up with the Brotherhood's Brenice Lee Smith." *OC Weekly.* December 10, 2009.

42. United States Senate. "Project MKULTRA: The CIA's Program of Research in Behavior Modification." Joint Hearing Before the Select Committee on Intelligence and the Subcommittee on Health and Scientific Research of the Committee on Human Resources 95th Congress 1st Session. August 3, 1977. Washington, DC: U.S. Govt. Print. Off., 1977.

43. United States Congress. House Un-American Activities Committee (HUAC). "Subversive Influences in Riots, Looting, and Burning." Washington, D.C.: GPO, (1967, 1968). Part 1.

Chapter 9

1. Valentine, Douglas. *The Strength of the Pack: The Personalities, Politics and Espionage Intrigues That Shaped the DEA.* Walterville, OR: Trine Day, 2009. Print.

2. U.S. Congress House Committee on Un-American Activities. "Communist Activities in the Central California Area." Hearings, 90th Congress, 1st session. July 12, 1964 and April 27 and 28, 1966. Print.

3. Lee, Martin A., Bruce Shlain, and Andrei Codrescu. *Acid Dreams: The Complete Social History of LSD: The CIA, the Sixties, and beyond.* London: Pan, 2001. Print. 132.

4. Ibid., 128.

5. Buckman, J. "Social and Medical Aspects of Illicit Use of LSD." *International Journal of Social Psychiatry* 17.3 (1971): 163–76. Print.

6. Suchman, Edward. "The 'Hang-Loose' Ethic and the Spirit of Drug Use." *Journal of Health and Social Behavior.* Special Issue on Recreational Drug Use. 9.2 (1968): 146–55. Print.

7. Klee, Hilary. *Amphetamine Misuse: International Perspectives on Current Trends.* Amsterdam: Harwood Academic, 1997. Print.

8. Lee, Martin A., Bruce Shlain, and Andrei Codrescu. *Acid Dreams: The Complete Social History of LSD: The CIA, the Sixties, and beyond.* London: Pan, 2001. Print. 22, 128, 129.

9. Solis, G.D. *Marines and Military Law in Vietnam: Trial by Fire.* Washington, D.C.: Headquarters, U.S. Marine Corps, 1989. Print. 74.

10. Parks, W.H. "Statistics Versus Actuality in Vietnam." *Air University Review* 32.4: (1981) Print. 86.

11. Solis, G.D. *Marines and Military Law in Vietnam: Trial by Fire.* Washington, DC: Headquarters, U.S. Marine Corps, 1989. Print. 126–127.

12. Brush, P. "Higher and Higher: Drug Use Among U.S. Forces in Vietnam." *Vietnam* 15.4: (2002) Print. 46–53, 70.

13. Zinberg, N.E. "G.I.'s and O.J.'s in Vietnam." *New York Times Magazine* (December 5, 1971) Print. 120.

14. Ibid.

15. Massing, Michael. *The Fix.* New York: Simon & Schuster, 1998. Print. 107–111.

16. Torgoff, Martin. *Can't Find My Way Home: America in the Great Stoned Age, 1945–2000.* New York: Simon & Schuster, 2004. Print.

17. McCoy, Alfred W. *The Politics of Heroin: CIA Complicity in the Global Drug Trade, Afghanistan, Southeast Asia, Central America, Colombia.* Chicago: Lawrence Hill, 2003. Print.

18. Solis, G.D. *Marines and Military Law in Vietnam: Trial by Fire.* Washington, DC: Headquarters, U.S. Marine Corps, 1989. Print. 126–127.

19. Brush, P. "Higher and Higher: Drug Use Among U.S. Forces in Vietnam." *Vietnam* 15.4: (2002) Print. 46–53, 70.

20. Cockburn, Alexander and Jeffrey St. Clair. *Whiteout: The CIA, Drugs, and the Press.* London: Verso, 1999. Print.

21. U.S. Treasury Department, Bureau of Narcotics. *Traffic in Opium and Other Dangerous Drugs for the Year Ending December 31, 1965.* Washington, DC: U.S. Government Printing Office, 1966. Print. 45.

22. McCoy, Alfred W. *The Politics of Heroin: CIA Complicity in the Global Drug Trade, Afghanistan, Southeast Asia, Central America, Colombia.* Chicago: Lawrence Hill, 2003. Print.

23. Statement of John E. Ingersoll, Director, Bureau of Narcotics and Dangerous Drugs, before the National Commission on Marijuana and Drug Abuse, New York City, February 24, 1972, p. 5. In McCoy, Alfred W. *The Politics of Heroin: CIA Complicity in the Global Drug Trade, Afghanistan, Southeast Asia, Central America, Colombia.* Chicago: Lawrence Hill, 2003. Print.

24. Ibid.

25. Paulson, Daryl S., and Stanley Krippner. *Haunted by Combat: Understanding PTSD in War Veterans Including Women, Reservists, and Those Coming Back from Iraq.* Westport, CT: Praeger Security International, 2007. Print. xii.

26. "Gangland." *Mongol Nation.* History Channel. Episode 21(8). May 15, 2008. Television.

27. "Motorbike Gangs to Lose Their Bad Name—Starting with the Mongols." *The Times | UK News, World News and Opinion.* October 23, 2008. http://www.timesonline.co.uk/tol/news/world/us_and_americas/article4996010.ece. Accessed on September 7, 2010.

28. Frenkel, S. I., D. W. Morgan, and J. Greden. "Heroin Use Among Soldiers in the United States and Vietnam: A Comparison in Retrospect." *Substance Use and Misuse* 12.8 (1977): Print. 1143–1154.

29. United States. Department of Justice. Office of Justice Programs. *Veterans in State and Federal Prison, 2004.* By Margaret E. Noonan and Christopher J. Mumola. Vol. NCJ 217199. Washington, DC: Bureau of Justice Statistics Special Report, 2007. Print. 9.

30. Massing, Michael. *The Fix.* New York: Simon & Schuster, 1998. Print. 114–116.

31. Jacobson, Mark. *American Gangster and Other Tales of New York.* New York: Blac Cat, 2007. Print.

32. Ibid.

33. McCoy, Alfred W. *The Politics of Heroin: CIA Complicity in the Global Drug Trade, Afghanistan, Southeast Asia, Central America, Colombia.* Brooklyn, NY: Lawrence Hill, 1991. Print.

34. Chepesiuk, Ron. *The War on Drugs: An International Encyclopedia.* Santa Barbara, CA: ABC-CLIO, 1999. Print. 2.

35. McCoy, Alfred W., Cathleen B. Read, and Leonard P. Adams. *The Politics of Heroin in Southeast Asia.* New York: Harper & Row, 1972. Print.

36. McCoy, Alfred W. *The Politics of Heroin: CIA Complicity in the Global Drug Trade, Afghanistan, Southeast Asia, Central America, Colombia.* Chicago: Lawrence Hill, 2003. Print.

37. Eshleman Jr., Russell E. "Probe in PA Nets Massive Cocaine Ring." *Inquirer* [Harrisburg] August 9, 1986. http://articles.philly.com/1986-08-09/news/26065033_1_cocaine-air-america-american-pilots. Accessed on September 7, 2010.

38. Rice, Berkeley. *Trafficking: The Boom and Bust of the Air America Cocaine Ring.* New York: Scribner, 1989. Print.

39. McCoy, Alfred W. *The Politics of Heroin: CIA Complicity in the Global Drug Trade, Afghanistan, Southeast Asia, Central America, Colombia.* Brooklyn, NY: Lawrence Hill, 1991. Print. 23.

Chapter 10

1. Bowden, Charles, and Julián Cardona. *Murder City: Ciudad Juárez and the Global Economy's New Killing Fields.* New York: Nation, 2010. Print.

2. Guillermoprieto, Alma. "Letter from Mexico: Days of the Dead." *The New Yorker* November 10, 2008. http://www.newyorker.com/reporting/2008/11/10/081110fa_fact_guillermoprieto. Accessed on August 25, 2010.

3. Ryo, Emily. "Through the Back Door: Applying Theories of Legal Compliance to Illegal Immigration During the Chinese Exclusion Era." *Law & Social Inquiry* 31.1: (2006) Print. 109–46.

4. Astorga, Luís. "Drug Trafficking in Mexico: A First General Assessment." Management of Social Transformations—MOST, United Nations Educational, Scientific and Cultural Organization. Discussion Paper No. 36. http://www.unesco.org/most/astorga.htm. Accessed on March 1, 2008.

5. Astorga, Luis, A. "El Siglo de Las Drogas." Espasa-Calpe Mexicana. Mexico DF, 1996. Print. 15–28.

6. Guillermoprieto, Alma. "Letter from Mexico: Days of the Dead." *The New Yorker* November 10, 2008. http://www.newyorker.com/reporting/2008/11/10/081110fa_fact_guillermoprieto. Accessed on August 25, 2010.

7. Shannon, Elaine. *Desperados: Latin Drug Lords, U.S. Lawmen, and the War America Can't Win.* New York: Penguin Group, 1989. Print. 63.

8. Astorga, Luís. "Drug Trafficking in Mexico: A First General Assessment." Management of Social Transformations—MOST, United Nations Educational, Scientific and Cultural Organization. Discussion Paper No. 36. http://www.unesco.org/most/astorga.htm. Accessed on March 1, 2008.

9. Badillo, A. R., Carlos Magis-Rodríguez, R. Ortiz-Mondragón, R. Lozada-Romero, P. E. Uribe-Zúñiga. "Persons Who Injecting Drug in Treatment and Prisoners in Tijuana, Baja California, Mexico." Presentation at the XII International Conference on AIDS. Geneva, Switzerland. Abstract no. 23218. 1998. Print. 385.

10. Astorga, Luís. "Drug Trafficking in Mexico: A First General Assessment." Management of Social Transformations—MOST, United Nations Educational, Scientific and Cultural Organization. Discussion Paper No. 36. http://www.unesco.org/most/astorga.htm. Accessed on March 1, 2008.

11. Bucardo, Jesus, Kimberly C. Brouwer, Carlos Magis-Rodríguez, Rebeca Ramos, Miguel Fraga, Saida G. Perez, Thomas L. Patterson, and Steffanie A. Strathdee. "Historical Trends in the Production and Consumption of Illicit Drugs in Mexico: Implications for the Prevention of Blood Borne Infections." *Drug and Alcohol Dependence* 79.3: (2005) Print. 281–93.

12. Astorga, Luís. "Drug Trafficking in Mexico: A First General Assessment." Management of Social Transformations—MOST, United Nations Educational, Scientific and Cultural Organization. Discussion Paper No. 36. http://www.unesco.org/most/astorga.htm. Accessed on March 1, 2008.

13. Logan, Samuel. "Mexico's Internal Drug War." *Power and Interest News Report (PINR)* August 14, 2006. Print.

14. U.S. Senate Committee Report on Drugs, Law Enforcement and Foreign Policy. Subcommittee testimony of General Paul Gorman. Part Two. 1988. Print. 8, 27.

15. U.S. Senate Committee on Foreign Relations, Subcommittee on Terrorism, Narcotics and International Operations. "Drugs, Law Enforcement, and Foreign Policy." 100th Congress Second Session. December 1988. Committee Print. 1.

16. Wallace-Wells, B. "How America Lost the War on Drugs." *Rolling Stone.* December 2007. http://www.rollingstone.com/politics. Accessed on August 25, 2010. http://www.rollingstone.com/politics/story/17438347/how_america_lost_the_war_on_drugs

17. Guillermoprieto, Alma. "Letter from Mexico: Days of the Dead." *The New Yorker.* November 10, 2008. http://www.newyorker.com/reporting/2008 /11/10/081110fa_fact_guillermoprieto. Accessed on August 25, 2010.

18. U.S. Department of State. "2008 International Narcotics Control Strategy Report." http://www.state.gov/p/inl/rls/nrcrpt/2008/index.htm. Accessed on August 25, 2010.

19. Diaz, Lizbeth. "Mexico Death Industry Thrives on Drug War Killings." Reuters.com. November 1, 2008. http://www.reuters.com/article/worldNews/idUSTRE4A01QZ20081101. Accessed on August 25, 2010.

20. Mohan, G. "Mexico Under Siege: The Drug War at our Doorstep." *Los Angeles Times.* July 25, 2010. http://projects.latimes.com/mexico-drug-war/#/its-a-war. Accessed on August 25, 2010.

21. Lloyd, Marion. "New fear in Mexico: Army Soldiers Fleeing for Cartels." *Houston Chronicle.* June 18, 2007. http://www.chron.com/disp/story.mpl/front/4897648.html. Accessed on August 25, 2010.

22. Rabasa, Angel, and Peter Chalk. *Colombian Labyrinth: the Synergy of Drugs and Insurgency and Its Implications for Regional Stability.* Santa Monica, CA: Rand, 2001. Print.

23. Diaz, Lizbeth. "Mexico Death Industry Thrives on Drug War Killings." Reuters.com. November 1, 2008. http://www.reuters.com/article/worldNews/idUSTRE4A01QZ20081101. Accessed on August 25, 2010.

24. Roebuck, Jeremy. "Violence the Result of Fractured Arrangement, Authorities Say." *Brownsville Herald.* March 9, 2010. http://www.brownsvilleherald.com/news/say-109525 -arrangement-violence.html. Accessed on August 31, 2010.

25. Shachtman, Noah. "Danger Room Debrief: Gang Threat Could Top Al Qaeda, Mr. President-Elect." Wired.com. November 17, 2008. http://blog.wired.com/defense/2008/11/ john-p-sullivan.html. Accessed on August 25, 2010.

26. U.S. Department of Justice Press Release. "175 Alleged Gulf Cartel Members and Associates Arrested in Massive International Law Enforcement Operation." September 17, 2008. http://www.fbi.gov/pressrel/pressrel08/cartel091708.htm. Accessed on August 25, 2010.

27. United States Department of Defense, Mexico Section 1004, Counter-Drug Assistance 2006. Office of Freedom of Information. Freedom of Information Act Request by Marina Walker Guevara, Ref: 06-F-0839. Washington: September 26, 2006. Print.

28. Just the Facts. Center for International Policy, the Latin America Working Group Education Fund. Washington Office on Latin America. http://justf.org. Accessed on August 25, 2010.

29. McCaffrey, Barry. "The President's Foreign Policy Inbox: U.S.-Mexico Relations." *Council on Foreign Relations.* February 10, 2009. General meeting transcript. http://www.cfr. org/publication/18593/presidents_foreign_policy_inbox.html. Accessed on August 25, 2010.

30. Quinones, Sam, and A. Serrano. "Mexico's Drug War: Mexico Drug Wars Spill Across the Border." *Los Angeles Times.* http://www.latimes.com/news/nationworld/nation/ la-na-cartels16-2008nov16,0,1692616.story?page=1. Accessed on August 25, 2010.

31. Pruden, Wesley. "The Missing Troops on the Border." *Washington Times.* June 30, 2006. http://www.washingtontimes.com. Accessed on August 25, 2010.

32. Bello, David Anthony. *Opium and the Limits of Empire: Drug Prohibition in the Chinese Interior, 1729–1850.* Cambridge, MA: Harvard University Asia Center, 2005. Print. 9.

33. Inskeep, Stephen. "As the Drug War Rages On, Will Mexico Surrender?" NPR: National Public Radio: Morning Edition. http://www.npr.org/templates/transcript/transcript .php?storyId=129009629. Accessed on August 25, 2010.

34. Ibid.

35. "Mexico Drugs War Murders Data Mapped" Guardian.co.uk. July 7, 2011. http:// www.guardian.co.uk/news/datablog/2011/jan/14/mexico-drug-war-murders-map.

36. Google Fusion Tables: Data Download from Mexican Government Database. July 7, 2011. http://www.google.com/fusiontables/DataSource?dsrcid=393962.

37. Luhnow, David, and Jose Cordoba. "A New Spate of Violence Roils Mexico." *The Wall Street Journal.* August 29, 2010. A6.

38. Hanson, Stephanie. "Mexico's Drug War." *Council on Foreign Relations.* November 20, 2008. http://www.cfr.org/publication/13689/. Accessed on August 25, 2010.

39. "Drug Violence in Mexico: Data Analysis from 2001–2009." Trans-Border Institute at the University of San Diego. http://www.sandiego.edu/peacestudies/tbi/. Accessed on August 25, 2010.

40. "Mexico Blames Cartel for Police Chief Murder." MSNBC.com. http://www.msnbc .msn.com/id/24594471/. Accessed on August 25, 2010.

41. Sanchez-Ruiz, Juan A. "Narcotrafficking in Mexico." Pentagon Report No. A942903. http://www.stormingmedia.us/94/9429/A942903.html. Accessed on August 25, 2010.

42. Guillermoprieto, Alma. "Letter from Mexico: Days of the Dead." *The New Yorker.* November 10, 2008. http://www.newyorker.com/reporting/2008/11/10/081110fa_fact_ guillermoprieto. Accessed on August 29, 2010.

43. Magaloni, Ana Laura. "The Justice Debate in Mexico: The Reform and Future Challenges." *Woodrow Wilson International Center for Scholars.* http://www.wilsoncenter.org/index.cfm?topic_id=5949&fuseaction=topics.event_summary&event_id=405271. Accessed on August 26, 2010.

44. Lee, Martin A., Bruce Shlain, and Andrei Codrescu. *Acid Dreams: The Complete Social History of LSD: the CIA, the Sixties, and beyond.* London: Pan, 2001. Print. 238.

45. Cockburn, Alexander and Jeffrey St. Clair. *Whiteout: The CIA, Drugs, and the Press.* London: Verso, 1999. Print. 348, 352.

46. McCaffrey, General Barry R. "After Action Report Mexico Visit December 5–7, 2008." United States Military Academy. International Affairs. December 29, 2008. http://www.afa.org/EdOp/AAR-Mexico2008.pdf. Accessed on August 29, 2010.

47. Iliff, Lawrence. "Mexico's Drug Czar Accused of Taking Money from Cartel." *The Dallas Morning News.* November 21, 2008. http://www.dallasnews.com/sharedcontent/dws/dn/latestnews/stories/112208dnintmexico.1d65030a5.html. Accessed on August 25, 2010.

48. Preston, Julia. "Drugs Connect Mexico Leaders to Abductions." *The New York Times.* March 9, 1997. http://www.nytimes.com/1997/03/09/world/drugs-connect-mexico-leaders-to-abductions.html?ref=jesus_gutierrez_rebollo&pagewanted=1. Accessed on August 29, 2010.

49. "Mexico Suspects Ex-Drug Czar Took Huge Bribes from Traffickers." CNN.com. CNN Mexico. November 21, 2008. http://www.cnn.com/2008/WORLD/americas/11/21/mexico.arrest/index.html. Accessed on August 29, 2010.

50. Becerra, Oscar. "New Traffickers Struggle for Control of Mexican Drug Trade." *Jane's Intelligence Review.* September 1, 2004. Print.

51. Thompson, Ginger. "Mexico Fears Its Drug Traffickers Get Help from Guatemalans." *The New York Times.* http://www.nytimes.com/2005/09/30/international/americas/30mexico.html?_r=2. Accessed on September 30, 2005.

52. Bunker, R. *Networks, Terrorism and Global Insurgency.* London: Routledge, 2005. Print. xv.

53. Subcommittee on Crime, Terrorism, and Homeland Security. "Weak Bilateral Law Enforcement Presence at the U.S. Mexico Border." November 2005. Print.

54. Grayson, George W. "Los Zetas: The Ruthless Army Spawned by a Mexican Drug Cartel." Foreign Policy Research Institute—FPRI. http://www.fpri.org/enotes/200805.grayson.loszetas.html. Accessed on August 26, 2010.

55. Thompson, Ginger. "Mexico Fears Its Drug Traffickers Get Help from Guatemalans." *The New York Times.* http://www.nytimes.com/2005/09/30/international/americas/30mexico.html?_r=2. Accessed on September 30, 2005.

56. U.S. Department of Justice. "National Drug Threat Assessment 2009." Washington, DC: National Drug Intelligence Center. http://www.usdoj.gov/dea/concern/18862/ndic_2009.pdf. Accessed on August 20, 2010.

57. Carter, Sara, A. "FBI Warns of Drug Cartel Arming: Cites Order to Hold Turf." *The Washington Times.* October 26, 2008. http://washingtontimes.com/news/2008/oct/26/fbi-warns-of-cartel-arming. Accessed on August 25, 2010.

58. "Italy Nabs 300 Mobsters, Reveals New Mob Structure: Ndrangheta, Mafia, Crime Now." TheMonitor.com. Associated Press. July 13, 2010. http://www.themonitor.com/articles/ndrangheta-40760-mafia-crime.html. Accessed on August 29, 2010.

59. Conery, Ben. "DEA Arrests 175 Drug-Smuggle Suspects." *The Washington Times.* September 18, 2008. http://washingtontimes.com/news/2008/sep/18/dea-operation-nets-175-drug-smuggle-suspects. Accessed on August 29, 2010.

60. "Border-Town Killing Sends Message." Los Angeles Times. June 10, 2005. Print.

61. Suverza, Alejandro. "Los Zetas, una Liesadilla Liara el Cartel del Golfo." *El Universal.* January 12, 2008. Print. 1.

62. Wilkinson, Tracy. "Mexico: Suspected Drug Lord Captured in Mexico State." *Los Angeles Times.* August 30, 2010. http://www.latimes.com/news/nationworld/world/la -fg-mexico-barbie-20100831,0,5384395.story. Accessed on August 31, 2010.

63. Associated Press. "Mexico Captures Reported Drug Lord 'The Barbie.'" NPR: National Public Radio. August 31, 2010. http://www.npr.org/templates/story/story .php?storyId=103181125. Accessed on August 31, 2010.

64. Luhnow, David, and Jose de Cordoba. "The Drug Lord Who Got Away: Mexican Capo Unleashes Mayhem on U.S. Border; The Making of a Legend." *The Wall Street Journal.* June 13, 2009. http://online.wsj.com/article/NA_WSJ_PUB:SB124484177023110993.html. Accessed on August 31, 2010.

65. Lawson, Gary. "The War Next Door: As Drug Cartels Battle the Government, Mexico Descends into Chaos." *Rolling Stone.* March 20, 2009. http://www.rollingstone.com/politics/ story/24012731/the_war_next_door.

66. Bowden, Charles, and Julián Cardona. *Murder City: Ciudad Juárez and the Global Economy's New Killing Fields.* New York: Nation, 2010. Print.

67. Smith, Phillip. "Murder City by Border Cognoscenti Charles Bowden." Stop the Drug War. July 29, 2010. http://stopthedrugwar.org/chronicle/2010/jul/29/ murder_city_border_cognoscenti_c.

68. Bowden, Charles, and Julián Cardona. *Murder City: Ciudad Juárez and the Global Economy's New Killing Fields.* New York: Nation, 2010. Print.

69. "Mexico Police Detain Their Own Commander at Gunpoint." BBC News. August 8, 2010. http://www.bbc.co.uk/news/world-latin-america-10910068.

70. "Federal Police Comandante on Sinaloa Cartel Payoff List." *Borderland Beat.* August 10, 2010. http://www.borderlandbeat.com/2010/08/federal-police-comandante-on-sinaloa .html. Accessed on August 29, 2010.

71. Bowden, Mark. *Killing Pablo: The Hunt for the World's Greatest Outlaw.* New York: Penguin Books, 2002. Print.

72. "Hallan Tres Cabezas Humanas en Plaza Pública de Puerto Palomas." Diario.com. mx: Edición Cd. Juárez. http://www.diario.com.mx/nota.php?notaid=e5bdcf33b687740 f915a644cfedd043a. Accessed on August 8, 2010.

73. "Severed Heads Discovered in Mexico State." UPI International News. July 28, 2010. http://www.upi.com/Top_News/International/2010/07/28/Severed-heads-discovered-in -Mexico-state/UPI-44281280339783/. Accessed on August 30, 2010.

74. Guillermoprieto, Alma. "Letter from Mexico: Days of the Dead." *The New Yorker.* November 10, 2008. http://www.newyorker.com/reporting/2008/11/10/081110fa_fact_ guillermoprieto. Accessed on August 29, 2010.

75. Lawson, Gary. "The War Next Door: As Drug Cartels Battle the Government, Mexico Descends into Chaos." *Rolling Stone.* November 13, 2008. http://www.rollingstone .com/politics/story/24012731/the_war_next_door. Accessed on March 10, 2009.

76. Ibid.

77. Wald, Elijah. *Narcocorrido: A Journey into the Music of Drugs, Guns, and Guerrillas.* New York: Rayo, 2002. Print.

78. Roberts, Chris. "Intelligence Chief Sees Border as Terrorist Entryway." *El Paso Times.* March 27, 2009. http://www.elpasotimes.com/ci_6683672?IADID=Search-www .elpasotimes.com-www.elpasotimes.com. Accessed on May 1, 2009.

79. "Congresswoman Raises Red Flag on Hezbollah-Cartel Nexus on U.S. Border." FOXNews.com. August 25, 2010. http://www.foxnews.com/politics/2010/06/25/ congresswoman-raises-red-flag-hezbollah-cartel-nexus-border. Accessed on July 1, 2010.

80. Roberts, Chris. "Intelligence Chief Sees Border as Terrorist Entryway." *El Paso Times*. March 27, 2009. http://www.elpasotimes.com/ci_6683672?IADID=Search-www .elpasotimes.com-www.elpasotimes.com. Accessed on July 1, 2010.

81. Stewart, Scott. "Hezbollah Radical, but Rational." Stratfor Global Intelligence Security Weekly Report. August 12, 2010. http://www.stratfor.com/weekly/20100811_ hezbollah_radical_rational. Accessed on August 30, 2010.

82. Ibid.

83. Carter, Sara A. "Hezbollah Uses Mexican Drug Routes into U.S." *Washington Times*. March 27, 2009. http://www.washingtontimes.com/news/2009/mar/27/hezbollah-uses -mexican-drug-routes-into-us/. Accessed on April 15, 2009.

84. Luhnow, David, and Jose Cordoba. "A New Spate of Violence Roils Mexico." *Wall Street Journal*. August 29, 2010. http://online.wsj.com/article/SB2000142405274870414780 4575455663134960250.html. Accessed on August 31, 2010.

85. Michaels, Jim. "U.S. Military Works with Mexico to Fight Drug Traffickers." *USA Today* [Washington, DC]. April 6, 2010. http://www.usatoday.com/news/military/2010 -04-06-Mexico_N.htm. Accessed on July 13, 2011.

86. Memo from the Washington Office on Latin America, The Merida Initiative and Citizen Security in Mexico and Central America. March 18, 2008. http://www.wola.org/ index. Accessed on August 20, 2010.

87. Associated Press. "Clinton: U.S. Drug Use Fuels Border Violence." MSNBC.com. http://www.msnbc.msn.com/id/29875572/. Accessed on August 26, 2010.

88. "CIA—The World Factbook." Central Intelligence Agency. https://www.cia.gov/ library/publications/the-world-factbook/fields/2086.html. Accessed on August 25, 2010.

89. Scott, Peter Dale. *Drugs, Oil, and War: The United States in Afghanistan, Colombia, and Indochina*. Lanham, MD: Rowman & Littlefield, 2003. Print. 89.

90. Mills, James. *The Underground Empire: Where Crime and Government Embrace*. New York: Dell, 1986. Print. 1135, 1181.

91. Bowden, Charles. "U.S.-Mexico 'War on Drugs' a Failure." http://www.cnn.com /2010/OPINION/03/31/bowden.ciudad.juarez.cartels/index.html. Accessed on April 10, 2010.

92. Luhnow, David, and Jose Cordoba. "A New Spate of Violence Roils Mexico." *Wall Street Journal*. August 29, 2010. http://online.wsj.com/article/SB2000142405274870414780 4575455663134960250.html. Accessed on August 31, 2010.

93. "U.S. Embassy Mexico American Citizens Services, Mexico Security Update." http:// mexico.usembassy.gov/eng/eacs_MexicoSecurityUpdate.html. Accessed on August 1, 2010.

94. Ibid.

95. Luhnow, David, and Jose Cordoba. "A New Spate of Violence Roils Mexico." *Wall Street Journal*. August 29, 2010. http://online.wsj.com/article/SB2000142405274870414780 4575455663134960250.html. Accessed on August 31, 2010.

96. Ibid.

97. Inskeep, Stephen. "As the Drug War Rages On, Will Mexico Surrender?" NPR: National Public Radio: Morning Edition. http://www.npr.org/templates/transcript/transcript .php?storyId=129009629. Accessed on August 25, 2010.

98. Finlay, Brian. "WMD, Drugs, and Criminal Gangs in Central America: Leveraging Nonproliferation Assistance to Address Security/Development Needs with UN Security

Council Resolution 1540." A report from the Stimson Center and the Stanley Foundation. 2010. Print. 3.

99. United Nations Office on Drugs and Crime. "Crime and Development in Central America: Caught in the Crossfire." May 2007. Print.

100. United States Joint Forces Command. "Joint Operating Environment 2008: Challenges and Implications for the Future Joint Forces." 2008. http://www.jfcom.mil/newslink/storyarchive/2008/JOE2008.pdf. Print. 35–36.

Chapter 11

1. United Nations Office on Drugs and Crime. "Addiction, Crime, and Insurgency: The Transnational Threat of Afghan Opium." October 2009.1. http://www.unodc.org/documents/data-and-analysis/Afghanistan/Afghan_Opium_Trade_2009_web.pdf. Accessed on July 1, 2010.

2. Asad, Amir Zada, and Robert Harris. *The Politics and Economics of Drug Production on the Pakistan-Afghanistan Border: Implications for a Globalized World.* Hampshire, England: Ashgate, 2003. Print.

3. Ibid.

4. Ibid.

5. Scott, Peter Dale. *The Road to 9/11: Wealth, Empire, and the Future of America.* Berkeley: U of California, 2007. Print. 73–75.

6. Lifschultz, Lawrence. "Pakistan: The Empire of Heroin." In McCoy, Alfred W. and Alan A. Block. *War on Drugs: Studies in the Failure of US Narcotics Policy.* Boulder, CO: Westview, 1992. Print. 319–352.

7. Scott, Peter Dale. *The Road to 9/11: Wealth, Empire, and the Future of America.* Berkeley: U of California, 2007. Print. 73–75.

8. Beaty, Jonathan and S. C. Gwynne. *The Outlaw Bank: A Wild Ride into the Secret Heart of BCCI.* New York: Random House, 1993. Print. 291, 315.

9. Beaty, Jonathan, S. C. Gwynne, Cathy Booth, Jay Branegan, and Helen Gibson. "B.C.C.I.: The Dirtiest Bank of All." *Time.* July 29, 1991. http://www.time.com/time/magazine/article/0,9171,973481-2,00.html. Accessed on September 2, 2010.

10. United States House Committee on Intelligence. "Investigation of Allegations of Connections Between CIA and the Contras in Drug Trafficking to the United States: Prepared Statement of Frederick P. Hitz, Inspector General, Central Intelligence Agency." Volume I, The California Report. March 16, 1998. Washington, DC. http://www.odci.gov/cia. Accessed on March 1, 2010.

11. "Pakistan at a Glance." *The New York Times.* August 18, 1988. Print. A10.

12. Murphy, Richard McGill. "The Rise and Fall of a Drug Lord." Forbes. October 16, 1997. http://www.forbes.com/1997/10/16/feat_side1.html. Accessed on September 4, 2010.

13. Scott, Peter Dale. *The Road to 9/11: Wealth, Empire, and the Future of America.* Berkeley: U of California, 2007. Print. 124–125.

14. Asad, Amir Zada, and Robert Harris. *The Politics and Economics of Drug Production on the Pakistan-Afghanistan Border: Implications for a Globalized World.* Hampshire, England: Ashgate, 2003. Print.

15. Rupert, James, and Steve Coll. "U.S. Declines to Probe Afghan Drug Trade: Rebels, Pakistani Officers Implicated." *The Washington Post.* May 13, 1990. Print.

16. Maurus, Veronique, and Marc Rock. "The Most Dreaded Man of the United States, Controlled a Long Time by the CIA." Translated by Google Translate. *Le Monde (Paris).*

September 14, 2001. In Giraldo, Jeanne K., and Harold A. Trinkunas. *Terrorism Financing and State Responses: A Comparative Perspective*. Stanford, CA: Stanford UP, 2007. Print.

17. Scott, Peter Dale. *The Road to 9/11: Wealth, Empire, and the Future of America*. Berkeley: U of California, 2007. Print. 124–125.

18. Peters, Gretchen. *Seeds of Terror: How Heroin Is Bankrolling the Taliban and Al Qaeda*. New York: Thomas Dunne, 2009. Print. 44.

19. Scott, Peter Dale. *The Road to 9/11: Wealth, Empire, and the Future of America*. Berkeley: U of California, 2007. Print. 124–125.

20. McCoy, Alfred W. *The Politics of Heroin: CIA Complicity in the Global Drug Trade, Afghanistan, Southeast Asia, Central America, Colombia*. Chicago: Lawrence Hill, 2003. Print. 461.

21. Cooley, John K. *Unholy Wars: Afghanistan, America, and International Terrorism*. London: Pluto, 2002. Print. 105–107.

22. Asad, Amir Zada, and Robert Harris. *The Politics and Economics of Drug Production on the Pakistan-Afghanistan Border: Implications for a Globalized World*. Hampshire, England: Ashgate, 2003. Print. xi.

23. Peters, Gretchen. *Seeds of Terror: How Heroin Is Bankrolling the Taliban and Al Qaeda*. New York: Thomas Dunne, 2009. Print. 44.

24. United Nations Office on Drugs and Crime. "Addiction, Crime, and Insurgency: The Transnational Threat of Afghan Opium." October 2009. http://www.unodc.org/documents/data-and-analysis/Afghanistan/Afghan_Opium_Trade_2009_web.pdf. Accessed on July 1, 2010. 1.

25. Lifschultz, Lawrence. "Pakistan: The Empire of Heroin." In McCoy, Alfred W. and Alan A. Block. *War on Drugs: Studies in the Failure of US Narcotics Policy*. Boulder, CO: Westview, 1992. Print. 336–337.

26. Lowinson, Joyce H., and David F. Musto. "Drug Crisis and Strategy." *The New York Times*. May 22, 1980. A35.

27. "70% of Heroin Sold in U.S. Comes from Pakistan." *The Muslim*. January 18, 1984. Quoted in Lifschultz, Lawrence. "Pakistan: The Empire of Heroin." In McCoy, Alfred W. and Alan A. Block. *War on Drugs: Studies in the Failure of US Narcotics Policy*. Boulder, CO: Westview, 1992. Print. 319.

28. Asad, Amir Zada, and Robert Harris. *The Politics and Economics of Drug Production on the Pakistan-Afghanistan Border: Implications for a Globalized World*. Hampshire, England: Ashgate, 2003. 19.

29. United Nations Drug Control Program. "Afghanistan Annual Opium Poppy Survey." 2000. Print.

30. Mustikhan, Ahmar. "Killing the 'Living Dead': A Special Report on the Pakistani Drugs Trade." *New Internationalist*. October 1999. http://findarticles.com/p/articles/mi_m0JQP/is_317/ai_30143255/. Accessed on September 2, 2010.

31. Ibid.

32. "LTTE Fall Will Alter Drug Trade in India." *Times of India*. May 20, 2009. http://timesofindia.indiatimes.com/city/mumbai/LTTE-fall-will-alter-drug-trade-in-India/articleshow/4595554.cms#ixzz0wQLERgxo. Accessed on August 10, 2010.

33. Aryasinha, R. "Time to Act: The LTTE, Its Front Organizations, and the Challenge to Europe." EU US International Seminar on the LTTE, The Hague. December 9 and 10, 2008. http://www.priu.gov.lk/ltte_report/chapter6.html. Accessed on September 4, 2010.

34. Gavrilis, George. "The Good and Bad News about Afghan Opium." Council on Foreign Relations. February 10, 2010. http://www.cfr.org/publication/21372/good_and_bad_news_about_afghan_opium.html. Accessed on March 25, 2010.

35. Asad, Amir Zada, and Robert Harris. *The Politics and Economics of Drug Production on the Pakistan-Afghanistan Border: Implications for a Globalized World.* Hampshire, England: Ashgate, 2003. 9–10.

36. Peters, Gretchen. *Seeds of Terror: How Heroin Is Bankrolling the Taliban and Al Qaeda.* New York: Thomas Dunne, 2009. Print.

37. Gavrilis, George. "The Good and Bad News about Afghan Opium." Council on Foreign Relations. February 10, 2010. http://www.cfr.org/publication/21372/good_and_bad_news_about_afghan_opium.html. Accessed on March 25, 2010.

38. United States Government Accountability Office. Report to Congressional Committees. "Afghanistan Drug Control: Despite Improved Efforts, Deteriorating Security Threatens Success of U.S. Goals." GAO-07-78. Washington, DC. November 2006. Print.

39. U.S. Drug Enforcement Administration. "Afghan Drug Kingpin Charged with Financing Taliban Terrorist Insurgency." DEA Public Affairs Press Release. October 14, 2008. Print.

40. Garamone, Jim. "Progress Must Continue in Afghanistan, Commander Says." United States Department of Defense. March 2, 2007. http://www.defenselink.mil/news/newsarticle.aspx?id=3243. Accessed on September 4, 2010.

41. United Nations Office of Drug and Crime. "Afghanistan Opium Survey." August 2008. Print. vii.

42. Peters, Gretchen. *Seeds of Terror: How Heroin Is Bankrolling the Taliban and Al Qaeda.* New York: Thomas Dunne, 2009. Print. 94.

43. "CIA—The World Factbook." Central Intelligence Agency. September 1, 2009. https://www.cia.gov/library/publications/the-world-factbook/fields/2086.html.

44. Schweich, Tom. "U.S. Counternarcotics Strategy for Afghanistan." August 2007. Print.

45. United Nations Office on Drugs and Crime. "2009 Afghanistan Opium Survey: Summary Findings." 2010. Print.

46. United Nations Office on Drugs and Crime. "2009 Afghanistan Cannabis Survey." April 2010. Print. 46.

47. Ibid., 6.

48. Ibid., 6, 153, 194.

49. Ibid., 5.

50. Ibid., 3–5.

51. Ibid., 3–5.

52. Nelson, Soraya Sarhaddi. "Drug Addiction, and Misery, Increase in Afghanistan." National Public Radio. April 16, 2009. http://www.npr.org/templates/story/story.php?storyId=102984398. Accessed on April 30, 2009.

53. United Nations Office on Drugs and Crime. "Drug Use in Afghanistan 2009 Survey: Executive Summary." 2010. Print. 3.

54. "2009 International Narcotics Control Strategy Report (INCSR) on Kazakhstan—United States Diplomatic Mission to Kazakhstan." U.S. Government Reports. February 27, 2009. http://kazakhstan.usembassy.gov/incsr2009.html. Accessed on September 4, 2010.

55. United Nations Office on Drugs and Crime. "Addiction, Crime and Insurgency: The Transnational Threat of Afghan Opium." October 2009. Print. 1.

56. McCoy, Alfred W. *The Politics of Heroin: CIA Complicity in the Global Drug Trade, Afghanistan, Southeast Asia, Central America, Colombia.* Chicago: Lawrence Hill, 2003. Print. 477.

57. Cooley, John K. *Unholy Wars: Afghanistan, America, and International Terrorism.* London: Pluto, 2002. Print. 110–111.

58. Ibid.

59. Risen, James. "Reports Link Karzai's Brother to Afghan Heroin Trade." *The New York Times.* October 4, 2008. http://www.nytimes.com/2008/10/05/world/asia/05afghan .html?_r=1&ref=asia. Accessed on October 20, 2008.

60. Smith, Graeme. "Afghan Officials in Drug Trade Cut Deals Across Enemy Lines." *Globe and Mail.* March 21, 2009. http://v1.theglobeandmail.com/servlet/story/ LAC.20090321.AFGHANDRUGS21/TPStory/Afghanistan. Accessed on December 1, 2010.

61. Farmer, Ben. "General Daud Daud and at Least Two German Soldiers Killed by Suicide Bomb." *The Telegraph.* May 28, 2011. http://www.telegraph.co.uk/news/worldnews/ asia/afghanistan/8543955/General-Daud-Daud-and-at-least-two-German-soldiers-killed -by-suicide-bomb.html. Accessed on July 13, 2011.

62. Smith, Graeme. "Afghan Officials in Drug Trade Cut Deals Across Enemy Lines." *Globe and Mail.* March 21, 2009. http://v1.theglobeandmail.com/servlet/story/ LAC.20090321.AFGHANDRUGS21/TPStory/Afghanistan. Accessed on December 1, 2010.

63. Ibid.

64. Ibid.

65. Partlow, Joshua. "Karzai Brother's Killer Had Been Taliban Foe: Police Commander Had Shared Intelligence with U.S., Relatives Say." *Washington Post.* July 15, 2011. A1, A9.

66. Filkins, Dexter, Mark Mazetti, and James Risen. "Brother of Afghan Leader Said to Be Paid by C.I.A." *The New York Times* October 27, 2009. http://www.nytimes.com/2009/10/28/ world/asia/28intel.html. Accessed on July 13, 2011.

67. "Wali Karzai: Drugs Baron, CIA Agent or Afghan Defender?" *Pakistan National News.* July 12, 2011. http://www.pakistannationalnews.com/worl/wali- karzai-drugs-baron -cia-agent-or-afghan-defender/. Accessed on July 13, 2011.

68. "Attorney: Chicago Restaurant Sparked Karzai Brother's Political Interest." *Chicago Tribune.* July 12, 2011. http://www.chicagotribune.com/news/local/breaking/chi-assassinated -halfbrother-of-karzai-once-ran-chicago-restaurant-20110712,0,7593493.story. Accessed on July 13, 2011.

69. "Wali Karzai: Drugs Baron, CIA Agent or Afghan Defender?" *Pakistan National News.* July 12, 2011. http://www.pakistannationalnews.com/worl/wali- karzai-drugs-baron -cia-agent-or-afghan-defender/. Accessed on July 13, 2011.

70. Shaughnessy, Larry. "WikiLeaks: Karzai's Brother Denies Drug Dealing, Remembers Chicago." *CNN.* November 30, 2010. http://articles.cnn.com/2010-11-30/us/. Accessed on July 13, 2011.

71. Shulman, Daniel. "WikiLeaks: US Considers Prosecuting President Karzai's Brother." *Mother Jones Magazine.* December 3, 2010. http://m.motherjones.com/politics/2010/12/ wikileaks-cable-us-considered-prosecuting-ahmed-wali-karzai. Accessed on July 13, 2011.

72. Filkins, Dexter, Mark Mazetti, and James Risen. "Brother of Afghan Leader Said to Be Paid by C.I.A." *The New York Times.* October 27, 2009. http://www.nytimes.com/2009/10/28/ world/asia/28intel.html. Accessed on July 13, 2011.

73. "Attorney: Chicago Restaurant Sparked Karzai Brother's Political Interest." *Chicago Tribune.* July 12, 2011. http://www.chicagotribune.com/news/local/breaking/chi-assassinated -halfbrother-of-karzai-once-ran-chicago-restaurant-20110712,0,7593493.story. Accessed on July 13, 2011.

74. United States Government Accountability Office. Report to Congressional Committees. "Afghanistan Drug Control: Despite Improved Efforts, Deteriorating Security Threatens Success of U.S. Goals." GAO-07-78. Washington, DC. November 2006. Print. 8–9.

75. Peters, Gretchen. *Seeds of Terror: How Heroin Is Bankrolling the Taliban and Al Qaeda.* New York: Thomas Dunne, 2009. Print. 218–233.

76. White House. Transcript of President Barack Obama's prepared speech. March 27, 2009. Print.

77. Associated Press. "7,000 Marines Patrolling Southern Afghan Desert." June 8, 2009. http://www.npr.org/templates/story/story.php?storyId=105114403. Accessed on August 9, 2010.

78. Warlord, Inc. Extortion and Corruption Along the U.S. Supply Chain in Afghanistan, Rep. John F. Tierney, Subcommittee on National Security and Foreign Affairs, June 2010, 36.

79. Kamminga, Jorrit. "The Political History of Turkey's Opium Licensing System for the Production of Medicines: Lessons for Afghanistan." The Senlis Council Security and Development Policy Group. 2006. http://www.icosgroup.net/documents/Political_History_Poppy_Licensing_Turkey_May_2006.pdf. Accessed on July 10, 2010.

80. United Nations Office on Drugs and Crime. "Drug Use in Afghanistan 2009 Survey: Executive Summary." 2010. Print. 3.

81. Stanisławski, Bartosz Hieronim. "Definition and Backgrounds Global Black Spots-Mapping Global Insecurity." Global Black Spots-Mapping Global Insecurity Program. Moynihan Institute, Syracuse University. http://www1.maxwell.syr.edu/moynihan/gbs/Definition_and_Background/. Accessed on September 4, 2010.

82. Asad, A.Z. and R. Harris. *The Politics and Economics of Drug Production on the Pakistan-Afghanistan Border.* Hampshire, England, Ashgate, 2003. xii.

83. United Nations Office on Drugs and Crime. "2009 Afghanistan Opium Survey: Summary Findings." 2010. Print. v.

84. Ibid.

85. United States Joint Forces Command. "Joint Operating Environment 2008: Challenges and Implications for the Future Joint Forces." 2008. Print. 35–36. http://www.jfcom.mil/newslink/storyarchive/2008/JOE2008.pdf.

86. United Nations Office on Drugs and Crime. "Crime and Development in Central America: Caught in the Crossfire." May 2007. Print.

87. Oppel, Richard E. "U.N. Sees Afghan Drug Cartels Emerging." *The New York Times.* September 1, 2009. http://www.nytimes.com/2009/09/02/world/asia/02afghan.html. Accessed on July 14, 2011.

88. United States Joint Forces Command. "Joint Operating Environment 2008: Challenges and Implications for the Future Joint Forces." 2008. Print 35–36. http://www.jfcom.mil/newslink/storyarchive/2008/JOE2008.pdf.

89. U.S. Senate Committee on Foreign Relations. "Confirmation Hearings for Secretary of State Hillary Clinton." January 13, 2009. http://www.cfr.org/publication/18214/hillary_clintons_confirmation_hearing_statement.html. Accessed on October 1, 2009.

90. United Nations Office on Drugs and Crime. "2009 Afghanistan Opium Survey: Summary Findings." 2010. Print. vii.

Chapter 12

1. Tanielian, Terri, and Lisa H. Jaycox, Eds. "Invisible Wounds of War: Psychological and Cognitive Injuries, Their Consequences, and Services to Assist Recovery." Monograph MG-720, RAND Corporation. 2008. http://www.rand.org/pubs/monographs/2008/RAND_MG720.pdf. Accessed on May 1, 2010.

2. Paulson, Daryl S., and Stanley Krippner. *Haunted by Combat: Understanding PTSD in War Veterans, Including Women, Reservists, and Those Coming Back from Iraq.* Westport, CT: Praeger Security International, 2007. Print. xii.

3. Colonel C. Castro, and J. Kupersmith. "Addressing Substance Abuse and Comorbidities Among Military Personnel, Veterans, and Their Families: A Research Agenda." Sponsored by the National Institute on Drug Abuse, Bethesda, MD. January 6, 2009. Personal observation.

4. McCarroll, J. E., R. J. Ursano, C. S. Fullerton. "Symptoms of PTSD Following Recovery of War Dead: 13–15 Month Follow-Up." *American Journal of Psychiatry* 152: (1995) Print. 939–941.

5. Tanielian, Terri, and Lisa H. Jaycox, Eds. "Invisible Wounds of War: Psychological and Cognitive Injuries, Their Consequences, and Services to Assist Recovery." Monograph MG-720, RAND Corporation. 2008. http://www.rand.org/pubs/monographs/2008/RAND_MG720.pdf. Accessed on May 1, 2010.

6. Stam, Rianne. "PTSD and Stress Sensitization: A Tale of Brain and Body: Part 1: Human Studies." *Neuroscience & Biobehavioral Reviews* 31.4: (2007) Print. 530–557.

7. Violanti, John M., Cecil M. Burchfiel, Tara A. Hartley, Luenda E. Charles, and Diane B. Miller. "Post-Traumatic Stress Symptoms and Cortisol Patterns Among Police Officers." *Policing: An International Journal of Police Strategies and Management* 30.2: (2007) Print. 189–202.

8. Faust, Drew Gilpin. *This Republic of Suffering: Death and the American Civil War.* New York: Vintage, 2008. Print. 41.

9. United States Army. "Army Health Promotion Risk Reduction Suicide Prevention Report." 2010. Print. i.

10. Centers for Disease Control and Prevention. "Web-Based Injury Statistics Query and Reporting System (WISQARS)." National Center for Injury Prevention and Control, CDC. 2005. www.cdc.gov/ncipc/wisqars/default.htm. Accessed on March 1, 2010.

11. Tyson, Ann Scott. "Soldiers' Suicide Rate on Pace to Set Record." *Washington Post.* September 5, 2008. Print.

12. United States Army. "Army Health Promotion Risk Reduction Suicide Prevention Report." 2010. Print. i.

13. Fuchsman, Kenneth. "Traumatized Soldiers." *The Journal of Psychohistory* 36.1: (2008) Print. 72–84.

14. Bray, Robert, John A. Fairbank, and Mary Ellen Marsden. "Stress and Substance Use Among Military Women and Men." *American Journal of Drug and Alcohol Abuse* 25.2: (1999) 239–256. DOI: 10.1081/ADA-100101858.

15. United States Army. "Army Health Promotion Risk Reduction Suicide Prevention Report." 2010. Print. i.

16. Kahn, Joseph P. "For Addicted Veteran, Regulation Is Enemy." *The Boston Globe.* August 27, 2010. http://www.boston.com/yourtown/braintree/articles/2010/08/27/for_addicted_veteran_regulation_is_enemy/. Accessed on September 1, 2010.

17. United States Army. "Army Health Promotion Risk Reduction Suicide Prevention Report." 2010. Print. 55.

18. Ibid.

19. McCanna, Shaun. "It's Easy for Soldiers to Score Heroin in Afghanistan." *Salon.* August 7, 2007. http://www.salon.com/news/feature/2007/08/07/afghan_heroin. Accessed on September 5, 2010.

20. Goldsmith, K. S. Testimony presented to U.S. Congress. May 15, 2008.

21. White N. M. "Addictive Drugs as Reinforcers: Multiple Partial Actions on Memory Systems." *Addiction* 91.7: (1996) Print. 921–949, 951–965.

22. Miller, G. "'Go' Pills for F-16 Pilots Get Close Look / Amphetamines Prescribed in Mission That Killed Canadians." *Los Angeles Times.* January 4, 2003.

23. Ibid.

24. "Air Force Rushes to Defend Amphetamine Use." *The Age Australia.* January 8, 2003. http://www.theage.com.au/articles/2003/01/17/1042520778665.html. Accessed on May 2, 2010.

25. United States Army. "Army Health Promotion Risk Reduction Suicide Prevention Report." 2010. Print.

26. United States Department of Defense. "Survey of Health Related Behaviors Among Active Duty Military Personnel." Research Triangle Institute. December 2006. Print.

27. Stahre, Mandy A., Robert D. Brewer, Vincent P. Fonseca, and Timothy S. Naimi. "Binge Drinking Among U.S. Active-Duty Military Personnel." *American Journal of Preventive Medicine* 36.3: (2009) Print. 208–217.

28. Sean Thomas is a pseudonym to protect the veteran's personal identity. Interview conducted at Syracuse University on October 15, 2008.

29. Schneider, Eric C. *Vampires, Dragons, and Egyptian Kings: Youth Gangs in Postwar New York.* Princeton, NJ: Princeton UP, 1999. Print.

30. "Army to Report Record Number of Suicides." CNN.com. January 1, 2009. http://www.cnn.com/2009/US/01/29/army.suicides/index.html?iref=newssearch. Accessed on September 5, 2010.

31. Adam, David. "Ecstasy Trials for Combat Stress." *The Guardian.* February 17, 2005. http://www.guardian.co.uk/science/2005/feb/17/usnews.drugsandalcohol. Accessed on March 1, 2009.

32. Hardman, H. F., C. O. Haavik, and M. H. Seevers. "Relationship of the Structure of Mescaline and Seven Analogs to Toxicity and Behavior in Five Species of Laboratory Animals." *Toxicology and Applied Pharmacology* 25.2: (1979) Print. 299–309.

33. United States Drug Enforcement Agency. "Controlled Substance Schedules." http://www.justice.gov/dea/pubs/scheduling.pdf. Accessed on July 1, 2010.

34. Mithoefer, Michael. "MDMA-Assisted Psychotherapy in the Treatment of Posttraumatic Stress Disorder (PTSD): Ninth Update on Study Progress." *Multidisciplinary Association for Psychedelic Studies (MAPS)* 17.3: (2007) 14–15.

35. Baard, Erik. "The Guilt-Free Soldier: New Science Raises Specter of World Without Regret." *Village Voice.* January 22, 2003. http://www.villagevoice.com/2003-01-21/news/the-guilt-free-soldier/1. Accessed on June 6, 2009.

36. Ibid.

37. Committee on Veterans Compensation for Posttraumatic Stress Disorder. "PTSD Compensation and Military Service." Institute of Medicine and National Research Council. 110th Congress, 1st Session. July 25, 2007. Print.

38. Solheim, Bruce Olav. *The Vietnam War Era: A Personal Journey.* Westport, CT: Praeger, 2006. Print. 208.

39. United States Army. "Army Health Promotion Risk Reduction Suicide Prevention Report." 2010. Print. ii.

40. National Council on Disability. "Invisible Wounds: Serving Service Members and Veterans with PTSD and TBI." March 4, 2009. Print.

41. Committee on Veterans Compensation for Posttraumatic Stress Disorder. "PTSD Compensation and Military Service." Institute of Medicine and National Research Council. 110th Congress, 1st Session. July 25, 2007. Print.

Chapter 13

1. Rifkin, Jeremy. *Time Wars: The Primary Conflict in Human History.* New York: Simon & Schuster, 1987. Print.

2. Brave Heart, Maria Yellow Horse, and Lemyra M. DeBruyn. "The American Indian Holocaust: Healing Historical Unresolved Grief." *American Indian and Alaska Native Mental Health Research* 8.2: (1998) Print. 60–82.

3. U.S. Department of Health and Human Services. Indian Health Service. *Trends in Indian Health, 2000–2001 Edition.* Washington, DC: February 2004. Print.

4. Faludi, Susan. *The Terror Dream: Fear and Fantasy in Post-9/11 America.* New York: Metropolitan Books, 2007. Print.

5. McConnell, J. Michael. "Annual Threat Assessment of the Director of National Intelligence for the Senate Select Committee on Intelligence." Senate Select Committee on Intelligence. February 5, 2008. http://intelligence.senate.gov/080205/mcconnell.pdf. Accessed on May 8, 2010.

6. Smith, David L. *The Most Dangerous Animal: Human Nature and the Origins of War.* New York: St. Martin's Press, 2007. Print.

7. Mueller, G.O.W. "Transnational Crime: Definitions and Concepts." *Transnational Organized Crime* 4.13–21: (1998) Print.

8. Hermann, N., and G. Eryvac. "Delayed Onset Post-Traumatic Stress Disorder in World War II Veterans." *Canadian Journal of Psychiatry* 39.7: (1996) Print. 439–41.

9. National Coalition for Homeless Veterans—Background & Statistics. http://www.nchv.org/background.cfm. Accessed on May 6, 2010.

10. Trocki, Carl A. *Opium, Empire, and the Global Political Economy: A Study of the Asian Opium Trade, 1750–1950.* London: Routledge, 1999. Print. xiv.

11. Kushlick, Danny. "Drug Policy That Promotes Security: The Paradox of De-Securitisation." Transform Drug Policy Foundation. April 2011.

12. Elwood, William N. *Rhetoric in the War on Drugs: The Triumphs and Tragedies of Public Relations.* Westport, CT: Praeger, 1994. Print. 33.

13. MacAllister, William B. *Drug Diplomacy in the Twentieth Century: An International History.* London: Routledge, 2000. Print. 46–50.

14. Kushlick, Danny. "Drug Policy That Promotes Security: The Paradox of De-Securitisation." Transform Drug Policy Foundation. April 2011.

Index

About the Author

Dessa Bergen-Cico, Ph.D., is an assistant professor in the Department of Public Health, and lead faculty of Addiction Studies at Syracuse University. She teaches international courses on drug policies and holds a research appointment at the Syracuse Veterans Affairs Medical Center. Dr. Bergen-Cico is a Certified Addiction Specialist (CAS) and has worked in the field of alcohol and other drug prevention and treatment for nearly 20 years. Prior to becoming a member of the faculty, she served as the director of a sexual assault services center and director of substance abuse prevention and counseling programs. From 1996 to 2000, she directed the National Security Studies health promotion programs for senior civilian and military leaders. In addition to her research on the effects of posttraumatic stress disorder (PTSD) and substance abuse, Dessa teaches and studies the benefits of cognitive behavioral stress reduction and mindfulness-based practices for those affected by violence, trauma, anxiety, and substance abuse.

On a personal note, Dessa has competed in several marathons, holds a black belt in Tae Kwon Do, and lives in Manlius, New York, with her husband, John. Their daughter, Rachael, works in education policy reform, and their son, John, is a cinematographer.